WOMEN AND TRAVEL

Historical and Contemporary Perspectives

Advances in Hospitality and Tourism

WOMEN AND TRAVEL

Historical and Contemporary Perspectives

Edited by
Catheryn Khoo-Lattimore, PhD
Erica Wilson, PhD

Apple Academic Press Inc. | Apple Academic Press Inc.
3333 Mistwell Crescent | 9 Spinnaker Way
Oakville, ON L6L 0A2 | Waretown, NJ 08758
Canada | USA

©2017 by Apple Academic Press, Inc.
Exclusive worldwide distribution by CRC Press, a member of Taylor & Francis Group
No claim to original U.S. Government works
Printed in the United States of America on acid-free paper
International Standard Book Number-13: 978-1-77188-468-6 (Hardcover)
International Standard Book Number-13: 978-1-315-36587-9 (CRC Press/Taylor & Francis e Book)
International Standard Book Number-13: 978-1-77188-469-3 (AAP eBook)

Library and Archives Canada Cataloguing in Publication

Women and travel : historical and contemporary perspectives / edited by Catheryn Khoo-Lattimore, PhD, Erica Wilson, PhD.

(Advances in hospitality and tourism book series)
Includes bibliographical references and index.
Issued in print and electronic formats.
ISBN 978-1-77188-468-6 (hardcover).--ISBN 978-1-315-36587-9 (PDF)
   1. Women travelers. 2. Tourism--Social aspects. 3. Travel--Social aspects. I. Khoo-Lattimore, Catheryn, 1974-, editor
II. Wilson, Erica, 1974-, editor III. Series: Advances in hospitality and tourism book series

G156.5.W66W64 2017   306.4'819   C2016-907919-8   C2016-907920-1

Library of Congress Cataloging-in-Publication Data

Names: Khoo-Lattimore, Catheryn, 1974- editor.
Title: Women and travel : historical and contemporary perspectives / editors, Catheryn Khoo-Lattimore, PhD, Erica Wilson, PhD.
Description: Toronto : Apple Academic Press, 2017. | Includes bibliographical references and index.
Identifiers: LCCN 2016054881 (print) | LCCN 2016056944 (ebook) | ISBN 9781771884686 (hardcover : alk. paper) | ISBN 9781315365879 (ebook)
Subjects: LCSH: Women travelers.
Classification: LCC G156.5.W66 W66 2017 (print) | LCC G156.5.W66 (ebook) | DDC 910.82--dc23
LC record available at https://lccn.loc.gov/201605488

Apple Academic Press also publishes its books in a variety of electronic formats. Some content that appears in print may not be available in electronic format. For information about Apple Academic Press products, visit our website at **www.appleacademicpress.com** and the CRC Press website at **www.crc-press.com**

ABOUT THE EDITORS

Catheryn Khoo-Lattimore, PhD

Catheryn Khoo-Lattimore holds a PhD in Consumer Behavior from the University of Otago, New Zealand and has worked in Malaysia, United States, and now Australia. She was a 2013/14 Fulbright Scholar with residency at the University of Florida, and is now Senior Lecturer in the Department of Tourism, Sport and Hotel Management at Griffith University. Catheryn's current research interest is on tourist and guest behavior, with a passionate focus on women, families, and young children. She is also particularly interested in understanding these segments from an Asian perspective, and how their travel experiences and behaviors differ cross-culturally. Catheryn serves on the editorial boards of the *Journal of Hospitality and Tourism Education*, the *Journal of Hospitality and Tourism Management*, *Tourism Review* and *Anatolia*. She is an executive committee member of The Council for Australasian Tourism and Hospitality Education (CAUTHE) and board member of the Asia Pacific Council on Hotel, Restaurant, and Institutional Education (APacCHRIE). She is also the founder and chair of Women Academics in Tourism (WAiT). Catheryn lives in a bayside suburb with her husband and their three young children, and attempts furniture upcycling in her spare time, when, she can find any.

Erica Wilson, PhD

Erica Wilson is Associate Professor and Deputy Head in the School of Business and Tourism, Southern Cross University. Her doctoral thesis (Griffith University) was an interpretive, qualitative exploration into the constraints faced by Australian solo women travelers. Erica also holds a postgraduate diploma in environmental studies (Adelaide University), and a first-class honors degree in tourism (James Cook University). Her scholarly publications and research interests focus on critical pedagogy in tourism, gender and tourism, leisure constraints and negotiation, sustainable tourism in protected/World Heritage areas, and qualitative methodologies. Erica currently sits on the Editorial Advisory Boards for *Hospitality and Society*, *Journal of Tourism and Development*, and the *Annals of*

Leisure Research. She is a co-coordinator of the Critical Approaches in Tourism and Hospitality Special Interest Group within CAUTHE. Erica lives "off the grid" on a rural property in northern New South Wales, with her partner and two children. She would love to have more time to be an independent woman traveler, but is content to stay put for a while and work in her veggie patch.

CHAPTER AUTHORS

Fiona Eva Bakas has a PhD in Tourism Gender and Economics from the University of Otago, New Zealand and a Master of Science in Ecotourism from Portsmouth University, UK. She is currently a postdoctoral research fellow at the University of Aveiro, Portugal. She is also an associate member of NGO Equality in Tourism and a member of the GOVCOPP research group.

Maria Manuel Baptista has a PhD in the philosophy of culture. She is an Assistant Professor and researcher of Portuguese Culture Area in the Department of Languages and Cultures of the Aveiro University, Portugal. She is also Director of the PhD in Cultural Studies in the Department of Languages and Cultures of the Aveiro University (3rd cycle taught in collaboration with the Minho University, Portugal).

Sue Beeton is a travel researcher, writer, blogger and Foundation Chair of the College of Eminent Professors at William Angliss Institute. She has conducted research into community development, film-induced tourism, and nature-based tourism, along with advising government in areas of public land management. As well as producing numerous academic papers and related media articles, she has published numerous books, including *Ecotourism: A Practical Guide for Rural Communities; Community Development through Tourism; Film-Induced Tourism*, and *Tourism and the Moving Image*. She founded the Asia Pacific chapter of the Travel and Tourism Research Association (TTRA) and is a Board Member of TTRA International as well as an Honorary Associate Professor at Latrobe University, Australia.

Gisele Carvalho holds a Master of Science in Education and Environmental Management of the University of Brasilia, Brazil. She is Effective Professor of the Federal Institute of Education, Science and Technology of Pará State, IFPA. She is currently a PhD candidate in the Doctoral Program in Tourism at Aveiro University, Portugal, under the Gisele is also a member of the GOVCOPP research group.

Carlos Costa is Full Professor and Director of the Department of Economics, Management, Industrial Engineering, and Tourism at the

University of Aveiro, Portugal. He holds a PhD and a Master of Science in Tourism from the University of Surrey, UK, and a Bachelor of Science in Urban and Regional Planning from the University of Aveiro. He is Director of the Doctoral Program in Tourism, editor of the *Journal of Tourism and Development*, and a member of the executive board of the Research Unit on Governance, Competitiveness, and Public Policy. He is also the technical-scientific Director of the spin-off tourism company "idtour-unique solutions".

Bente Heimtun is Associate Professor at the UiT, The Arctic University of Norway. Bente's research interests are the sociology of tourism, gender studies, life course theories, the interface between the philosophies of feminist social sciences and the practices of tourism research, tourism employment, and place attachment. Recently she has turned her attention to winter tourism, with a focus on Northern Lights tourism performances situated in material, cultural, and social structures.

Magdalena Hoffmann completed a nursing degree and obtained a postgraduate Master in hospital management and a MBA in health service management simultaneous to her employment as a registered nurse followed by a Master's degree in public health. During her professional engagement, she filled the roles of ward manager as well as nursing expert in organizational development in a geriatric hospital. She is currently employed by the Medical University Graz and writing her dissertation. Her past and present fields of research are public health, communication in intensive care units, geriatrics, health tourism, and health literacy.

Margret Jaeger completed her PhD research on women's health politics in Austria and Brazil at the University of Graz, Austria. She worked as senior research scientist at the Department of Public Health & HTA at UMIT, University for Health and Life Sciences in Vienna until 2014. The study about health tourism and the evaluation of a health touristic facility was realized between 2013 and 2015 and supported by the Tyrolean Fund of Science. She currently works as independent researcher and teacher. Her research interests are cancer rehabilitation, health tourism and gender, and the development of transcultural competence for health professionals.

Kelley A. McClinchey has a PhD in geography specializing in urban social and cultural geography. She is currently a part-time lecturer in the Department of Geography and Environmental Studies at Wilfrid Laurier University, Waterloo, Ontario, Canada. Kelley studies the philosophies of place in the context of tourism. Using a framework of sensuous and emotional geographies, she relates these specifically to literary travel, tourism and leisure mobilities, the tourism-migration nexus, and ethno-cultural urban festivals. She has published articles in academic journals, book chapters in edited volumes, and presented at several tourism and geography conferences.

Paolo Mura is Senior Lecturer in Tourism and Program Director of the Postgraduate Programs at Taylor's University, Malaysia. His research interests include tourist behavior, gender, young tourists, deviant behavior on holiday, and ethnographic approaches to research.

Linda M. Myers is an independent researcher living in Northern Scotland. Her background is in women's and girls' physical and outdoor education. As a mature student, she completed her PhD in Department of Tourism, at the University of Sunderland, UK. She received an ESRC research grant to present her work in South Korea at the World Leisure Conference. Her studies focus on women's travel, with emphasis upon independent, backpacker, and gay women travelers. Her research interests include the value of travel to women, identity development, and identity reassessment resulting from the travel journey itself and from adventurous activity undertaken. Her publications include book chapters in Backpacker Tourism, Beyond Backpacker Tourism, International Sports Events and Annals of Leisure Research Australia and NewZealand Association.

Maria Oprodovsky teaches in the registered nurses program and is lecturer in the bachelor's degree program in the Campus Social Medical Center South of Vienna belonging to the Vienna Hospital Association. She is a registered nurse and has been working at a surgical ward before she went through a training program in pedagogics for nurses. She has earned a Bachelor Degree in Nursing Science and a Master Degree in Health Science from the private university UMIT in Hall, Tyrol.

Mandy Rowe began her working life as a psychologist for the RAAF, which is where she met her husband. Together, they have had two long sojourns overseas and returned to Australia in 2002, settling in rural Victoria. For the next eight years, Mandy owned a luxury bed and breakfast. Inspired by her worldwide group of very good friends, she founded Broads Abroad Travel Network (a global female-only online hospitality exchange), and has had published two books: a memoir, *Broads Abroad: One Woman's Journey,* and a quirky travel compilation, *Broads Abroad: Worldly Wise.*

Agnieszka Rydzik is Senior Lecturer in Tourism at the University of Lincoln, UK. Her research focuses on four key areas: tourism employment; mobilities, gender and migration; working lives and career trajectories of women, and visual and participatory methodologies. She completed her PhD at the Welsh Centre for Tourism Research, Cardiff Metropolitan University. Her interdisciplinary doctoral study, underpinned by visual and participatory methodologies, explored the employment experiences, trajectories and identities of Central and Eastern European female migrants working in UK tourism.

Heike Schänzel is Senior Lecturer in international tourism management at Auckland University of Technology, New Zealand. Heike's doctoral thesis examined family holiday experiences for the whole family group from a New Zealand perspective from which she has published extensively. She is passionate about better understanding family fun (along with the avoidance of conflict) as well as the facilitation of sociality within the context of tourism and hospitality. Her research interests include families and children in tourism, tourist experiences, sociality in tourism, innovative and qualitative research methodologies, and critical theory development in tourism and hospitality.

Jennie Small is Honorary Associate in the Business School at the University of Technology, Sydney. Her specific teaching and research interest is tourist behavior from a Critical Tourism approach, with a focus on feminism, gender, and tourism. Her publications relate to women's and girls' holiday experiences across the life course, women's experiences of motherhood and tourism, and women's experiences of embodiment on holiday. She is recognized for her contribution to the development of the feminist research method, "memory-work." She is a coordinator of the *Critical Approaches in Tourism and Hospitality* Special Interest Group of the Council for Australasian University Tourism and Hospitality Education (CAUTHE).

Davina Stanford is Senior Lecturer at Leeds Beckett University, Leeds, UK where she is course leader for the Responsible Tourism Management MSc. Her research interests include responsible tourist behavior, destination management, and responsible tourism transport in protected areas. Davina has worked as a tourism consultant for a range of clients, including destination management organizations, local authorities, regional, national, and international agencies (e.g. VisitEngland, Natural England, UNEP, and UNWTO).

Rokhshad Tavakoli is a Lecturer at the School of Hospitality, Tourism and Culinary Arts, Taylor's University, Malaysia. She has completed her doctoral studies in tourism at Taylor's University, Malaysia. Her PhD explored social capital within the context of Malaysian homestays. Her research interests include tourist behavior, gender, 2D and 3D social networks, virtual tourism, contemporary issues in tourism and ethnographic approaches to research.

Stephen Wearing is Conjoint Professor in the Newcastle Business School at the University of Newcastle, Australia. His research and projects are in the area of leisure and tourism studies, with a PhD focused on sustainable forms of tourism. Stephen has made seminal contributions in many areas including ecotourism, volunteer tourism and community development. The importance of community-based approaches in the leisure, recreation, and tourism sector has formed the focus of his research. His practical experience as a town planner, environmental and park planner at local, state, and international level have provided him with real world experiences that he brings to his teaching and research. He has been project director for a range of social sciences in natural resource management projects and research and a team leader for a variety of ecotourism, volunteer tourism, and outdoor education activities internationally.

Jude Wilson is a tourism researcher at Lincoln University in New Zealand. The New Zealand OE was the subject of her PhD thesis and she has also published *Flying Kiwis: A History of the OE*. Jude's other research interests include tourism and climate change, the impacts of cruise tourism on host communities, cycle tourism, and tourist decision_making. She also works with the New Zealand Tourism Industry Association (TIA) and Statistics New Zealand to produce an annual *State of the Industry* report.

Elaine Chiao Ling Yang is a PhD candidate in tourism at Griffith University. Her main area of interest is gender studies in tourism in the Department of Tourism, Sport and Hotel Management. Her current doctoral research focuses on Asian solo female travelers and their perception of risk in the gendered and ethnicized tourism space. She is also currently involved in research on girlfriend getaway holidays. Her other research interests include qualitative research methods, postcolonial feminist research, Asian tourist behavior, tourist risk perception and food studies.

CONTENTS

LIST OF CONTRIBUTORS

Fiona Eva Bakas
Department of Economics, Management, Industrial Engineering and Tourism, University of Aveiro, Portugal. E-mail: fiona.bakas@ua.pt

Maria Manuel Baptista
Department of Languages and Cultures, Aveiro University, Portugal. E-mail: mbaptista@ua.pt

Sue Beeton
William Angliss Institute, Australia. E-mail: s.beeton@outlook.com

Gisele Carvalho
Department of Economics, Management, Industrial Engineering and Tourism, University of Aveiro, Portugal / Federal Institute of Education, Science and Technology of Pará State, IFPA, Brazil. E-mail: gisele.maria@ua.pt

Carlos Costa
Department of Economics, Management, Industrial Engineering and Tourism, University of Aveiro, Portugal. E-mail: ccosta@ua.pt

Bente Heimtun
Department of Tourism and Northern Studies, UiT, The Arctic University, Norway. E-mail: bente. heimtun@uit.no

Magdalena Hoffman
Medical University Graz, Austra. E-mail: magdahoffmann@gmail.com

Margret Jaeger
Health Tourism Consultant, Austria. E-mail: margretjaeger@yahoo.com

Catheryn Khoo-Lattimore
Department of Tourism, Sport and Hotel Management, Griffith Business School, Griffith University, Australia. E-mail: c.khoo-lattimore@griffith.edu.au

Kelley A. McClinchey
Department of Geography and Environmental Studies, Wilfrid Laurier University, Canada. E-mail: kelleymcclinchey@yahoo.ca

Paolo Mura
School of Hospitality, Tourism and Culinary Arts, Taylor's University, Malaysia. E-mail: paolo. mura@taylors.edu.my

Linda M. Myers
Department of Tourism, University of Sunderland, UK. E-mail: lindammyers@hotmail.com

Maria Oprodovsky
Campus Social Medical Center, Vienna, Austria. E-mail: maria.oprodovsky@wienkav.at

Mandy Rowe
Broads Abroad Travel Network. E-mail: mandy@broadsabroad.net

Agnieszka Rydzik
Lincoln International Business School, University of Lincoln, UK. E-mail: ARydzik@lincoln.ac.uk

Heike A. Schänzel
School of Hospitality and Tourism, Auckland University of Technology, New Zealand. E-mail: heike.schanzel@aut.ac.nz

Jennie Small
UTS Business School, University of Technology, Sydney, Australia. E-mail: jennie.small@uts.edu.au

Davina Stanford
School of Events, Tourism, Hospitality and Languages, Leeds Beckett University, Leeds, UK. E-mail: D.J.Stanford@leedsbeckett.ac.uk

Rokhshad Tavakoli
School of Hospitality, Tourism and Culinary Arts, Taylor's University, Malaysia. E-mail: rokhshad.tavakoli@taylors.edu.my

Stephen Wearing
Newcastle Business School, The University of Newcastle, Australia. E-mail: stephen.wearing@uts.edu.au

Erica Wilson
School of Business and Tourism, Southern Cross University, Australia. E-mail: erica.wilson@scu.edu.au

Jude Wilson
Department of Tourism, Sport and Society, Lincoln University, New Zealand. E-mail: jude.wilson@lincoln.ac.nz

Elaine Chiao Ling Yang
Department of Tourism, Sport and Hotel Management, Griffith Business School, Griffith University, Australia. E-mail: elaine.yang@griffithuni.edu.au

LIST OF ABBREVIATIONS

AQR	Association for Qualitative Research
ASTA	American Society of Travel Agents
BATN	Broads Abroad Travel Network
CEE	Central and Eastern Europe
FITs	free independent travelers
GGAs	girlfriend getaways
GTM	grounded theory methodology
ISPA	International Spa Association
OE	overseas experience
OVC	Overseas Visitors Club
T-MONA	Tourismus Monitor Austria
UK	United Kingdom
VFR	visiting friends and relatives
WAAC	Women's Auxiliary Army Corps
WW2	World War Two

ADVANCES IN HOSPITALITY AND TOURISM BOOK SERIES BY APPLE ACADEMIC PRESS, INC.

Editor-in-Chief:
Mahmood A. Khan, PhD
Professor, Department of Hospitality and Tourism Management, Pamplin
College of Business, Virginia Polytechnic Institute and State University,
Falls Church, Virginia, USA
Email: mahmood@vt.edu

Books in the Series:
Food Safety: Researching the Hazard in Hazardous Foods
Editors: Barbara Almanza, PhD, RD, and Richard Ghiselli, PhD

**Strategic Winery Tourism and Management: Building Competitive
Winery Tourism and Winery Management Strategy**
Editor: Kyuho Lee, PhD

**Sustainability, Social Responsibility and Innovations in the
Hospitality Industry**
Editor: H. G. Parsa, PhD
Consulting Editor: Vivaja "Vi" Narapareddy, PhD
Associate Editors: SooCheong (Shawn) Jang, PhD,
Marival Segarra-Oña, PhD, and Rachel J. C. Chen, PhD, CHE

**Managing Sustainability in the Hospitality and Tourism Industry:
Paradigms and Directions for the Future**
Editor: Vinnie Jauhari, PhD

**Management Science in Hospitality and Tourism: Theory, Practice,
and Applications**
Editors: Muzaffer Uysal, PhD, Zvi Schwartz, PhD, and
Ercan Sirakaya-Turk, PhD

Tourism in Central Asia: Issues and Challenges
Editors: Kemal Kantarci, PhD, Muzaffer Uysal, PhD, and
Vincent Magnini, PhD

Poverty Alleviation through Tourism Development: A Comprehensive and Integrated Approach
Robertico Croes, PhD, and Manuel Rivera, PhD

Chinese Outbound Tourism 2.0
Editor: Xiang (Robert) Li, PhD

Hospitality Marketing and Consumer Behavior: Creating Memorable Experiences
Editor: Vinnie Jauhari, PhD

Women and Travel: Historical and Contemporary Perspectives
Editors: Catheryn Khoo-Lattimore, PhD, and Erica Wilson, PhD

Wilderness of Wildlife Tourism
Editor: Johra Kayeser Fatima, PhD

Medical Tourism and Wellness: Hospitality Bridging Healthcare (H2H)©
Editor: Frederick J. DeMicco, PhD, RD

Sustainable Viticulture: The Vines and Wines of Burgundy
Claude Chapuis

The Indian Hospitality Industry: Dynamics and Future Trends
Editors: Sandeep Munjal and Sudhanshu Bhushan

ABOUT THE SERIES EDITOR

Mahmood A. Khan, PhD, is a Professor in the Department of Hospitality and Tourism Management, Pamplin College of Business at Virginia Tech's National Capital Region campus. He has served in teaching, research, and administrative positions for the past 35 years, working at major U.S. universities. Dr. Khan is the author of seven books and has traveled extensively for teaching and consulting on management issues and franchising. He has been invited by national and international corporations to serve as a speaker, keynote speaker, and seminar presenter on different topics related to franchising and services management. He is the author of *Restaurant Franchising: Concepts, Regulations, and Practices, Third Edition, Revised and Updated*, published by Apple Academic Press, Inc.

Dr. Khan has received the Steven Fletcher Award for his outstanding contribution to hospitality education and research. He is also a recipient of the John Wiley & Sons Award for lifetime contribution to outstanding research and scholarship; the Donald K. Tressler Award for scholarship; and the Cesar Ritz Award for scholarly contribution. He also received the Outstanding Doctoral Faculty Award from Pamplin College of Business.

He has served on the Board of Governors of the Educational Foundation of the International Franchise Association, on the Board of Directors of the Virginia Hospitality and Tourism Association, as a Trustee of the International College of Hospitality Management, and as a Trustee on the Foundation of the Hospitality Sales and Marketing Association's International Association. He is also a member of several professional associations.

ACKNOWLEDGMENTS

This book on women's travel began with an idea from Catheryn Khoo-Lattimore; its culmination has been the result of serendipity, supportive organizations, and the work of many good people.

In the order of events relating to the publication of the book, Catheryn would like to thank the Bureau of Educational and Cultural Affairs of the United States Department of State, and the Malaysian–American Commission on Educational Exchange for the Fulbright award that led her to the initial idea for this book. Catheryn would also like to thank Professor Mahmood Khan at Virginia Tech for his encouragement and this opportunity, and her co-editor Associate Professor Erica Wilson, for her guidance, collegiality, professionalism, and faith in her. Catheryn acknowledges all of the chapter authors for their hard work and contribution of passionate ideas, the Griffith Institute for Tourism (GIFT) for its financial support, and her husband who holds the fort whenever "his woman" travels. Finally, Catheryn thanks her friends, colleagues, and students who have assisted both directly and indirectly in the preparation of this book.

Erica would like to thank all of the intrepid and humble women out there—both past and present—who embark upon journeys and lead paths all around the world. She would also like to thank Catheryn in particular for inviting her to come along on this writing adventure. It has been a pleasure working with Catheryn, and all of the co-authors on this women's travel book; the process has very much been a joint effort! Erica would like to acknowledge the School of Business and Tourism at Southern Cross University and her colleagues there for a supportive environment in which to work and edit this book. Erica thanks her partner, Noah, and her children, Maya and Solomon, for always "keeping it real," and for their ongoing support in creating space and time for travel, writing, and work.

Finally, both Catheryn and Erica would like to acknowledge the very fine editing and proofreading skills of Mun Yee Lai at Griffith University, and to Mahmood Khan and the team at Apple Academic Press for their professional support and wise advice during their time editing this book.

CHAPTER 1

INTRODUCTION: WOMEN AND TRAVEL, PAST AND PRESENT

CATHERYN KHOO-LATTIMORE[1*] and ERICA WILSON[2]

[1]*Department of Tourism, Sport and Hotel Management, Griffith Business School, Griffith University, Australia*

[2]*School of Business and Tourism, Southern Cross University, Australia*

Corresponding author. E-mail: c.khoo-lattimore@griffith.edu.au

CONTENTS

A Lady an explorer? A traveller in skirts?
The notion's just a trifle too seraphic:
Let them stay and mind the babies, or hem our ragged shirts;
But they mustn't, can't, and shan't be geographic.
(from a cartoon in *Punch* magazine, 1893, cited in Robinson, 1994, p 1)

1.1   WOMEN ON THE MOVE

In the opening ditty above, published in the British *Punch* magazine in 1893, we see the satirical rejection of a woman traveling, and the notion reiterated of travel as a primarily masculine venture. During this era, well over 100 years ago, it was not socially acceptable for women to travel, and certainly not on their own, without family or husband. It was around this time, in the late 1800s, where debates were sparking regarding the admission of women as fellows into the Royal Geographic Society—a debate which raged for over 20 years until 1913, when the Society finally admitted women for the first time (Bell & McEwan, 1996). Despite the controversies among geographical societies, many (Western) women defied societal and gendered conventions by traveling, often solo, and both at home and abroad. They negotiated, resisted, found ways of doing so. And in doing so, they defied traditional ideologies of "woman," and "woman at home" (Wilson & Little, 2005).

Moving forward into the twenty-first century, things have changed for women—and been fought for—in many parts of the world; a recent resurgence in the publication of women's travel narratives, for example, attests to the fact that women continue to travel, adventure, move, explore, and pioneer. As we explore later in this Introduction, however, and as also demonstrated by many chapters in this book, women still need to negotiate their freedoms on an everyday basis, let alone when traversing the globe. The stigma around women's travel—and women's solo travel in particular—still remains, and women's travel more generally remains a site open to discussion, discourse, and problematization.

Within the contemporary tourism industry, women are now widely recognized as a "growing force" (Ćurcic et al., 2009). For example, a significant increase in business travel was recorded among women—from 1% in 1970 to 25% in 1991; and then to almost 50% around a decade later in 2010 (Brownwell, 2011). Consistent with this rise of women's participation in business, women not only undertake travels and journeys, but they also make the majority of household decisions on travel choices. Purchasing decisions for vacations, which were once determined by men, are becoming less husband-oriented in more contemporary families as wives are becoming more significant in calling the cards in some of the household aspects, particularly family holidays; research shows that 92% of travel decisions are now made by women (Silverstein & Sayre, 2009).

The leisure and pleasure travel market has also witnessed a rising trend of females in its traveler demographics (Marzuki et al., 2012). Indeed, research shows that women are predominant in some travel markets such as adventure tourism and ecotourism (Cole et al., 2013; Weaver, 2001) but also in volunteer tourism (Mostafanezhad, 2013). There are increasing numbers of females choosing to travel alone and "solo" without the assistance or company of partners, husbands or packaged tour groups. The latest statistics by Booking.com indicate that 72% of American women are interested in solo travel while recent studies document the rise of all-women travel (Khoo-Lattimore & Gibson, 2015; Khoo-Lattimore & Prayag, 2015) as a $6 billion market (AAA, 2007). It is also interesting to see this phenomenon reflecting in Asia, where the ratio of male to female travelers has been shifting dramatically in favor of women; from around 90:10 ratio (males to females) 30 years ago, to around 60:40 ratio (males to females) in 2005 (Mastercard, 2005). Many more region-specific reports abound on the increase of women's travel, and their travel behaviors, desires, and experiences. For example, a recent Australian report revealed that 60% of the 5000 Australian women polled have been on at least one overseas trip in the past 12 months (Gentle, 2013).

1.2 STRUCTURE OF THE BOOK: A GENDERED APPROACH

The opportunities for women travelers have inadvertently opened up discourses around resistance, independence, empowerment, and individual agency. At the same time, women's travel may differ from men's in many ways; thus it is important to understand female travelers' motivations, needs, preferences, and behaviors. This book on Women and Travel offers a compilation of work that explores and examines the discourses, debates, and discussions about women, travel, and tourism.

Our book on women's travel is built upon the premise that all tourism experiences and activities, like all social, cultural, and political interactions, are gendered. We deliberately foreground women's travel as a gendered "phenomenon", drawing on Kinnaird and Hall's proposal of a gender-aware framework, introduced into the tourism discourse over two decades ago (Kinnaird & Hall, 1994, 1996). This framework explicitly recognizes that we do not live in a gender-free society, and that all aspects of society are, inherently, gendered. Operating within and through this framework are gendered tourists, gendered hosts and gendered tourism industries. Under this banner of gender-aware research may sit studies about women, studies about men, but also studies about both men and women and their inter-relationships (Swain, 1995; Kinnaird & Hall, 1994).

Three important works produced in the mid-1990s brought "gender"—and women—to the forefront of the tourism research agenda. These were a literature synthesis on gender and tourism prepared by Norris & Wall (1994), a special edition on gender and tourism in the *Annals of Tourism Research* by Margaret Byrne Swain (1995), and a book edited by Kinnaird and Hall (1994) titled "Tourism: A Gender Analysis." Almost a decade later, Pritchard, Morgan, Ateljevic, and Harris's *Tourism and Gender: Embodiment, Sensuality and Experience* re-energized the discussion on women, travel, and embodiment through a critical, gendered lens (Pritchard et al., 2007). While emphasizing women's experience as producers and consumers of tourism, these publications also pointed to the interaction of gender with other important social factors, such as ethnicity, class, and race. The authors of these publications called for tourism researchers to consider the importance of the intersectionality between the multiple dimensions and layers of gender and power when studying the social complexities of tourism-related activity.

And very recently, we see renewed studies of gender in tourism, with Small et al. (2015) and Figeuroa-Domecq et al. (2015) finding that despite well over two decades of gender-aware research and recognition, not much seems to have changed. A state of "gender-stagnation" remains, whereby the majority of papers focusing on or featuring gender remain non-crit-ical, androcentric in focus, and largely gender-blind in both method and academic authorship. In writing this book, we take on Figeuroa-Domecq et al.'s (2015) clarion call to move (again) toward an agenda of "gender-ignition", whereby feminist, gender-aware approaches are furthered and embraced (Figeuroa-Domecq et al., 2015). Women's travel does not take place in a social, cultural, or political vacuum; it always has, and always will remain, very much a gendered phenomenon.

To provide structure to these varied voices and experiences, we have divided the book into five Sections. These sections cover historical accounts of women's travel (Section A, Chapters 2 and 3); issues and constraints faced by women travelers (Section B: Chapters 4–6); gendered approaches to studying women's travel (Section C: Chapters 7–9) and contemporary experiences of the female traveler (Section D: Chapters 10–13). The final part, Section E, incorporates two chapters focusing on industry perspectives on women's travel (Chapters 14 and 15).

1.2.1 SECTION A: HISTORICAL ACCOUNTS OF WOMEN'S TRAVEL

Travel and pioneering have long been construed as the sole preserve of men (Dann, 1999; Tinling, 1989), with women and their travel achievements generally overlooked in the history of exploration (Towner, 1994). Our opening verse from *Punch* revealed the level of societal scorn toward Victorian women travelers. Women in the Victorian era were bound by the ethic of care (Gilligan, 1982), relegating them to the primary care for others because of their assumed nurturing abilities. As a result, a woman who chose to travel alone faced criticism for daring to "outstep her proper sphere" (Jones, 1997, p. 209), a sphere which was limited to the domestic, the private and the secluded.

We begin this book chronologically, starting with two chapters in Section A dedicated to exploring the historical accounts for (predominantly Western) women travelers. In Chapter 2, Davina Stanford analyzes the writings of early Victorian women travelers, and then compares these themes with the experiences of contemporary female tourist. It is interesting here to see how the historical experiences faced by Victorian women endure today, despite significant shifts in the political and gendered expectations of women's role in and contribution to society. In Chapter 3, Jude Wilson writes about the travel experiences of New Zealand women on overseas working holidays in the 1950s, 1960s, and 1970s. These holidays, also referred to in New Zealand as the OE (or overseas experience), were dominated by a female market. Wilson demonstrates how these travelers have added to and impacted on the OE practices today of both women and men. Setting the scene with these two historical chapters, we attempt to redress what has been termed by some historians as "a major omission in the historical record" (Towner, 1994; p 725), the omission being women's involvement and contribution to travel and tourism.

1.2.2 SECTION B: WOMEN'S TRAVEL CONSTRAINTS AND ISSUES

As shown in Section A, while women have been traveling alone for centuries, their explorations were not without constraint, challenge, and resistance. The discussions by Stanford and Jude Wilson on constrictions experienced by early women travelers continue in Section B as we explore the different roles and identities performed by women today. In Chapter 4, Heike A. Schänzel investigates how the role of woman as mother and primary caregiver intersects with travel for contemporary women. Schän-zel's chapter offers an understanding on how motherhood in particular impacts on women's attitude toward and feelings about family holiday time. Her findings reveal that similar to early women's travel, women today must continue to resist an enduring "motherhood" discourse. In doing so, these women construct for themselves, and arguably for women after them, a new definition of what it is to be a "good mother" on holiday.

Moving away from a Western perspective, we see the next two chapters explore women's travel constraints from a Brazilian and Iranian (Muslim) perspective, respectively. In Chapter 5, Gisele Carvalho, Carlos Costa, Maria Manuel Baptista, and Fiona Bakas explore Brazilian women's performances in independent travels. While all young, adult, and mature women saw the benefits of travel for the development of the self, they also experienced negative feelings of fear and of being sexualized, harassed, disrespected, and humiliated. They attributed these discouraging experi-ences partly to public stereotypes portraying Brazilian women as being "sexually appealing." In Chapter 6, the authors set out to enlighten readers on women's travel from the Muslim world. As an Iranian Muslim woman herself, Rokhshad Tavakoli applies her own experiences, observations, and reflections to the issues surrounding travel for Iranian women. Together with her co-author Paolo Mura, they provide readers with a detailed over-view of the historical and political shifts in Iran that have restricted the way Iranian women can travel today. Not too dissimilar to the Victorian standards where the idea of a woman who traveled alone seemed to be particularly aberrant, worthy of ruining a "lady's" highly regarded social reputation (Robinson, 1990), many married Iranian women today require their husband's permission to apply for a passport. The chapter concludes with some encouraging examples of how these women are proactively seeking and discussing their right to travel through online social networks.

1.2.3   SECTION C: GENDERED APPROACHES TO STUDYING WOMEN'S TRAVEL

In line with our premise of a gendered approach, Section C includes chapters which firmly bring to the fore feminist and gendered ideas and methods for studying women's travel. In Chapter 7, Jennie Small and Stephen Wearing acknowledge gendered inter-relationships in their analysis of the women's experience as tourists. Identifying the tourist destination as an interactive, alive, and changing space, Small and Wearing demonstrate how a woman tourist should be framed as a creative, interacting, *choraster*, challenging the long-standing assumption of women travelers as mere objects of the tourist gaze (or the *flaneur*). Indeed, such interactions discussed by Small and Wearing are also evident in Chapter 8. Here, Kelley A. McClinchey explores American, Canadian, and Australian women's travel narratives of Paris, and at different stages of their lives. Using a literary travel approach, McClinchey seeks answers as to why there are so many women's travel books written on the city of Paris. More importantly, she wanted to see if there were common stories and experiences among these texts. What emerged from McClinchey's analysis was a focus on emotion, yet as she demonstrates, these women's emotions are very much the result of the interactions of diverse social, cultural, and even historical factors that have, in turn, constructed their different notions of Paris.

In Chapter 9, Elaine Chiao Ling Yang employs an innovative, autoethnographic account of her recent solo travels. She acknowledges the social and cultural factors that firstly underpin Asian gender norms, which in turn influence her experience of travel as an Asian woman. She connects these wider, external factors to her own personal factors such as gut feeling, common sense and intuition in coping with the complexities of traveling solo. Like Small and Wearing, Yang further concludes that travel is a reflexive project in which individuals have the agency to choose, conform, and reconstruct their social identities.

1.2.4 SECTION D: CONTEMPORARY WOMEN TRAVELERS: EXPERIENCES AND TRENDS

Tourism researchers have long claimed that women are the primary deci-sion-makers regarding family holidays but women are also becoming more prominent in their consumption of other types of travel, a reflec-tion of expanding numbers of women in the workforce worldwide. As a consequence, much of the existing tourism research attempts to better understand women as travelers by studying different markets. Specifically, scholars have investigated niche segments such as solo women travelers (Jordan & Gibson, 2005; Wilson & Little, 2008), senior women travelers (Stone & Nichol, 1999), educated women travelers (Pennington-Gray & Kerstetter, 2001), women cruisers (Jennings, 2005), businesswomen trav-elers (Alamdari & Burrell, 2000), and more recently, women traveling with other women, also known as the girlfriend getaway market (Berdy-chevsky et al., 2013; Gibson et al., 2012; Khoo-Lattimore & Gibson, 2015; Khoo-Lattimore & Prayag, 2015). These studies presuppose that the female travel market is heterogeneous, thus Section D extends this by featuring further discussion on the varied experiences of contemporary women travelers.

In Chapter 10, Linda Myers interviews 60 independent women trav-elers between the ages of 17 and 75 on their experiences with nature-based and adventure activities in New Zealand. Her findings reiterate that women's motivations, needs, and preferences in travel and tourism activi-ties differ from those of men, and show how women carve out space and time for travel in different ways. Myers found that even when participating in "extreme" nature-based activities, women tend to be reflective and spir-itual about the experiences, as opposed to competitive and exploitative. Interestingly, the older women in her study who had inherited stereo-typical gendered roles also expressed the feeling of empowerment and a strong sense of freedom and personal achievement during these indepen-dent, nature-based travels.

Despite existing studies on the different types of women's travel, our understanding of migrant women is still limited. Agnieszka Rydzik's work in Chapter 11 highlights the mobility of migrant women tourism workers from the less affluent nations of Central and Eastern Europe, and follows their new lives in the United Kingdom. Rydzik moves deftly and quickly away from considering migrant women only in the context of family reunification, and in doing so also challenges the conventional portrayal of migrant women as the oppressed. With over 105 million migrant women worldwide, this chapter adds to a need for an urgent understanding a relatively invisible group of women travelers.

From looking at migrant women in their new homes, Chapter 12 explores midlife single women and their conception of "real holidays" that take place at home. Findings from Bente Heimtun's work with 30 women challenge our assumption that touristic activities and experiences must almost always occur away from home. For the women in her study, fulfilling and rewarding holiday experiences can happen at home even when they revolve around domestic chores and caring for the elderly, evidencing that everyday life and tourism may not necessarily be categorized into two separate worlds. This research on home holidays adds a new dimension to the literature on laid-back motilities (Haldrup & Larsen, 2010; Larsen, 2008) and second home holidays (Haldrup, 2004) in leisure studies.

In this book, we also wanted to explore existing market opportunities that focus on women travelers, thus the last chapter of Section D is dedicated to highlighting these. In Chapter 13, Margaret Jaeger and her colleagues Magdalena Hoffmann and Maria Oprodovsky, explore insights into the European wellness and health tourism industry, where women have not yet been fully recognized as a target market. Interestingly, the women in Jaeger et al.'s study recommended that wellness centers incorporate facilities for sports and fitness activities, which contradict qualities typically associated with wellness such as calmness, meditative, and indulgence. Like research on women's preferences of accommodation attributes (Khoo-Lattimore & Prayag, 2015; Lutz & Ryan, 1993; Sammons et al., 1999), female wellness customers in this study also expressed inclinations for female-only designated areas such as the sauna. The study identified two main groups of female customers for the industry and recommended that wellness packages be designed and catered to both groups.

1.2.5   SECTION E: INDUSTRY PERSPECTIVES

Finally, we are conscious that the tourism industry has responded to the growth of women's travel through its offering of not only tour and accommodation packages but also travel information and contemporary travel experiences. Section E features two chapters highlighting an industry perspective on women travel. In Chapter 14, Sue Beeton takes the discussion on independent women's travel further to focus on safety, and considers recent media reports of attacks on women tourists in India. The inspiration for her work came after her own attendance at the Indian chapter of the American Society of Travel Agents (ASTA) as a keynote speaker, her observations from regular visits to India and somewhat frustration with representatives from the Indian government that would not engage with other tourism stakeholders in addressing these issues of violence against women travelers. Findings from her survey with over a hundred women shed light for tourism authorities worldwide—the women provided constructive and practical suggestions to their own governments and other tourism providers on how best to continue catering to the international, educated, independent women traveler. In the final chapter of the book (Chapter 15), and also the final industry highlight, Mandy Rowe, who owned and operated a bed and breakfast for eight years and later started a global female-only online hospitality exchange platform known as the Broads Abroad Travel Network, provides insight into the network's members and operations. Rowe's chapter provides some explanations for the increasing preference for private accommodation over commercial providers.

1.3   CONCLUSION

This book explores women and travel, through an exploration from past to present. In doing so, we reveal the enduring connections, opportunities and constraints between historic and contemporary women's travel. Our goal was to bring light to perspectives from different countries, cultures, backgrounds, and religions, and utilizing different methods, approaches and styles of presentation. It was our deliberate aim that when calling for contributions on women's travel, we featured a variety of voices, stretching beyond the traditional Western, white, predominantly Christian female experience which has tended to dominate the literature. In editing this book, we were pleased to see and welcome work on Muslim women, Asian women, for example. We were also hopeful to extend stagnant binaries of home/away, and we can see this coming through in this book, with chapters exploring home holidays, family holidays, and working migrants as travelers.

We also encouraged methodological and stylistic playfulness, which can be seen in a range of chapters which draw on both written and visual methodologies, and which incorporate women's direct voices, poetry, historical excerpts, and both qualitative and quantitative data. Further, while aiming to write a largely academic book with an academic publisher (and no doubt to a primarily academic audience), as editors we wanted to hear what was happening with women's travel in the industry, and from an industry perspective. As humble editors, who act merely as the guide in bringing our contributors' work to the published page, we were pleased to be able to achieve all of our initial goals with this book, and to welcome such a varied, interesting and important set of studies on women, gender, and travel.

KEYWORDS

- **Victorian women travellers**
- **Constraints**
- **Empowerment**
- **Historical perspectives on travel**

REFERENCES

AAA. AAA Girlfriend Travel Research. 2007, Retrieved 26 February 2014, from http://aspi-remarketing.com/girlfriend-getaway-report-conducted-by-aaa-and-aspire-marketing/

Alamdari, F.; Burrell, J. Marketing to Female Business Travelers. *JATWW.* **2000,** *5*(2), 3–18.

Bell, M.; McEwan, C. The Admission of Women Fellows to the Royal Geographical Society, 1892–1914: The Controversy and the Outcome. *Geogr. J. 1996, 162*(3), 295–312.

Berdychevsky, L.; Gibson, H. J.; Bell, H. L. Girlfriend Getaways and Women's Well-Being. *J. Leis. Res.* **2013,** *5*(5), 602–623.

Brownwell, J. Creating Value for Women Business Travelers: Focusing on Emotional Outcomes. *Cornell Hosp. Reports.* **2011,** *11*(12), 6–17.

Cole, E.; Rothblum, E. D.; Tallman, E. M. *Wilderness Therapy for Women: The Power of Adventure;* Routledge: New York, 2013.

Ćurcic, N.; Zakic, L.; Galantić, M. Segmentation of Tourist Markets: Women as Consumers. *Geogr. Temisiensis.* **2009,** *19*(1–2), 67–74.

Dann, G., Writing Out the Tourist in Space and Time. *Ann. Tour. Res.* **1999**, *26*, 159–187.

Figeuroa-Domecq, C.; Pritchard, A.; Segovia-Perez, M.; Morgan , N.; Villace-Molinero, T. Tourism Gender Research: A Critical Accounting. *Ann. Tour. Res.* **2015**, *52*, 87–103.

Gentle, N. *2012 Female Travel and Lifestyle Report*; 2013. Available at http://www.lastminute.com.au/femaletravelandlifestylereport

Gibson, H. J.; Berdychevsky, L.; Bell, H. L. Girlfriend Getaways Over the Life Course: Change and Continuity. *Ann. Leis. Res.* **2012**, *15*(1), 38–54.

Gilligan, C. *In a Different Voice: Psychological Theory and Women's Development;* Harvard University Press: Cambridge, MA, 1982.

Haldrup, M. Laid-Back Mobilities: Second-Home Holidays in Time and Space. *Tour. Geogr.* **2004**, *6*(4), 434–454.

Haldrup, M.; Larsen, J. *Tourism, Performance and the Everyday: Consuming the Orient;* Routledge: London, 2010.

Jennings, G. R. Caught in the Irons: One of the Lived Experiences of Long-Term Ocean Cruising Women. *Tour. Review Int.* **2005**, *9*(2), 177–193.

Jones, A. D. 'When a Woman so far Outsteps her Proper Sphere': Counter-Romantic Tourism. In *Women's Life-Writing: Finding Voice/Building Community;* Coleman. L. S., Ed.; Bowling Green State University Press: Bowling Green, OH, 1997; pp 209–237.

Jordan, F.; Gibson, H. 'We're not Stupid . . . But we'll not Stay Home either': Experiences of Solo Women Travelers. *Tour. Review Int.* **2005**, *9*(2), 195–211.

Khoo-Lattimore, C.; Gibson, H. J. Understanding Women's Accommodation Experiences on Girlfriend Getaways: A Pragmatic Action Research Approach. *Curr. Issues Tour.* **2015**, 1–19. http://www.tandfonline.com/doi/full/10.1080/13683500.2015.1068745

Khoo-Lattimore, C.; Prayag, G. The Girlfriend Getaway Market: Segmenting Accommodation and Service Preferences. *Int. J. Hosp. Manage.* **2015**, *45*, 99–108.

Kinnaird, V.; Hall, D. Understanding Tourism Processes: A Gender-Aware Framework. *Tour. Manage.* **1996**, *17*, 95–102.

Kinnaird, V.; Hall, D. *Tourism: A Gender Analysis;* John Wiley & Sons: Chichester, West Sussex, 1994.

Larsen, J. De-Exoticizing Tourist Travel: Everyday Life and Sociality on the Move. *Leis. Stud.* **2008**, *27*(1), 21–34.

Lutz, J.; Ryan, C. Hotels and the Business Woman: An Analysis of Businesswomen's Perceptions of Hotel Services. *Tour. Manage.* **1993**, *14*(5), 349–356.

Marzuki, A.; Tan, L. C.; Razak, A. A. What Women Want: Hotel Characteristics Preferences of Women Travelers. In *Strategies for the Tourism Industry: Micro and Macro Perspectives;* Kasimoglu, M., Aydin, H., Eds.; Open access book, InTech: Rijeka, Croatia, 2012; pp 143–164.

Mastercard. Women Travelers of Asia/Pacific: A New Powerhouse. *Insights, 1st Quarter,* 2005, pp 1–4, Retrieved from: http://www.mastercard.com/cn/wce/PDF/insights/2005/1st_Quarter/Insights_Women_V4_en.pdf

Mostafanezhad, M. 'Getting in Touch with your Inner Angelina': Celebrity Humanitarianism and the Cultural Politics of Gendered Generosity in Volunteer Tourism. *TWQ.* **2013**, *34*(3), 485–499.

Norris, J.; Wall, G. Gender and Tourism. In *Progress in Tourism, Recreation and Hospitality Management;* Cooper C. P., Lockwood, A ., Eds.; John Wiley & Sons: Chichester, 1994;Vol. 6, pp 57–78.

Pennington-Gray, L. A.; Kerstetter, D. L. What do University-Educated Women Want from their Pleasure Travel Experiences? *J. Travel Res.* **2001,** *40*(1), 49–56.

Pritchard, A.; Morgan, N.; Ateljevic, I.; Harris, C. Eds.; *Tourism and Gender: Embodiment, Sensuality, and Experience;* CABI: Wallingford, Oxfordshire, UK, 2007.

Robinson, J. *Unsuitable for Ladies: An Anthology of Women Travellers;* Oxford University Press: Oxford, 1994.

Robinson, J. *Wayward Women: A Guide to Women Travelers;* Oxford University Press: Oxford, 1990.

Sammons, G.; Moreo, P.; Benson, L. F.; Demicco, F. Analysis of Female Business Travelers' Selection of Lodging Accommodations. *J. Travel Tour. Mark.* **1999,** *8*(1), 65–83.

Silverstein, M. J.; Sayre, K. The Female Economy. *Harvard Business Rev.* **2009,** *87*(9), 46–53.

Small, J.; Harris, C.; Wilson, E. In *Gender on the Agenda? The Position of Critical Tourism Studies in Gender Research,* Paper Presented at the 10th Critical Tourism Studies Conference, Opatija, Croatia, 2015.

Stone, G. J.; Nichol, S. Older, Single Female Holidaymakers in the United Kingdom - Who Needs Them? *J. Vacat. Mark.* **1999,** *5*(1), 7–17.

Swain, M. B., Gender in Tourism. *Ann. Tour. Res.* **1995,** *22,* 247–266.

Tinling, M. *Women into the Unknown: A Sourcebook on Women Explorers and Travelers;* Greenwood: New York, 1989.

Towner, J. Tourism History: Past, Present and Future. In *Tourism: The State of the Art;* Seaton, A.V., Ed.; John Wiley & Sons: Chichester, 1994; pp 721–728.

Weaver, D. *Ecotourism;* John Wiley & Sons: Brisbane, Queensland, 2001.

Wilson, E.; Little, D. E. A 'Relative Escape'? The Impact of Constraints on Women who Travel Solo. *Tour. Rev. Int.* **2005,** *9*(2), 155–175.

Wilson, E.; Little, D. E. The Solo Female Travel Experience: Exploring the 'Geography of Women's Fear'. *Curr. Issues Tour.* **2008,** *11*(2), 167–186.

SECTION I
Historical Accounts of Women's Travel

CHAPTER 2

WOMEN AND THE TOURIST GAZE: HISTORICAL AND CONTEMPORARY ISSUES FOR WOMEN TRAVELING IN MALE-DOMINATED PUBLIC SPACE

DAVINA STANFORD

School of Events, Tourism, Hospitality and Languages, Leeds Beckett University, Leeds, UK

E-mail: D.J.Stanford@leedsbeckett.ac.uk

CONTENTS

2.1   INTRODUCTION

Women have traveled throughout history both widely and independently (Morris, 1993; Robinson, 1990), and this chapter focuses in the first instance on the experiences of the so called "Victorian lady travelers." These women "...defied the strictures of femininity..." (Enloe, 1989, p. 23) and by choosing adventure travel, entered both the "uncharted" territory of the world and the unchallenged territory of men. Through an analysis of their writing the chapter will explore some of the problems and constraints that they faced when venturing out into what was, at that time, very much a man's world, and some of the coping strategies that they developed in response. The chapter continues to illustrate that these issues and strategies are not that far removed from the experiences of women today. It will also discuss how opportunities to travel may still be restricted; how tourism is gendered; how women are advised to behave as tourists and how they actually do behave as tourists.

Drawing on a number of academic sources the paper documents the historical position of Victorian women travelers and compares this to the experience of the women who travel today. Evidence is further gathered for our understanding of the contemporary experiences of women from a range of media including news items, gray literature, guidebooks, marketing material, and literary sources. Interwoven in this narrative is an auto-ethnographic reflection, linking cultural and social constructions to the experiences of author. This arises from my own experiences as a woman traveler, from the questions that I asked myself about my own experience and behavior, and also from a curiosity about how different (or similar) my experience was from that of my predecessors. In doing this, I am ultimately trying to answer the question, "how far have we come" as women travelers?

This chapter brings originality by connecting together the experiences of historical and contemporary women, highlighting the similarities in their experience. Our assumptions about both rhetoric, responsibility and reality are challenged and questions raised regarding the role of women as agents of change in patriarchal societies as well as the line that women tread when compromising their feminist principles in order to be a polite guest. Greater exploration of the role of gender and values as women continue to travel alone and in groups into societies with very different understanding of gender from their own would be fertile ground for further research.

2.2 VICTORIAN WOMEN TRAVELERS

In Victorian society "...bourgeois culture evolved the home as the temple of femininity..." (Rojek & Urry, 1997) while public space was dominated by men (Wolff, 1985). The male *Flâneur* (identified by Urry (1990), as the forerunner of the modern tourist) enjoyed the freedom to wander the city and enjoy its visual pleasures (Wearing & Wearing, 1996), while in the wider world Victorian men were occupied with colonizing and exploring (Buzzard, 1993; Rojek & Urry, 1997) or enjoying the "sexual promise" of the Orient (Said, 1978, p. 188). For women who wished to enter this male-dominated space faced accusations of neglected familial duties and selfishness (Foster, 1990); indeed, many women could only travel after the death of an elderly parent released them from their responsibility as carer or nurse (Hall & Kinnaird, 1994; Middleton, 1965). Being in a "man's world" also brought the Victorian woman's moral character into question and for a woman to be alone without a male chaperone was widely thought of as "unrespectable" behavior (Buzzard, 1993; Craik, 1997; Wolff, 1985) compromising not only her reputation, but also her safety (Deem, 1996). The issues mentioned above are socially constructed difficulties; however, these women also faced practical challenges in their travel. For example Fiefer documents such essential paraphernalia as a collapsible rope-and-pulley fire escape and mahogany-rimmed chamber pot disguised as a bonnet box (Fiefer,1985), while Foster describes the extreme physical difficulties encountered (Foster,1990).

Having outlined some of the issues faced by Victorian women travelers, I would like to return to my title and briefly discuss how they were able to leave their "recognized" space of the home and enter public space to travel (of the question of finance, like Dorothy Middleton, I too assume that these women had access to "private means" (Middleton, 1965, p. 6)). To counter allegations of selfishness, Foster comments that many women "...traveled ostensibly in a spirit of service and self-sacrifice..." for example, spreading the word of the Bible or nursing lepers. Foster continues however, that "...motives of self-gratification may underlie the most honorable humanitarian ones" (Foster, 1990, p. 10). In other words, travel for altruistic purposes may have enabled travel for self-fulfillment. As regards the question of morals and traveling as an "unprotected" woman, many Victorian women were able to travel under the respectable chaperoning of Thomas Cook (Buzzard, 1993; Craik, 1997; Enloe, 1989).

If, however, a reliable chaperone was not available then women could find protection disguised as men (Foster, 1990; Wolff, 1985), or were allowed the position of "honorary man" (Hall & Kinnaird, 1994). Conversely, some women abhorred the idea of wearing trousers and maintained strict dress codes, they also considered themselves safe as long as they conducted themselves "...with suitable decorum" (Foster, 1990, p. 15).

Victorian women travelers were also able to depart for foreign shores in ways similar to that of their male counterparts, particularly with regards to the development of the empire. During the era of Colonialism, although exploration was largely a male endeavor, women certainly played their part. Enloe sees women travelers as agents of "imperial pride" bringing word of the empire, through writings or lectures, to the women at home (Enloe, 1989, p. 24). However, Singh sees women travelers bringing "Victorian domesticity" to the colonies—tutoring Indian women in the patriarchal values of being "...good wives, mothers, daughters" (Singh, 1996, p. 94). The writing of the colonial era is seen by Said as constructing the orient as the "Other" and disempowering the inhabitants (Said, 1978). Mills, however, believes that despite female collusion in colonialism, in general their writings do not fit easily into the model of Orientalism as described by Said, and that they demonstrate a greater engagement with local peoples (Mills, 1993). Foster concurs, focusing on the individual experience of Alexandra David-Neel who traveled in Tibet, where "... national and racial differences [were] passed over in a desire for integration and relationship" (Foster, 1990, p. 168). Women's experiences differed from those of the men, but this was not always a negative thing, and women were often afforded experiences to which men did not have access. Women, for example, could visit places such as the harem, the nursery or the kitchen, gaining access to "...spheres of foreign life from which men were excluded or discouraged" (Foster, 1990, p. 16). Ironically, then, having excluded women from the public sphere to relegate them to domestic space at home, men abroad found themselves excluded from these intimate and private areas.

2.3   CONTEMPORARY WOMEN TRAVELERS

While several typologies of travelers exist according to their psychological profile or behavior (e.g., Sharpley, 1999), this chapter chooses not to use these traditional definitions (which included clearly gendered definitions such as "explorer" [Cohen (1972), cited in Sharpley (1999)]). Instead, I concentrate on a category defined by women who travel unchaperoned by a male companion. The main focus of the chapter is the lone "independent" traveler, or one who is not on an organized packaged tour, traveling in less developed countries. This section draws on the travel writings of contemporary women and applying an autoethnographic approach, my own anecdotal experience, this includes sources of information and advice for the female traveler offered through guidebooks and websites.

Like the Victorian women travelers, a study of today's women travelers would benefit from an examination of how their position in public/domestic space and society in general may influence some women when venturing further from home and traveling in "a man's world." Woodward and Green observe that "...women's proper place has traditionally been seen as the home..." and that a woman entering into a perceived male public area such as the pub, may be deemed not to be "respectable" (Woodward & Green, 1988, p. 134). Enloe agrees that the gendering of public/private space exists, whereby a woman who travels away from "...the ideological protection of 'home' and without the protection of an acceptable male escort is likely to be tarred with the brush of 'unrespectability'"; furthermore she will be blamed should any harm befall her (Enloe, 1989, p. 21).

In *Ways of Escape,* Rojek refers to the early capitalist street as an area where there "...[was] the fear of robbery", an area "that *was* regarded as a place of menace" (Rojek, 1993, p. 79). Unfortunately, however, it seems that women's leisure and activity is still restricted due to a fear of being alone at night (Deem, 1986; Green et al., 1990; Fanghanel, 2014). A recent report (ESRC, 2013) shows that in the United Kingdom, more women than men feel unsafe walking after dark in public spaces (15% of women aged 16–30; 17% of women aged 31–60 and 34% of women aged >61, this compares to 1% of men aged 16–30; 2% of men aged 31–60 and 9% of men aged >61). This fear of relatively familiar public space in a known country may affect women's decisions to travel even further afield.

Women may also feel their entitlement to leisure restricted by their role as carer for others with Woodward and Green (1988) commenting that most women internalize the idea that they have the primary responsibility for the care of others, not only for children or partners, but also elderly relatives. The role of carer is not an easy one to forego and Deem (1996) and McGehee et al. (1996), observe that many women find it difficult to break away from this role. Carol Esslemont, who took a holiday without her partner or children, told a Guardian journalist she felt not only scared but also "a bit selfish" (The Guardian, 2000). While Sheila Keegan, writing in the book "Women Travel", chose to take her daughter along to India with her, reportedly being criticized by some as an irresponsible mother (Jansz & Davies, 1999). This is despite the clear educational value that the journey offered and the fact that it allowed mother and child unrestricted time together. Kahn concurs, observing that:

> ...gender remains vital in determining the liberty to travel. In leisure, women remain 'relatively' more constrained than men. Though other socio-demographic constraints operate on both genders, the extent of their influence varies. For men, employment is a major constraint to leisure travel, while for women, family responsibilities and spousal/ family dominance exacerbate the gender constraint. The 'doing gender', poses restrictions on the freedom of women (Khan, 2011, p. 116).

Writing in 1986, Deem reported that finances might be a further restricting factor on women's leisure and despite Equal Opportunities Legislation, women still earn, on average, less than men. In fact, according to recent Eurostat statistics, women earned an average of 16.4% less than men in the European Union in 2013 (The Telegraph, 2015). Anita Avery, again reported in The Guardian, 11 April, 2000, also goes on holiday alone, she says that she is only able to do this through her economic independence; that is, she has a job which pays her enough to have independent finances from her partner.

Contemporary women's travel may still be perceived as male domain "...infused with masculine ideas about adventure, pleasure and the exotic" (Enloe, 1989, p. 20) and travel for women is still restricted by "...the close association of women with the home and men with the limitless expanse of external space" (Rojek & Urry, 1997). Furthermore, Urry sees the tourist as a modern day *flâneur*, a *flâneur* who gazes on the sensual and visual pleasures of the city, and who, by definition can only be male (Urry, 1990). There is also a prevailing sense from women that solo travel is an inherently risky activity, "...shrouded with peril, challenge and harassment" (Wilson & Little, 2008, p. 172), though Wilson and Little provide evidence that these fears are based largely on societal and others' perceptions, and not always grounded in the reality of what is faced. Wilson and Little further cite an example from Australia which demonstrates that public safety for women has in fact increased and that most of acts of sexual violence against women are carried out by men they know (Wilson & Little, 2008). Yet despite carrying their backpacks along with various socially constructed baggage, women still choose to travel independently. Thus, how do they manage and negotiate?

When setting off on their journey, many women may first look for advice from guidebooks but in their handbooks for women travelers both McCarthy (1992) and Moss and Moss (1987) comment on how "invisible" women are in the average guide book—a glance at some popular guides shows this to be the case. The Lonely Planet standard format includes a short paragraph offering advice which deals mainly with the problems that women may encounter, for example sexual harassment, while the Footprints and Insights series do not offer a separate section for women at all. In guides for women, personal safety is a big issue and both set about giving practical and positive advice to women while attempting to reassure that the fear of rape or violent assault is probably greater than the reality of it actually happening. Guidebooks recommend a confident manner suggesting that one has every right to be by oneself without male "protection." McCarthy comments wryly that to give women a list of dos and don'ts, although useful, implies that if a women is attacked then it is her fault because she did or did not do something; the reality, however, is because "...some man got it into his head" (McCarthy, 1992). Moss and Moss also suggest that the invention of an imaginary husband, acting as chaperone by proxy may offer some protection (1987). Lonely Planet (1990, p. 71) also suggest inventing a husband, or say that using "...your best memsahib tone – may help" (compare this to the haughty "suitable decorum" advised to the Victorian traveler and draw your own conclusion as to the colonialist attitude of this post-colonial advice). That said, women travelers today do not have to rely solely on printed travel guides as their Victorian predecessors once did and can access useful and supportive online communities aimed at solo women travelers (see for example, http://www.journeywoman.com which provides practical and inspirational advice to solo women travelers, or the numerous blogs listed here https://www.flipkey.com/blog/2014/11/03/top-25-solo-female-travel-bloggers-to-follow-in-2015 /).

Women today may travel under the facilitating patronage of aid organizations and several of the contributors to Jansz and Davies's "Women Travel", have undertaken charitable work abroad (Jansz & Davies, 1999). Working for such organizations offers several benefits: For example, it may allow women to travel without feeling selfish, or it may allow women to be in a place where they might otherwise not be allowed (Sarah Beattie, in "Women Travel" reports that despite strict Taliban rulings she was allowed to undertake her work designing wheelchairs in an all-male workshop in Afghanistan). Alternatively, voluntary organizations may offer some feeling of security and lend an air of "respectability." For example, in 1998/1999, I traveled with the British Council to Peru as a volunteer English teacher. While at my posting in the Andean highlands, the problem that local men had with me traveling as a lone woman was nearly always solved by my saying I worked for the British Council. Having traveled simply for pleasure in other countries I have found the "imaginary husband" to be far less use in explaining my lone situation than the respectable chaperoning of the British Council. Out of 14 volunteers, only three were men and many of the women volunteers to whom I spoke said they would feel nervous traveling by themselves. Given the aid organization's role as travel facilitator, I suggest that further research into the motivation of aid workers from a gender point of view would prove interesting. I would pose two questions: Firstly to see if the work was seen as an altruistic end in itself or whether, in fact, it facilitated leaving home in some way. Secondly, given that there appears to be more women volunteers than men, for example, anecdotally women are more likely than men to volunteer abroad (Huffington Post, 2015). Is this women demonstrating their independence or an extension of taking their role as carer with them when they travel?

In the absence, however, of a suitable chaperone women may use the persona of "honorary man" when traveling. In "Women Travel" Nicki McCormick describes her journey through Pakistan on a motorbike. She writes "...unaccompanied young women on motorcycles are so far removed from people's concept of 'female' as to be impossible..." (Jansz & Davies, 1999, p. 465) and continues that the locals often solved the problem she posed to their culture as a lone female by treating her as an "honorary man." I, too, was awarded this status while traveling in Morocco. At meal times Moroccan women generally eat after they have served the men, they then eat whatever is left over. As a guest in a Moroccan household, my hosts clearly thought it would be impolite for their visitor to wait for leftovers, so as an "honorary man" I was waited on by the women and was allowed to eat first with the men. This was a situation in which I felt deeply uncomfortable and demonstrates for me how assuming the role of a man may not solve the problem of inequality. As Enloe observes, women assuming a masculinized role serves simply to pose no threat to male to privilege, rather than to actually challenge it (Enloe, 1989). There is of course an ethical issue as to how to a woman should behave when faced with a culture which clearly compromises her feminist ideologies. If, for example, I had insisted on taking my turn with the other women, would this have forced my hosts to re-examine their attitudes to gender, or would I simply have appeared rude? Furthermore, to what extent would I have had the right to challenge the beliefs of others and would doing so simply be an example of cultural arrogance working "...very much within the colonialist legacy of carrying enlightenment from the West to the rest of the world" (Loomba, 1998, p. 230). It is easy to make assumptions yet Nicki McCormick who, like her Victorian predecessors is invited into the private female area of the home, is surprised to discover that "...none of the women I met...expressed the slightest urge to mix in the 'men's world'" (Jansz & Davies, 1999, p. 469). Recent research from Ahmad on tourism's impact on gender equality studying ethnic Baluchi women in Iran has positive findings and may indicate that, in some cultures at least, women are starting to question their role in society and see tourism as enabling them to do so (Ahmad, 2015, p. 172). The women in Ahmad's study mention that from women can learn about the alternative lifestyles of women in different cultures and that this may help them in the "...fight to overcome the traditional culture such as rejecting the Baluchis men's polygamy."

Eleanor Simmons in "Women Travel," also experiences some of the dilemmas that women face when confronted with cultural differences, describing how she managed to present a positive example to the women she met. Eleanor was invited by a family friend, Govind, to visit his aid organization in India. Govind proudly introduced her to the village women as a "strong woman" with the courage to travel to a far country. The women were attentive hosts and Eleanor, who felt that she was not worthy of such attention, was guilty and embarrassed to be waited on by the women. She was further embarrassed by the luxury of her compara-tive wealth and lifestyle and felt humbled by the back breaking work that the women undertook daily. In conclusion she realized that she should accept hospitality in whatever way it was given and that simply by being there as an independent woman, she could act as a positive role model. She writes,

...they were stronger than anyone I've ever met, yet they did not have the freedom I take for granted: To argue with men, to travel outside wherever they want, to spend money as they pleased. If they were to break free, they needed to lose their sense of inferiority, and that was where getting to know me was – in Govind's view – an education (Jansz & Davies, 1999, p. 273).

Clearly, "getting to know" Eleanor would be impossible if she were to travel simply employing the "male" tourist gaze, a gaze which objectifies the other rather than actually gets acquainted with it. Wearing and Wearing develop the idea of a more interactive tourism, taking on the concept of an area or "*chora*" where a style of feminized interactive tourism may take place as an alternative to the masculinized tourist gaze (Wearing & Wearing, 1996). The "*chora*" (described by Plato as between being and becoming) is an area "...where people actually interact with each other and people from the host community, their subjective experiences may enlarge or enhance the self" (Wearing & Wearing, 1996, p. 231). Enhancing the self, one hopes, of both host and guest. Paraphrasing Grosz (1995), Wearing and Wearing postulate that the "*chora*" not only facilitates a two way positive exchange, but that its implicit female qualities offer a way of re-appropriating public space for women, making way for "... women to reoccupy places from which they have been re/displaced or expelled and also expose men's appropriation of the whole of space" (Wearing & Wearing, 1996, p. 234). Wearing and Wearing continue that the tourist space "...may allow a 'becoming' beyond that possible at home" (Wearing & Wearing, 1996, p. 239).

Meisch also sees the tourist space as a liminal area which offers women the chance to experiment with their gender roles (Meisch, 1995), while Pruit and LaFont cite liminality coupled with "new economic power" as enabling women to have "...an identity beyond the confines of the traditional gender scripts offered in their cultures" (Pruit & LaFont, 1995, p. 423). Both Pruit and LaFont, and Meisch document the romantic encounters of women travelers with local men and their findings open the floor to further questions which, unfortunately, are outside the scope of this chapter. For example, how do the affairs of these women differ from the typically male search to experience difference and the "other" through "sexual adventures?" (Jokinen & Veijola, 1997). Recent research also confirms that the liminal and anonymous space offered through travel allows women a sense of sexual freedom and liberation which they may find difficult to assert at home. Based on a study of women's sexual behavior in tourism, Berdychevsky et al. (2013, p. 83) observe:

> ...tourism constitutes an arena in which women can practice resistance to oppressive gender roles and in so doing empower themselves. Although, surveillance does not vanish in tourist experiences, it is different from everyday scrutiny. By offering a venue for the expression of repressed desires, tourist experiences may provide women with a context for self-exploration and self-discovery, either through the expression of the authentic self or by experimentation with alternative identities.

However, does being sexually liberated encourage the myth that Western women are "easy?" This last question is particularly pertinent in the globalized village of the 21st century where images of Western women in pornography and even mainstream Hollywood that have traveled east may suggest that the women who feature in these films are more sexually willing than the women of the culture where these films are shown. During the colonial era men identified two types of women, those at home who were sexually pure and the native women who were purely sexual. Like the native women of the colonial era contemporary Western women may now be seen as available and exotic in some countries where they travel. Meanwhile, women in countries such as Thailand may continue to be seen as sexually exotic by Western men. In general it seems that women have now become the "other" themselves, offering "sexual promise," excitement and difference. A further challenge for women travelers is how they can conduct themselves safely and with dignity in the face of the world-wide man-made reputation of their sexual availability that has been constructed for them. The main strategies which women may adopt are those such as accommodating to fit in, "...modifying their dress, fitting to local (female) norms of behavior, remaining constantly aware, or removing themselves from places where they felt fearful" (Wilson & Little, 2008).

2.4 CONCLUSION

This chapter has shown that tourists can and do act as agents of social change and Western women can provide positive role models to women who have yet to challenge their own patriarchal systems. Travel is a fulfilling and rewarding experience and women continue to prove that we have as much right to wander freely in the world as men. However, from the similarities of the experiences of Victorian women and contemporary women it should be apparent that the position of women in today's society has not changed as much as we would like to believe and opportunities for leisure and tourism are still restricted. As Beck comments "...consciousness has rushed ahead of conditions..." and while rhetoric suggests that women have achieved equality, the reality is somewhat different (Beck, 1992, p. 104). It is also apparent that I have raised more questions than I have answered and evidently there is need for further research into gender and tourism and I suggest some possible areas. Firstly, Moss and Moss have suggested quite bluntly that "...the fear of rape does more to keep women 'safely at home' than anything else" (Moss & Moss, 1987, p. 214). This is somewhat anecdotal evidence, so I suggest that there is a need for further research comparing perceived risk by women travelers with actual risk. Secondly, how do women feel about compromising their feminist principles in order to be a "polite" guest? Building on the work of Ahmad (2015), we need to explore and understand the extent to which women can or should act as agents of social change. I end this chapter with two final questions: Should women attempt to alter attitudes of clearly patriarchal societies? Is there is universal understanding of what it means to be an empowered woman and how can this be enacted through travel? These are ongoing questions which could drive future research on the contemporary independent woman traveler.

KEYWORDS

- experience
- development
- restricting factor
- responsibilities
- Victorian women travelers
- constraints
- empowerment
- historical perspectives on travel

REFERENCES

Ahmad, R. S. The Impact of Ethnic Tourism on Gender Equality: A Case Study of Iran's Baluchistan Women. *Tourism*. **2015**, *63*(2), 161–174.

Beck, U. *Risk Society: Towards a New Modernity;* Sage: London,1992; Vol. 17, p 272.

Berdychevsky, L.; Gibson, H.; Poria, Y. Women's Sexual Behavior in Tourism: Loosening the Bridle. *Ann. Tour. Res*. **2013**, *42*, 65–85.

Buzzard, J. *The Beaten Track: European Tourism, Leisure and the Ways to Culture, 1800–1918;* Oxford University Press: Oxford, UK, 1993.

Craik, J. The Culture of Tourism in Rojek. In *Touring Cultures: Transformations of Travel and Theory;* Craik, J., Urry, J., Eds.; Routledge: London, 1997; pp 113–136.

Deem, R. *All Work and No Play: The Sociology of Women and Leisure;* Open University Press: Milton Keynes, 1986.

Deem, R. Women, the City and Holidays. *Leis. Stud*. **1996**, *15*, 105–119.

Enloe, C. *Bananas, Beaches and Bases: Making Feminist Sense of International Politics*; University of California Press: Worcester, 1989; p 244.

ESRC. *Analysing the Fear of Crime Using the British Crime Survey*; ESRC: UK, 2013.

Fanghanel, A. Approaching/Departure: Effacement, Erasure and 'Undoing' the Fear of Crime. *Cult. Geogr*. **2014**, *21*(3), 343–361.

Fiefer, M. *Going Places: The Ways of the Tourist from Imperial Rome to the Present Day;* Macmillan: London,1985; p 288.

Foster, S. *New Worlds: Nineteenth Century Women Travelers and their Writings;* Harvester Wheat Sheaf: Loughborough, Hertfordshire, 1990.

Green, E.; Hebron, S.; Woodward, D. *Women's Leisure? What Leisure?* Macmillan: London, 1990.

Hall, D.; Kinnaird, V. *Tourism: Gender Perspectives*; John Wiley: Chichester, West Sussex, 1994. *Huffington Post 2015; Why do More Women Volunteer Abroad than Men?* http://www.huffingtonpost.com/ealan-parker/why-do-more-women-volunte_b_5483375.html (accessed May 8, 2015).

Jansz, N.; Davies, M. *Women Travel: First-hand Accounts from More than 60 Countries*; Penguin: London, 1999.

Jokinen, E. Veijola, S. The Culture of Tourism. In *Touring Cultures: Transformations of Travel and Theory;* Rojek, C., Urry, J., Eds.; Routledge: London, 1997; 23–51

Khan, S. Gendered Leisure: Are Women More Constrained in Travel for Leisure? *J. Tour*. **2011**, *6*(1), 105–121.

Lonely Planet.; *India*; Lonely Planet: Australia, 1990.

Loomba, A. *Colonialism/Post-Colonialism;* Routledge: London, 1998.

Meisch, L. Gringas and Otavaleños: Changing Tourist Relations. *Ann. Tour. Res*. **1995**, *22*(2), 441–462.

McCarthy, A. *Get up and Go: A Travel Survival Kit for Women;* Attic Press: Dublin, 1992.

McGehee, N. G.; Loker-Murphy, L.; Uysal, M. The Australian International Pleasure Travel Market: Motivations from a Gendered Perspective. *J. Tour. Stud*. **1996**, *7*(1), 45–57.

Middleton, D. *Victorian Lady Travelers*; Routledge & Kegan Paul: London, 1965.

Mills, S. *Discourses of Difference: An Analysis of Women's Travel Writing and Colonialism;* Routledge: London, 1993.

Morris, M. *Maiden Voyages*; Vintage Departures: New York, 1993.

Moss, G.; Moss, M. *Handbook for Women Travelers;* Piatkus: London, 1987.

Pruit, D.; La Font, A. For Love and Money: Romance Tourism in Jamaica. *Ann. Tour. Res.* **1995,** *22*(2), 422–440.

Robinson, J. *Wayward Women: A Guide to Women Travelers*; Oxford University Press: Oxford, UK, 1990.

Rojek, C. *Ways of Escape: Modern Transformations in Leisure and Travel*; Macmillan: London, 1993.

Rojek, C.; Urry, J. *Touring Cultures: Transformations of Travel and Theory*; Routledge: London, 1997.

Said, E. *Orientalism;* Routledge & Kegan Paul: London, 1978.

Sharpley, R. *Tourism, Tourists and Society;* ELM Publications: Huntingdon, Cambridgeshire, 1999.

Singh, J. G. *Colonial Narratives, Cultural Dialogues: 'Discoveries' of India in the Language of Colonialism;* Routledge: London, 1996.

The Guardian. Women: See You in a Week, Darling, April 11, 2000, pp 4–5.

The Telegraph. UK Has Sixth-Largest Male-Female Pay Gap in EU. http://www.telegraph.co.uk/finance/jobs/11453093/Britain-has-sixth-largest-male-female-pay-gap-in-EU.html (accessed May 8, 2015).

Urry, J. *Tourist Gaze: Leisure and Travel in Contemporary Societies;* Sage: London,1990.

Wearing, B.; Wearing, S. Refocusing the Tourist Experience: The *Flâneur* and the *Choraster*. *Leis. Stud.* **1996,** *15,* 229–243.

Wilson, E.; Little, D. The Solo Female Travel Experience: Exploring the 'Geography of Women's Fear'. *Curr. Issues Tour.* **2008,** *11*(2), 167–186.

Wolff, J. The Invisible *Flâneuse*: Women and the Literature of Modernity. *Theor. Cul.Soc.* **1985,** *2*(3), 37–47.

Woodward, D.; Green, E. 'Not Tonight Dear!' The Social Control of Women's Leisure. In *Relative Freedoms: Women and Leisure;* Wimbush, E., Talbot, M., Eds.; Open University Press: Milton Keynes, 1988; 131–146.

CHAPTER 3

OPPORTUNITY TO ESCAPE: THE OE AND NEW ZEALAND WOMEN TRAVELERS

JUDE WILSON

Department of Tourism, Sport and Society, Lincoln University, New Zealand

E-mail: jude.wilson@lincoln.ac.nz

CONTENTS

3.1   INTRODUCTION

Every year, for over six decades, thousands of young New Zealanders have departed on the travel and working holiday experience popularly known as the Overseas Experience ("OE"). The "classic OE" is a two-three year experience during which proponents live and work in the United Kingdom and travel extensively (Wilson, 2006). The OE began as a response to New Zealand's geographical and cultural isolation and developed into a travel phenomenon in its own right—so that "doing an OE" became the goal (Wilson, 2014). A noteworthy characteristic of the OE's early decades was a disproportionate number of female travelers taking this "opportunity to escape." The development of the OE and the establishment of a "travel template"—followed by thousands of other New Zealanders over subsequent decades—can be described through these women's travel experiences.

This chapter examines the experiences of women travelers on the OE during the 1950s, 1960s, and 1970s. Although the term "OE" did not come into use until the 1980s, those who traveled in earlier decades are comfortable with their travel experiences being encapsulated as such. The chapter is arranged in seven sections. The first two sections—Foundations of a Travel Phenomenon and The OE—are contextual. This is followed by an outline of the research methodology. Then, the three decades of the OE are described according to their underlying characteristics: the "opportunity to escape" that emerged in the 1950s; the "swinging sixties;" and the freedom of the 1970s. The chapter concludes with a discussion on the legacy of the OE, in respect of the women who went and for the OE phenomenon itself.

3.1.1   FOUNDATIONS OF A TRAVEL PHENOMENON

As a colonial nation, New Zealand was settled by people with a propensity to travel, but it was the Second World War and post-war migration in particular, which laid the foundations for the OE. In an era of expensive travel, going to war was the only way most people could gain a form of overseas experience and servicemen and women represented the largest group of New Zealand travelers to depart in the first half of the twentieth century. Of the 140,000 New Zealanders who served overseas during the course of the Second World War, however, only around 1400 were female.

Records show that 629 of these were nurses, 541 were Volunteer (nurse) Aids serving in the Women's Auxiliary Army Corps (WAAC) (Kendall & Corbett, 1990), and around 200 more served with WAAC in welfare and clerical roles (Hall, 2004). Rogers notes that the nurses who enlisted did so for the same reasons as their male counterparts—duty, patriotism, and "adventure" (Rogers, 2003).

New Zealand (men's) war travel tales are well documented: in *The Soldier Tourist,* for example, Brewer describes the 10 countries he visited during the war (Brewer,1999); others published accounts of their post-war return visits to the places they had served (e.g., Allison, 1961,1969; Mason, 1964). By contrast, few stories have been published of New Zealand women traveling during these years. The exception are those appearing in a number of volumes—often focused on issues of national identity—recounting the overseas experiences of the social and cultural elite who left New Zealand in order to further their talents and advance their careers (e.g., Harris, 1971; Grayland, 1972).

The first post-war decade introduced travel to the masses and, from the 1950s onward, the number of New Zealanders going overseas increased dramatically because of a combination of factors. New Zealand's links with Britain remained strong as assisted immigration brought many British migrants to New Zealand; throughout the 1950s and 1960s and into the 1970s the returning migrant ships provided easily accessible transport out of New Zealand. The reasons for these opportunities being taken up can be attributed to post-war economic growth and social change in New Zealand (Wilson, 2014). "Britain" is used throughout this chapter as it was not until the 1970s that "UK" was widely used in the New Zealand lexicon; UK has been used to denote the broader OE experience.

For residents of distant New Zealand, having available transport was key to travel facilitation. The 1960s represented the peak decade for passenger shipping (in 1967—the peak year—97,800 passengers traveled to and from New Zealand by sea). The decline in passenger shipping came rapidly as airfares and travel times fell as a result of changing aircraft technology and introduction of jet services. Measured in 2015 values, an Auckland–London return fare fell from $34,965 in 1950, to $19,753 in 1960 and to a mere $8633 in 1973 (Reserve Bank of New Zealand, 2015). A similar return fare today is around $2500. International travel (and the OE) became more egalitarian in the 1970s in response to these falling transport costs and increasing wealth and social change in New Zealand.

3.1.2   THE OE

It is difficult to estimate exactly how many people have been on an OE. In migration statistics they most likely equate to those recorded as New Zealand residents departing long-term (i.e., for more than 12 months). Figure 3.1 shows the increase in these departures through the 1950s, 1960s, and into the 1970s: annual departures averaged 8,200 in the 1950s and 18,600 in the 1960s. The 15–24 year age group (which would have included most OE departures) represented 24.3% of long-term departures in 1951, this proportion increasing to 30.2 and 39.5% in 1961 and 1970, respectively.

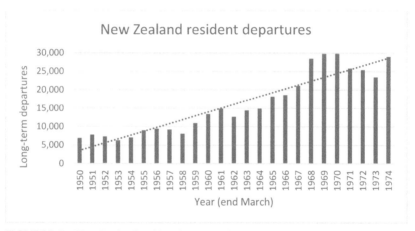

FIGURE 3.1   New Zealand resident long-term departures (Source: Statistics New Zealand, 2015).

Increases in the numbers traveling in the 1970s were directly related to the earliest of the baby boomer population cohort reaching adulthood. Although the sea journey had all but ceased, travel by air and land (along the Hippie Trail) delivered thousands of young New Zealanders to the United Kingdom and Europe. Average annual departures reached 27,000 in the first five years of the 1970s and, by 1973, the 20–24 year age group represented 49% of all long-term departures. Within the OE age departing population, females outnumbered males in 20 of the 25 years starting 1950.

Historical circumstances, geographical factors, and socio-cultural links established Britain (and London) as the foremost destination for these early travelers (Wilson, 2006). The New Zealand school syllabus and culture were strongly Anglocentric (Easthope, 1993). Until 1964, passports were labeled "British passport, New Zealand." New Zealanders could live and work in Britain with no restriction until the mid-1970s. Having a common language and similar qualifications were advantageous. As the descendants of migrants, many New Zealanders still had family connections in Britain. "British" family was commonly perceived to be useful as initial support and contact points. They also often provided the impetus to travel beyond London to more remote parts of the British Isles. Some found staying with family stifling and preferred their independence, others were excited to meet the unknown people who had sent cards and gifts at Christmas throughout their lives (Wilson, 2014). It was also reassuring for the parents back home in New Zealand that their offspring— particularly females—had someone to "keep an eye on them."

While OE experiences were facilitated by these colonial antecedents (with both the migrant ships and migrant population playing a role), an individual's OE experiences were driven and shaped in part by their New Zealand cultural identity. This included a perceived propensity to travel, having a can-do attitude, being adventurous, and being less constrained by social conventions than their forebears (although the latter was also facilitated by the OE taking them so far from the watching eyes of home) (Wilson, 2014).

3.2 METHODOLOGY

The chapter draws on data collected via in-depth interviews with 17 female OE travelers, the majority of whom departed New Zealand during the 1960s and 1970s (eight from each decade). Respondents were found via snowball sampling. It was more difficult to find respondents who departed during the 1950s as these women are currently aged in their 80s and 90s. As a result, 1950s OE departures are represented by only one interviewee, but are also described via the detailed OE account provided in the self-published volume of letters home sent by Mary Dudson (1995) and by several stories published in McCarter's OE collection (McCarter, 2001). A search of the library holdings, particularly in New Zealand reference collections, provided additional material. The chapter draws on seven published accounts of individual OEs and several volumes of collected OE stories pertaining to women OE travelers in these decades. When reporting interview data names have been changed, square brackets refer to a respondent's year of departure (e.g., Rose, 1950). The author-ship of published material is attributed in the normal way. Both interview and published data were supported by travel ephemera associated with these early OE travel experiences. This ephemera included the tickets, brochures, and other souvenirs kept by respondents, as well as material found in the National Library Archives in New Zealand. In addition, the chapter draws on travel data published in newspapers (e.g., passenger ship departures and ticket prices) in both New Zealand and London. The *NZ UK News* (an expatriate London publication) also provided records of employment opportunities, travel information, and social events relating to these decades.

3.3   OPPORTUNITY TO ESCAPE

In the 1950s, the OE offered New Zealand women their opportunity to escape—both from geographic isolation and the restrictions of New Zealand society. The travel stories of returning soldiers had fueled their interest in the world beyond New Zealand shores. Mary Dudson left New Zealand in 1950 and in 1995, at the insistence of her grandchildren, published her weekly letters home. In these she noted that "the whole spirit of the letters was to allay her [*mother's*] fears that I was not starving, or cold, or beset by danger and that the world out there, which she never knew, was full of the most diverse, entertaining and wonderful people" (Dudson, 1995, p.1).

Going on an OE was overwhelmingly an adventure into the unknown. In some ways it was easier for women to depart than it was for men: men were expected to devote their energies to establish a career and saving to purchase either a house or a piece of land—with a plan to build a house—before they married. To go overseas on a working holiday, taking casual jobs would be irresponsible. For women the OE presented a "time filler" before their (inevitable) marriage. It was not uncommon for women to get engaged before going on their OE, leaving their fiancés behind.

The cost of travel was a major obstacle for many: a one-way fare in a six-berth cabin on the Rangitikei in 1951, for example, cost the equivalent of NZ$4275 in 2015 value (Wilson, 2006). For many female travelers, gaining the requisite parental permission presented an even bigger hurdle. In 1950, Rose wanted so badly to travel that when her father offered her the choice of either money or having a party for her 21st birthday, she did not hesitate before picking the money. However, she then had to find someone to accompany her, as her parents would not let her go alone. She eventually left two years later with a girl she worked with—their departure was announced in the local newspaper.

For these early travelers the travel experience (and excitement) started the minute they departed New Zealand on the long ship voyage. Rose, for example, was not only leaving home for the first time, but it was her first time on a ship ("you didn't even know if you were a decent sailor or not"). She recalled that there were many more girls than boys on the ship, reflecting "I think the boys had to stay at home and work;" of the 57 passengers who joined the *RMS Orion* in New Zealand for her voyage, 27 were listed as a "Miss" and only 10 were listed as a single "Mr" (married couples were listed as a couple). It was common for unmarried couples to travel on different ships.

Time on the 4–6 week ship journey was fully occupied by deck sports, entertainment, and other social events. There was the much anticipated party to celebrate crossing the equator and port calls to exotic places. In 1950 Mary Dudson traveled via Panama ("so different from home") and Curacao (where she noted the "newness of the cars"); Rose's Orient Line voyage (departing Sydney) went "the other way," visiting Melbourne, Adelaide, Freemantle, Colombo, Aden ("I remember all the flies"), Port Said, Sicily, Marseille, and Gibraltar before sailing down the Thames to the Royal Albert Docks. The cheaper ships of the Greek and Italian shipping lines reduced both the time and cost of sea travel. However, while younger passengers would happily go on the cheaper ships, their parents (who sometimes contributed to the ticket purchase) were often a little fussier, insisting they sail on the "English" ships of the P&O Orient and Shaw Savill lines, or with the New Zealand Shipping Company.

The cost of the voyage to Britain (and the length of time it took) determined that these early travelers were away from New Zealand for several years, necessitating working for at least some of their time away. The common female professions of the era—nursing, teaching, and secretarial work—proved to be excellent travel jobs. Mary Dudson wrote that her mother was reassured by Mary having a pre-arranged job in England. The British "teach yourself book," *Traveling Abroad* included a chapter on "traveling for adventure;" the author illustrated the importance of having solid qualifications using four New Zealand girls as an example (Dunbar, 1957). These girls, united by the motive to travel, had found work teaching, in retail and in secretarial positions; it was noted that their employers admired their enterprise and looked favorably on them when they requested extra time off to travel (Dunbar, 1957).

Live-in jobs were conducive to saving for travel and often also ensured better living conditions than found in rented flats. However, flatmates were easily found among friends and acquaintances from home and new friends met on-board ship on the way over. Adjusting to life in Britain was challenging. London in the 1950s was dirty (compared with New Zealand) and war damage was still visible. As Mary Dudson noted, "rationing was still in force but different from our New Zealand arrangement" (Dudson,1995, p.23). While many sought jobs in the country areas which were "more like home," London had considerable appeal for outings to enjoy cultural and sporting outings and meeting friends. Before departing New Zealand young travelers were often recommended the Overseas Visitors Club (OVC) as a budget London accommodation option. Established in 1954 in Earl's Court by two South Africans and an Australian, in its heyday the OVC provided accommodation, restaurants and bars, a nightclub, an employment agency, a *post-restante* office, a theatre booking office, and a travel agency.

Currency restrictions in the post-war decades also made travel difficult. In New Zealand, Reserve Bank permission was required to take money out of the country. In 1968, for example, the daily allowance was $14 with a maximum of $1400 allowed per trip (Reserve Bank of New Zealand, 1968). In Britain a basic personal allowance for travel abroad of £100 per year was introduced in 1945 with the amount varying according to the balance of payments situation (Bank of England, 1967). Mary Dudson wrote of how she "wangled the money" needed for a European trip by buying some of a friend's unused allowance. Paying in advance for a tour was a way around these restrictions, although such tours attracted relatively few other young travelers. Rose paid £57.15s.0d for a 15-day European tour in 1951. This equates to a 2014 income equivalent of £5571 (Officer & Williamson, 2014). The Belgian, German, and Italian visas she needed cost an additional £3.4s.9d (~£312 in 2014). She recalled being pleased that the son of one of the families on the tour was able to chaperone her and her friend to nightclubs and other places, to which otherwise, as single females, they would have been unable to go.

Independent travel held the most appeal for these young—and budget conscious—New Zealanders. While Mary Dudson traveled "independently" in Europe in the early 1950s she recounts spending the morning at Thomas Cook and Sons making decisions about her route and organizing the required train tickets and accommodation in youth hostels. The 1950s travelers relied heavily on the Youth Hostel handbook and map, and on word of mouth information from other travelers. To save money hitchhiking was common: Rose hitched extensively around Britain, but switched to public transport in Ireland because her relatives there did not approve of girls hitchhiking.

In *The Big OE* Nigel McCarter retells several female travel stories from the 1950s (McCarter, 2001). In one, three girls purchased bicycles and fitted them out with pannier bags and carriers telling the shop owner they were "going to explore Europe by bike. That caused quite a stir. It just wasn't done for three girls to go off cycling around Europe. But we were Kiwis and we could do anything" (McCarter, 2001, p.15). In another tale, after disembarking their ship in Naples, two New Zealand girls set off to hitchhike the rest of the way to London; in later travels the same pair took a ship to Bergen in Norway before hitchhiking back through Scandinavia and France. Mary Dudson recalls "first studying maps in [*the*] German [*language*] in Austria and setting off to hitch on the '*Eisenbahn*' only to discover it was the railway, hence we took the train" (Dudson, 1995, p.340).

By the end of the 1950s a handful of published travel accounts appeared describing early (and somewhat adventurous) travel experiences. One of these New Zealand travelers was Louise Sutherland who, in 1951, set out from London to cycle through Europe and the Middle East to India. In her account of the trip, *I Follow the Wind,* she wrote "After all, I thought to myself as I cycled, I HAD left home to see the world. There was £40 in my pocket. My entire savings since I had arrived in England nine months before. My time was entirely my own" (Sutherland, c.1960, p. 1). Louise was a nurse and, having arrived penniless in Beirut, easily found work for a few months. Another published travel account told the story of *Four Kiwis and a Falcon* traveling overland for 94,000 miles, through 50 countries in 21 months; two of the four were female (Harford, 1970).

The standard of living rose sharply throughout the 1950s in Britain with increased private car ownership, the introduction of paid holidays and development of package tours contributing to a growing demand for travel. Package tours gradually became cheaper, more flexible and catered to increasingly diverse, but often specialized, markets. One of the first youth tours was a 21-day "Young Commonwealth Special" tour of the Continent in 1958; the company running the tour was based in the OVC and suggests an increasing number of young colonials traveling from a London base (Wilson, 2014).

The 1950s OE experience was equal parts escape and adventure although, as the numbers departing New Zealand increased and a range of services emerged to cater for their needs, the adventure aspect was becoming diluted. The home (escape) and away (adventure) facets of the OE were also presented in different ways. As might be expected, published accounts focused on more adventurous (away) experiences of the OE, whereas interview data included considerable reflection on the escape (from home) aspect of the OE.

3.3.1 THE "SWINGING SIXTIES"

By the 1960s the OE had become a much easier proposition from a New Zealand perspective; as Anne (1962) explained, there was still an "expectation of working—not really in a career job—simply to fill in time until getting married" and the OE had become an accepted way to fill in that time. These OE travelers were very young. Brenda (1962) recalled that because she was under 21, and a woman, she had to have a guarantor—her father had to sign a form to say he would be responsible for any bills she had. Gwen (1968) was only 20 when she left on her OE but "at that time people were getting married at 21, so you still had to fit it into a window of freedom." Statistics New Zealand data show that the average age of women entering their first marriage in 1960 was 21.9 years; in 2014 it was 30.4 years. Colleen (1968) had left a romance in New Zealand ("the boyfriend was letting me do it, but he didn't want to go") and was heartbroken when "he didn't want to stay the distance." Claire (1965) went overseas because "it's what you did. I had been nursing and had no prospects at that stage of being married—so the next thing was to go overseas." Brenda (1962) agreed, noting that "The only way girls could leave home—without it being a slur on their parents' name—was to either go to another city to study or go overseas." Brenda added that she planned to be away for about two years, "but you didn't look too far ahead because if you did all you saw was suburbia and nappies and predictability and it just didn't bear thinking about—you put all that off."

Alongside the increasing social acceptance of the OE in New Zealand was a growing cultural confidence. Colleen (1968) reflected:

> I think we went because New Zealand was so isolated and even television was fairly new then – so our window on the world was very, very limited. The freedom of being overseas was a bonus but it wasn't just that – we were armed with confidence as we came from a land of full employment – we were armed with bravado, but it wasn't a false one.

Anne (1962) recalled the sense of security she felt having been given a year leave of absence from her job in New Zealand; arriving in London she went to the OVC, took a job with the same insurance firm she had worked for in New Zealand and traveled to remote places (all of which she described as being "just what you did"). She recalled London being "looser than New Zealand" and of being "aware of the drug scene in Amsterdam."

The OVC was a focal point around which an extensive OE support network was developing. By the 1960s Earl's Court had become popularly known as "Kangaroo Valley" because of the number of young colonials living and socializing in the area. Attitudes toward the OVC (and Earl's Court) were mixed, with some enjoying the expatriate community experience and others seeking more authentic English experiences. Most recognized their own "foreignness." Bella (1966) recalled being "a special case within the class system" and that the only time her and her flatmates ate meat "was when the family sent it from New Zealand." Many of these girls reported feeling like "country bumpkins" when they arrived in London, but as Linda (1964) commented "London was swinging in the 1960s—with the Beatles and Mary Quant and Carnaby Street—it was a good time to be there." London was less intimidating because they had the support of flatmates, many of whom were New Zealanders; each also had individual New Zealand friends and extensive expatriate social networks developed.

These young colonials were part of a growing youth travel phenomenon. The first guide in the "Let's Go" series was published in 1961 and, although very American-focused, was the first practical guide book aimed at youth travelers. For young colonials, independent travel was still popular and taking one's own vehicle became more common. While couples traveling together purchased cars, the joint purchase of a van made more sense for groups of friends. All-female groups were also a common occurrence. Bella (1966) recalled her group being so poor traveling that "we stopped and stole food from fields—I still managed to buy leather boots when we got to Italy though!" Others recalled horrendous break-down stories that curtailed trips. Most of the other people met traveling were other colonials. With increasing numbers of young travelers based in London, some of the entrepreneurial among them seized on the opportunity to fund their own travels by taking others "on tour." The cheap camping tour of Europe was born and, while most tour companies were established by males, the passengers were mainly female. The first ever Contiki tour, for example, carried 10 females and only two males (one of whom was the driver/guide) (Anderson, 2010). Other tours were similar—in 1963 Brenda went on an eight-week Europe tour with "18 girls plus the driver and another man he brought along for moral support—neither got mixed up with any girl on the trip." Likewise, on Anne's 1962 tour there were only five or six males out of 22 passengers and with "six to a tent you were either going to be enemies or friends for life." Anne also recalled that tours were not very organized with passengers "dropped off in the middle of town squares in Europe and told to just walk around;" she bought her own guide book for each place they visited. One story in *The Big OE* describes the *ad hoc* nature of these tours, with passengers responsible for purchasing and cooking their own food (often with limited equipment) and setting up their own campsites (McCarter, 2001).

The 1960s also brought some changes in the OE work experience. Nursing, teaching, and secretarial skills were still considered important job skills, but an OE work experience that incorporated a novelty aspect was often sought after. Brenda (1962) worked for a time in the Scilly Isles picking daffodils rather than taking a well-paid nursing job, simply because "the last thing we wanted to do was recreate that nine to five thing we'd already had at home." One of the 1960s stories in *The Big OE* tells of two New Zealand girls being bored with the Scottish life and weather and, having heard of possibility of earning a lot of money working on the fishing fleet in Iceland, were on their way within two weeks. They were the first New Zealanders in the part of Iceland they worked (McCarter, 2001).

While word of mouth was an important source of both work and travel information in these early decades, travelers also relied on advertisements posted on notice boards at the OVC and at New Zealand House in London. The *NZ UK News* also published increasing amounts of practical information for the growing community of expatriate New Zealanders living in London.

3.3.2   FREEDOM OF THE 1970s

By the 1970s, as travel costs reduced and a large population cohort reached traveling age, the numbers going on OE increased significantly. In New Zealand the OE had become the norm (at least for some segments of the population) (Wilson, 2006). *Down Under in Europe*, the first OE-specific guide book appeared in 1973, normalized the OE even more (Miles & Bolot, 1973). This publication was notable for including advice on finding accommodation and work, as well as being a travel guide. For females, the guide noted that "mixed flatting is popular in London though not so popular with parents back home in the Antipodes" (p.17) and advised that female travelers not to write home and tell parents that they "intend becoming a barmaid (topless or otherwise), Bhuddist (sic), Hari-Krishna, hippie or drop-out" (p.58). Despite this advice, working behind a bar (particularly in London) became one of the more popular OE jobs for women. Bar jobs were easy to pick-up and convenient in that they offered free accommodation and did not have to be taken too seriously, or for too long (Wilson, 2006).

In the 1970s working on Israeli kibbutz became popular, joining the Iceland fish factory and flower picking in the Scilly Islands as jobs that were—in later decades—recognized as "legendary" OE jobs (Wilson, 2014). Published OE stories of the 1970s told of increasingly exotic OE work and life experiences. *The Big OE* stories include one girl working as a nanny for a Saudi Arabian princess, living in a harem at the king's palace. Another girl's first job in France was working for a Vicomtesse who was a former Europe champion horsewoman; finding it a bit lonely she eventually left the job for a "round of the usual pub and teaching jobs" (McCarter, 2001, p. 141). *Dancing Naked* tells the story of a New Zealand Sunday school teacher who became an erotic dancer in Amsterdam and then spent two years in the chorus line at the Folies Bergère ("wearing feather, jewels and gloves—and not much else") (Austin, 1998), back page. The story of a nurse, who traveling in the Middle East met and married a tour guide in Petra, is told in *Married to a Bedouin* (Van Gelder-malsen, 2006). Woodward Swinburn met her Iranian husband in London; her story of later moving to Iran with him is told in *The Scent of Rosewater* (Woodward Swinburn, 1998).

In Western Europe an ever-increasing number of tourists and tourism development made travel more expensive (and some destinations less appealing) for many of those on OE. Travel horizons were widened to incorporate the Middle East and countries along the Hippie Trail; the latter also, conveniently, provided an alternative method of travel between New Zealand and the OE at a time when passenger shipping was in decline and air travel was still expensive. *Down Under in Europe* described (and critiqued) the different ways of traveling the overland Asia route: best was by private vehicle, provided one was well equipped and prepared for anything; hitchhiking was risky and uncomfortable; and rail travel was "cheap and still adventuresome"(Miles & Bolot, 1973, p.12). The simplest way to travel was by bus tour, and although this option was much more expensive it still involved "roughing it" (p.13).

New Zealanders were well represented across all types of overland travel and accounts on www.overlandbiz.com (an overland website) suggest that female travelers were overrepresented on these overland bus tours. Meanwhile the European camping tours, while still popular, became both more sophisticated and expensive, reducing their appeal for many of those on OE. Miles and Bolot did, however, recommend them for travel to destinations beyond the Iron Curtain where independent travel was hampered by bureaucratic difficulties (Miles & Bolot, 1973).

3.3.3 THE LEGACY OF THE OE

The 1950s OE travelers went in search of adventure and—reflecting the social mores of that decade in both New Zealand and Europe—their OEs were relatively (at least compared to those of later decades) sedate, restrained, and serious. The 1960s took OE travelers from a relatively quiet (and socially repressed) New Zealand to "swinging sixties" London and their OEs reflect the excitement of encountering this new world. From the 1970s onwards, advances in gender equality in New Zealand extended to the OE. For men, the 1970s brought more freedom from career and adulthood responsibilities and the number of men going on OEs increased. The 1970s gave women greater social freedom both at home and across all aspects of the OE experience.

However, although women on OE in the 1970s enjoyed greater social freedom than their predecessors, the OE itself became more restrictive as a result of tightening British immigration regulations, associated with their entry into the European Union. The working holiday visa, introduced at the start of the 1970s, allowed a generous five-year stay but this was reduced to only two years by the end of the decade (Wilson, 2014). The terms of the working holiday visa also restricted those on OE to work that was secondary to their holiday. The number of other OE travelers around, the consolidation of an OE support network in London (which by the 1970s included many OVC type clubs, OE-specific employment agencies, and travel companies) and the increase in tourism more generally, also diminished the sense of adventure and excitement that had defined the OE in its earlier decades.

While by the 1970s many of the practices of the OE had become more prescribed, the same themes underpinned the OE throughout these three decades: the OE exposed one to social and cultural difference, it was a search for adventure, it involved roughing it and financial hardship and it was about experiencing, albeit temporally, a different life to that in New Zealand. Just how easy that was changed considerably over these three decades. Crucially, by the 1970s some of the challenge had gone from the OE experience—following a well-worn path to London, where thousands of other New Zealanders were already in residence, packaged the "opportunity" while restricting the degree of "escape" the OE could offer.

While both the practitioners and the practices of the OE changed significantly over time, these three decades were fundamental to the development of an OE template which has subsequently been followed by thousands of other New Zealanders, both men and women. Although the number of males departing on OE had increased, female dominance in OE departures continued. For example, since 1979, between 5 and 12% more females (than males) in the 20–30 year age group have departed long-term to the United Kingdom as country of next residence (Wilson, 2014). The world to which these young women were escaping also changed considerably, and this in turn impacted on the type of challenge the OE experience presented for its practitioners.

Perhaps the most challenging aspect of the OE which persists to this day is the return home. Returning to their (previous) New Zealand life was a significant challenge as these female travelers were (often irrevocably) changed by their OEs. It was common to arrive home with no money—in Mary Dudson's last letter to her mother (which she wrote from Freemantle) she asked that "You had better bring some extra money to Wellington with you when you come as I am likely to be quite short" (Dudson, 1995, p. 334). Colleen (1968) spent every penny she had on travel and eventually returned to New Zealand in debt to her parents. Another 1960s OE story told of a girl who got pregnant to a Scottish waiter on the *Northern Star*. Apparently she could not find the father again and eventually arrived home from her OE with—to her mother's surprise—a baby (NZ UK News, 2002, p. 4). One 1970s returnee recalled shocking her parents when she arriving back in Auckland wearing a Bedouin costume (McCarter, 2001). These return home experiences also reflect the underlying characteristics of each decade—the formality of the 1950s, the irresponsibility of the "swinging sixties" and the freedoms of the 1970s.

3.4   CONCLUSION

The history of the OE is a colorful history of women travelers and describes societal and cultural change in both New Zealand and in the countries these travelers visited. OE travelers provided the catalyst for the development of many travel businesses and opportunities that underpin contemporary youth travel practices. The OE is an important travel phenomenon in its own right and these early women travelers contributed significantly to its development. The OE is still widely practiced today and the OE is regarded as part of "ordinary" life in New Zealand for those participating in it, so much so that departure overseas on an OE is seen as an almost requisite "rite of passage" (Wilson, 2006).

The OE, and the escape and the opportunities it offered, also left a personal legacy to its many practitioners. As Jenny (1973) reflected "OE gave me a travel yen that has never abated and given me a permanent interest in international affairs and other cultures." Claire (1965) described how the OE "stretches your boundaries in ways that you cannot anticipate." Diane Brown's travel memoir of her 1970s OE was published as *Liars and Lovers*: on meeting her family at the airport on her return she writes "They don't know I'm not the same person any more" and then goes on to reflect that "Travel changes you, people say, and of course it does... [*but*] New Zealand had also changed in my absence, or was it just that I saw it differently?" (Brown, 2004, p. 240–241).

For these women travelers, the OE presented an escape from home and from New Zealand society that was unprecedented at the time. Historically, outbound travel from New Zealand had been male-dominated and associated with the patriotic duties of war and, as such, was easily assimilated into social expectations and constraints. Post-war, men were subject to greater social pressures in respect of their career and life responsibilities, while women had more freedom to experiment and to simply experience life, albeit with considerable social constraints. As a result, life overseas for these women travelers also presented a greater escape from home than it did for their male compatriots. The dominance of female travelers in its formative years both contributed to and impacted on the OE practices enjoyed by both genders in subsequent decades. These early female travelers also played a key role in the establishment of social expectations surrounding gender equality in New Zealand today.

KEYWORDS

- **travelers**
- **OE**
- **colonials**
- **New Zealand**
- **history**

REFERENCES

Allison, E. S. *Kiwi at Large;* Robert Hale Limited: London, 1961; Vol. 8, p 190.

Allison, E. S. *Kiwi Vagabond;* The Travel Book Club: London, 1969.

Anderson, J. *Only Two Seats Left;* The Great Gathering Company: Australia, 2010; p 304.

Austin, M. *Dancing Naked: An Exhibitionist Revealed;* Random House: Auckland, New Zealand, 1998; p 215.

Bank of England . The UK Exchange Control: A Short History. http://www.bankofengland.co.uk /archive/Documents/historicpubs/qb/1967/qb67q3245260.pdf (accessed April 27, 2015).

Brewer, Gunner. N. H. (Joe). *The Soldier Tourist: A Personal Account of World War 11;* Reed Books: Auckland, New Zealand, 1999; Vol. 8, p 231.

Brown, D. *Liars and Lovers: A the Tourist Gaze. Leisure and Travel in Contemporary Society Travel Memoir;* Random House: Auckland, New Zealand, 2004.

Dudson, M. *Oamaru to Europe: 'What Do You Want to Go There for?';* Kitchen Table Top Publishing: Christchurch, New Zealand, 1995; p 342.

Dunbar, J. *Travelling Abroad;* The English Universities Press Ltd: London, 1957; p 152.

Easthope, J. *Home Away from Home: The Recent History of Overseas Travel by New Zealanders to Britain, C. 1960–1975;* Unpublished Honors Research Paper, Victoria University: Wellington, New Zealand, 1993.

Grayland, E. *More Famous New Zealanders;* Whitcombe and Tombs Limited: Christchurch, New Zealand, 1972; p 174.

Hall, D. O. W. Women at War: The Women's Auxiliary Army Corps. In *Episodes & Studies Volume 1, Part of: The Official History of New Zealand in the Second World War 1939–1945;* The New Zealand Electronic Text Collection: Wellington, New Zealand, 2004. http://nzetc.victoria.ac.nz/tm/scholarly/tei-WH2-1Epi-c4-WH2-1Epi-c.html 2004. (accessed June, 10, 2015).

Harford, D. *4 Kiwis and a Falcon;* Robert Hale & Company: London, 1970; p 192.

Harris, N. *The Fly Away People;* Baynard-Hillier: London, 1971; p 192.

Kendall, S.; Corbett, D. *New Zealand Military Nursing – A History of the Royal New Zealand Nursing Corps, Boer War to Present Day;* S. Kendall & D. Corbett: Auckland, New Zealand, 1990; p 240.

Mason, M. J. *The Water Flows Uphill;* Blackwood & Janet Paul: Auckland, New Zealand, 1964.

McCarter, N. *The Big OE: Tales from New Zealand Travelers;* Tandem Press: Auckland, New Zealand, 2001; p 167.

Miles, S.; Bolot, P. *Down Under in Europe: A Survival Kit for Australians and New Zealanders in London and Thereabouts;* Pan Books: London, 1973; p 189.

NZ UK News. 'Memories'; New Zealand News UK: 75 Year Anniversary Supplement, New Zealand, 2002.

Officer, L. H.; Williamson, S. H. Six Ways to Compute the Relative Value of a U.K. Pound Amount, 1270 to Present, Measuring Worth, 2014. http://www.measuringworth.com/ukcompare (accessed June, 13, 2015).

Reserve Bank of New Zealand. *Exchange Control: Travel and Fares*; R.B.E.C. June 7, 1968.

Reserve Bank of New Zealand. *Exchange Calculator.* http://www.rbnz.govt.nz/monetary_policy/inflation_calculator (accessed April 15, 2015).

Rogers, A. *While You're Away: New Zealand Nurses at War 1899–1948*; Auckland University Press: Auckland, New Zealand, 2003.

Statistics New Zealand. *Population and Migration Statistics*; Annual Year Book Publications, New Zealand. www.stats.govt.nz (accessed June 10, 2015).

Sutherland, L. *I Follow the Wind;* Southern Cross Press: London, 1960; p 118.

Van Geldermalsen, M. *Married to a Bedouin;* Virago Press: London, 2006.

Woodward Swinburn, A. *The Scent of Rosewater: A New Zealand Bride in Iran;* Shoal Bay Press: Christchurch, New Zealand, 1998.

Wilson, J. 'Unpacking' the OE: An Exploration of the New Zealand 'Overseas Experience'. Ph.D. Dissertation, Lincoln University, Lincoln, New Zealand, 2006.

Wilson, J. *Flying Kiwis: A History of the OE;* Otago University Press: Dunedin, New Zealand, 2014.

SECTION II
Women's Travel Issues and Constraints

CHAPTER 4

A TIME AND SPACE OF ONE'S OWN: WOMEN'S RESISTANCE TO THE MOTHERHOOD DISCOURSE ON FAMILY HOLIDAYS

HEIKE A. SCHÄNZEL

School of Hospitality and Tourism, Auckland University of Technology, New Zealand

E-mail: heike.schanzel@aut.ac.nz

CONTENTS

4.1   INTRODUCTION

Tourism studies informed by a feminist research perspective have found that the gendered roles of mothers are mostly maintained on family holidays (Mottiar & Quinn, 2012). This means that the responsibility to feed, organize and emotionally look after the family does not leave on holiday. For many women, the continuation of domestic and caring responsibilities is merely transposed from home to another location (see Deem, 1996; Small, 2005), and is bound up with what is means to be a mother. Increasingly, women resist the social expectations created by the "ideology of motherhood" by redefining what it means to be a good mother through creating spaces to achieve their own happiness (Spowart et al., 2008). This includes seeking freedom from the care of children on family holidays (Small, 2005) and pursuing their own interests.

For a better understanding of gendered holiday experiences, a more holistic and critical approach is needed that is inclusive of the voices of all family members. A whole-family methodology was adopted for this study into domestic summer holiday experiences in New Zealand, based on 10 families (10 mothers, 10 fathers, and 20 children). The chapter is focused on the social experiences and meanings of family holidays over time for the family members, using gender, generation, and group dynamic perspectives. This chapter illustrates the findings relating to the gendered holiday experiences of mothers in relation to their children, husbands/partners, and family group dynamics.

4.2   TOURISM, MOTHERHOOD, AND RESISTANCE

Much of the initial research on tourism was concerned with the individual tourist and the part that holidays play in establishing self-identity and the "self" was presented as male (Wearing & Wearing, 2001). Pritchard and Morgan argued that this prevailing male bias in tourism research makes little allowance for gender difference and subsumes female experiences into those of the dominant male patterns (Pritchard & Morgan, 2000). Feminist writers have criticized those historical masculine ways of thinking about the world that have permeated tourism theory (e.g., Fullagar, 2002) and called for more nuanced and gendered ways of knowing. It is the pluralizing depictions of the tourist experience which are sensitive to gender that are needed, as stated by Uriely (2005). Gender considerations gained attention in the tourism literature in the 1990s (e.g., Kinnaird & Hall, 1994; Swain, 1995) which attest that men and women are involved differently in the construction and consumption of tourism, such as women's emphasis placed on family and kinship. However, the study of the behavior and experiences of women as tourists is still in its incipient stages compared with other fields of study (e.g., geography and cultural studies) (Harris & Wilson, 2007). Although some progress has been made in leisure research, tourism gender research remains marginal to tourism enquiry and disarticulated from wider feminist and gender-aware initiatives, as argued recently by Figueroa-Domecq et al. (2015). More research and debate on women and travel is therefore needed as this book production attests.

Historically the role of women as leisured consumers has been determined by traditional gender distinctions (Kinnaird & Hall, 1994) and centered on the home and family. The female emphasis of socializing and interactions with others is highlighted by Chaplin compared with the male emphasis on action and self (Chaplin, 1999). Selänniemi concluded that women experience more often their holiday through relationships while men seem more likely to let go into a liminoid float, free of everyday demands (Selänniemi, 2002). According to Wood, gender differences could be interpreted as the expressions of femininity or masculinity in relation to social interactions (Wood, 1994). Rather than gender per se, it is the presence and absence of children and partners that has an impact on travel behavior (Freysinger & Ray, 1994; Lin & Lehto, 2006), with women reporting more negative holiday experiences than men, due to the women's feelings of responsibility for others (Crawford et al., 1992). It is, thus, the social context that affects female travelers differently. From a gendered perspective, holiday leisure cannot necessarily be described as an escape from work when others (e.g., children) are involved. Instead of a break from home, holidays for women contain obligation, work, social disapproval, and responsibility (McCormack, 1998). A number of earlier studies on family holidays informed by feminist perspectives and focused on mothers' family holiday experiences (see Anderson, 2001; Davidson, 1996; Deem, 1996; Small, 2005) highlight the never-ending physical and emotional work of motherhood both at home and when traveling. More recently, Mottiar and Quinn confirmed that the genderized roles of mothers are mostly maintained on self-catering family holidays (Mottiar

& Quinn, 2012). Yet, more recent developments in leisure research point to an increasing resistance to the more traditional discourse of motherhood and the forever caring and laboring mother.

The largely feminist literature on women's leisure has debated whether leisure can be both empowering and constraining and if it differs between women (Hall et al., 2003). The constraints of leisure for mothers are associated with an "ethic of care" (Bialeschki, 1994; Henderson & Allen, 1991) and are based on Gilligan's (1982) initial approach on caring rooted in social contexts. Gilligan's research highlighted that women's greater concerns for social responsibility and relationships place a constraint upon their lives as "others" are often placed before self. This points to a relational aspect to time, in that a woman's time is never her own (Hilbrecht, 2013). Family leisure is thought to establish a sense of family through bonding and is deliberately used to provide opportunities for meaningful interactions. However, facilitating family leisure activities may not be freely chosen or intrinsically motivated by women, as there is often a sense of duty or responsibility associated with organizing and participating in these activities (Harrington, 2013; Shaw & Dawson, 2001). Overall, the literature presents a picture of family leisure as highly valued and a central component to family life, but also involving much work and a potential to cause stress or mental fatigue, particularly for women. Women already experience the everyday tasks of family life as more stressful than do men (Helms & Demo, 2005). It is not surprising, then, that women seek a break from the care of children on holiday (Small, 2005), which can be considered as a resistance to the motherhood discourse.

Resistance has emerged in the leisure literature in recent years as underlying premises about how women are no longer victims of their situations and have the power to challenge their circumstances and make active choices (Henderson & Hickerson, 2007). While resistance can occur in all settings and circumstances, leisure provides enhanced opportunities for resistant acts because of greater opportunities for self-expression and self-determination. Several leisure studies researchers have argued that women can and do resist by actively creating time out for themselves through engaging in their own leisure activities (e.g., Shaw, 2001). There is then increasing resistance of the ideology of motherhood through creating spaces to achieve their own happiness, such as in the case of snowboarding mums carving out time for themselves (Spowart et al., 2008). However, mothers do not just create spaces of freedom through active leisure, such as snowboarding and surfing, but leisure spaces can also entail more passive activities (Spowart et al., 2010). A recent study by Fountain et al. (2015) underlines how mothers visiting family attractions use the facilities there to create adult time for themselves and a break from everyday life through having a coffee while the children are playing or meeting up with other mothers. Indeed the notion emerges that leisure allows a situation of choice, control, and self-determination that permits mothers to enact change through demonstrating "resistance" when they choose to engage in their own leisure pursuits. The aim of this chapter is to provide insights into how mothers experience their holidays within the family.

4.3 WHOLE-FAMILY STUDY METHODOLOGY

The study in this chapter is based on aimed to understand the individual and collective experiences and meanings of family holidays over time for all family members. As a collective experience, investigation of family group behavior requires a more inclusive approach, and is in accordance with interdisciplinary trends (e.g., sociology and family studies) which advocate and integrate the inclusion of children and whole-family aspects within family research (Handel, 1996; Seymour & McNamee, 2012). Whole-family methodology was adopted from family research and applied to tourism (Schänzel, 2010). Ten New Zealand families made up of 10 fathers, 10 mothers, and 20 children were recruited through primary schools for the study. To maintain some homogeneity in terms of family life cycle stage and travel propensity (see Shaw et al., 2008) only families that had at least one child 8–12 years old were invited, resulting in the participation of 11 boys and 9 girls, ranging from 6–16 years to participate. To give a balanced gender perspective on parenthood, only two parent (male/female) families were selected which allowed for step-parents but no such "blended" families volunteered.

The participants were all white, New Zealand and middle-class, making the families relatively homogenous and not representative of the ethnic diversity of New Zealand society. The whole-family approach involved interviewing in their family homes, first, all family members together in a group interview and, then, each family member separately (children had the option of having a parent present). This was repeated three times, once before and twice after their summer holiday to capture their anticipation and short- and longer-term recollections of holiday experiences. Some statements from the children are included here in the findings to reflect on the role of the mother from the children's perspective. These might not be as profound as adults but this approach provided the children with an active voice that is not often heard.

The choice of methodology was underpinned by the philosophical perspective of interpretivism with the goal of understanding the complex world of lived experience from the point of view of those who live it (Denzin & Lincoln, 2000). A symbolic interactionist perspective was adopted for this study which focuses on the connection between symbols (i.e., shared meanings) and interactions (i.e., verbal actions and communications) and also formed the basis for a constructivist grounded theory methodology (GTM) (Charmaz, 2000) used for the analysis. This approach allowed a focus on interpersonal relations within the family group.

Case studies of families are mainly based on interviews and a small number of cases (Handel, 1991) and are almost always conducted in the home (LaRossa et al., 1994). The three stages of interviews were all digitally recorded and later transcribed. The GTM was carried out through manual coding in that data was initially coded by reading through the transcripts several times while making notes which were then sorted into themes (Charmaz, 2000). A comparative analysis of the stages was conducted after which all emerging data fitted into the main themes and theoretical saturation was deemed achieved (Morse, 1995). This resulted in a theoretical model of the sociality of family holiday experiences that center on "family time" and "own time," maintaining that successful family holidays contain a balance of togetherness and separateness and require the negotiation of the internal family group dynamics between the two (see Fig. 4.1). While there is the ideal of family togetherness in family time, every family member also seeks freedom from family commitments in their own time. Own time encapsulated freedom from those family commitments to pursue familiar interests alone or with peers, which increased in importance with age of the child(ren).

This chapter focuses primarily on the gendered differences in how holiday experiences are perceived by mothers in relation to their children, husbands/partners, and family group dynamics. Selected quotes from the interviews are used to illustrate the findings with New Zealand birds as pseudonyms for family names.

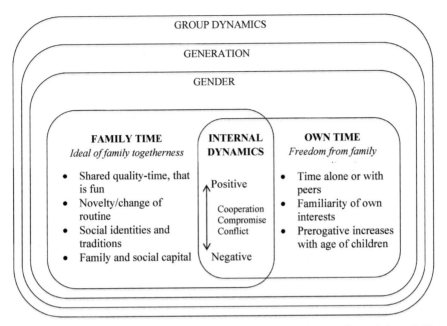

FIGURE 4.1 Model of the sociality of family holiday experiences. (From Schänzel, H. A.; Smith, K.A. *Leisure Sciences.* 2014, 36, 133.)

4.4 FINDINGS

What emerged from the findings with regards to the gendered experience of the mothers is their paramount desire or need for relaxation and for own time on holiday along with fun family time spent together. The discussion of the findings is structured around the different perspectives of how the mothers' holiday experiences of own time and relaxation are perceived by themselves and others in the family, as well as the facilitators and requirements to achieve a sense of relaxation in own time for the mothers.

4.4.1 MOTHER'S OWN TIME OR RELAXATION

All the mothers in this study were outspoken about their needs to get time out or own time during the family holiday in order to relax and immerse themselves in their own interests which in these cases were mainly reading, walking and going shopping, as illustrated here:

I suppose I need a bit more personal space rather than the rest of the family which is why I go off and do some of the stuff [*shopping*]. (Takahe mum)

And then me having a bit of time somewhere in that day also just relax and read a book and not have to deal with anyone else.... It is quite nice having a bit of time without the children during the holiday but that usually does not happen much. (Hoiho mum)

I liked having the time and space to be able to read my book actually. It was good. (Kea mum)

The women perceived the never-ending physical and emotional work of motherhood at home, at leisure, and when traveling as draining, and desired a time to read or go shopping by themselves. It extends the notion that women's magazines facilitate and legitimize "me-time" for women at home (Stevens et al., 2007) to women's general reading away from home. Reading provided the women with justification for relaxation instead of just sitting and "doing nothing." Reading at home and on holiday enabled the women to focus on their own needs and wants and to temporarily ignore the needs and wants of others, but could come at the expense of their husbands/partners.

4.4.2 FATHERS AS FACILITATORS OF MUM'S OWN TIME

The need for own time was reflected in mothers going off and pursuing their own interests. Unless there were other family members or child-care facilities available, the fathers ensured that the mothers could get some time for themselves. Fathers mainly became the facilitators for the mothers' own time, as illustrated below:

We went to the Butterfly house near the airport. [*Mum*] didn't do that. I just took the girls and we had a really nice time. [*Mum*] wanted to go shopping. We dropped her off. So that was nice just hanging out with the girls and they were pretty good. (Weka father)

I got a bit bored so I went around Hastings to look at shops. I did not stay at Splash Planet the whole time but I only went out for about 1 ½ hours. That was quite fun. (Takahe mother)

The activities-based parenting of the fathers on holiday enabled the mothers to get some relaxation. This meant that fathers were entertaining the children partly to enable the mothers to pursue their individual interests, for example, read or go shopping. This facilitation role was acknowledged by both parents in their final individual interviews:

> Father: I suppose at those campgrounds I would be happy to just sit in the chair and read but I realize that it is important for them [*children*] particularly to be entertained and have fun with me and do these sort of activities when I would personally be just as happy sitting and reading because (wife) tends to spend time during the [*school*] term with dealing with the children while I am at work.

> Mother: I really appreciate (husband) going off and doing things with the kids because that gives me a bit of time out when I am with them more the rest of the year.

The Hohio parents illustrate the contrasts of at-home and on-holiday roles and behavior and some of the gender role reversal taking place. The different environment available on holiday then allowed the women to carve out more time for themselves which was also linked to diminished domestic work.

4.4.3 GENDER DIFFERENCES IN RELAXATION NEEDS FOR THE PARENTS

The on-holiday engagement of fathers in more active leisure behavior with their children mirrors findings in the leisure literature (Kay, 2006). In contrast, mothers preferred a more passive and emotional involvement with their children and generally saw theme parks as more of a sacrifice, valued because of the children's enjoyment rather than their own.

> Hoiho Father: I did a lot of rides [*at Rainbow's End*] with the children. I was not a spectator so I accompanied the children on those rides. So I enjoyed those days as well because the children were enjoying themselves and just for their own sake. They were quite fun too.

> Hoiho Mother: And there are certain things that I don't enjoy as much but I would do anyway. It is not that I hate them because if my kids

are enjoying it then that is enough. Things like Rainbow's End do not particularly appeal to me at all.

The high adrenalin rides offered at theme parks then proved less appealing to the mothers who preferred more relaxing activities or having their own time, while the fathers went on the rides with their children. Theme parks provide an example of how high adventure and adrenalin is more prevalent for men, whereas women tend to experience relaxation on family holiday more through more passive and restful activities.

4.4.4 RELAXATION NEEDS FOR THE MOTHERS AS RECOGNIZED BY THE CHILDREN

How the mothers placed more importance on relaxation needs, instead of more active engagement with their children, was recognized by the children themselves who contrasted the activities and behaviors of their two parents on holiday. Including the perspective of the boys and girls in this study highlights gendered differences on holiday from the voice of the beneficiaries of the mother-child relationship, for example: "With mum it is more relaxing like playing card games; with dad it is more sailing and fishing." (10-years-old Kereru boy). "Mum doesn't really like running around and sports things. She is more of an organized, relaxing person. And dad is more of a fun, sporty type person." (10-years-old Kea girl). It emerged that mothers in their choice of engagement with their children on holiday seek more relaxing activities rather than having to be on the go and running around all the time or taking out a lot of time during the day for family leisure.

4.4.5 RELAXATION LINKED TO LESS RESPONSIBILITY

Other role reversals included cooking responsibilities, with fathers being more active on holiday which provided the mothers with a break from their domestic responsibilities, as illustrated here: "It is just [husband] doing the cooking and that is something I really appreciate. He does the barbecuing here but it is a bit different when we are camping. He can do more on that and he takes more responsibility than he would at home. Which is nice, it is a break for me." (Kea mother, post-interview). On holiday the men often took on the responsibility of the barbecue (BBQ) and cooking food for the family.

However, while there were some role reversals with regards to cooking responsibilities, the main domestic and emotional commitment remained with the mothers, such as making sure there was enough food available. The difference on holiday is that many responsibilities rather than being done alone are shared. A real break from domestic responsibilities and relaxation was only achieved when cooking and cleaning was taken care of, as this quote exemplifies: "When I go and hang out at [*my*] auntie's that is a holiday. They cook and clean and do the washing." (Weka mother, final interview).

This demonstrates why all-inclusive family resorts prove so popular especially for mothers, in that relaxation for women is linked to having less or ideally no domestic responsibilities on holiday. And why self-catering holidays where many of the tasks from everyday life such as cleaning, minding children, and cooking must still be undertaken, are perceived as a continuation of work by the mothers (Mottiar & Quinn, 2012).

4.4.6 RELAXATION LINKED TO SAFETY OF CHILDREN

In order for the mothers to feel relaxed it is also imperative for them to know that their children are safe and taken care of. This subscribes to more traditional notions of motherhood of protecting their children from harm but is an essential requirement for resistance to happen. One of the reasons why campgrounds are so popular is because they provide a safe space for the children to entertain themselves, as illustrated here: "Being at a camp ground and know that the kids are safe. They could run and meet some friends and we didn't have to worry about them." (Kea mother, post-interview).

However the perception of a lack of safety of the children leads to automatic feelings of stress for the mothers, as illustrated in this dialog with her teenage son:

Mother: I didn't really enjoy walking on Westshore beach which is very notoriously dangerous and I told the kids and so [*son*] had to go and have a try and walk right by the waves.

Son: I wasn't anywhere near the waves. I was the whole room away from the waves. You were having a panic attack.

Safety of the children is then considered an essential requirement on family holidays, as any accidents to the children would ruin the holiday and lead to more stress and responsibilities, as also emphasized by Khoo-Lattimore et al. (2015). The consideration that the children are safe is a paramount concern for the mothers and only when that is taking care can the mothers emotionally relax, enjoy their own time, and achieve resistance.

4.4.7 FAMILY HOLIDAY EXPERIENCES FOR THE MOTHERS

The mothers' holiday experiences largely confirm previous studies in leisure and tourism in that mothers' sought a break from their motherhood discourse (Small, 2005) or ethic of care commitments. Mothers were also more emotionally involved with their children and more deliberate about instilling social connectedness and social identity in their children than the fathers in this study. In their own time, mothers preferred less physical activities, such as shopping and more restful relaxation, such as reading. This correlates with a study on visits with their children to family attractions whereby mothers are more likely than fathers to be motivated by an opportunity to take a break from everyday life, if not from the everyday tasks of mothering (Fountain et al., 2015). The mothers in this study here voiced greater claims on personal time than the fathers and were more purposeful in how they used their free time, such as needing to shop rather than just wondering about. It confirms recent studies in leisure that women increasingly resist dominant motherhood roles and prioritize their leisure needs over others, such as their husbands/partners. The need for own time then was perceived as paramount and felt deserved by the women. The findings also highlight that women found it harder to get a break on holiday because their sense of relaxation was linked to not only less or ideally no domestic and caring responsibility but also knowing that the children are safe. Safety needs of the children then form an essential requirement for resistance to succeed.

4.5 CONCLUSION

The findings in this chapter reveal how family life on holiday requires dynamic interrelationships within which mothers carve out what they perceive as valuable and rare time and space for themselves, such as reading or going shopping. It is, however, not just more passive leisure activities but also active leisure, such as surfing, that can afford disruptive potentialities or spaces of freedom for mothers (Spowart et al., 2010). It is the freedom from family commitments to pursue own interests that is sought especially by the mothers, within the overarching purpose of spending time together on family holidays. To achieve own time and satisfy the mothers' needs for relaxation requires negotiations between family members, especially the fathers, potentially leading to some gender role reversals on holiday. The findings highlight a more assertive focus on women's needs and wants and invite a new definition of what it means to be a good mother on holiday. It confirms disruption of the myth of the forever caring, uncomplaining mother (Small, 2005) and demonstrates a form of resistance to the motherhood paradigm by prioritizing time out for themselves. The chapter then illustrates how traditional ideologies of "mothers" and her role in "the family" have shifted within the context of women's travel, as part of a movement toward more gender equality at work and at home. It also invites more debate about the different gendered roles on family holiday through a truer gender scholarship, in that the role of fathers as entertainers of the children and facilitators of the women's own time needs more acknowledgment (Schänzel & Smith, 2011). This debate must also be about the roles of mothers and fathers in today's society.

What, then, are the underlying reasons for mothers increasingly taking a more active voice on holiday about yearning for a time and space of their own? Does one explanation lie in the fact that mothers still spend more time with their children involving childcare and maintenance (Craig, 2006), and perceive more of a need for respite from these duties? Is it harder for mothers to switch off and feel relaxed on holiday because of the traditionally expected and more emotional concern about the well-being of the children, be it safety or nourishment? In 1929, the feminist writer Virginia Woolf stated that: "A woman must have money and a room of her own if she is to write fiction." She pointed to both a literal and figural space for women writers within a literary tradition dominated by patriarchy. Within the family leisure domain, this can be translated to a new definition of: "*A woman must have time and space for herself if she is to be a good mother*," pointing to a home and leisure life framed by patriarchal structures. Allowing women "time-out" from motherhood is not only beneficial for the whole family in that a "happy mum equals happy family" (Spowart et al., 2010) but is also part of a more just and equal world. It is in the interest of everyone involved in the family and society that mothers are afforded their own time through leisure and on holiday. As Figueroa-Domecq et al. (2015) state, none of us lives in a gender equal society and not one country has yet eliminated the gender gap. It is these gendered power relations that also permeate the lived tourism worlds and affect tourism experiences. There is then not just a need for more gender-oriented and feminist tourism scholarship but maybe we all need to become feminists in our everyday lives.

KEYWORDS

- mothers
- motherhood
- family
- fathers
- parents
- children

REFERENCES

Anderson, J. Mothers on Family Activity Holidays Overseas. In *Women's Leisure Experiences: Ages, Stages and Roles;* Clough, S., White, J., Eds.; Leisure Studies Association: Eastbourne, 2001; pp 99–112.

Bialeschki, M. D. Re-Entering Leisure: Transition within the Role of Motherhood. *J. Leis. Res.* **1994,** *26,* 57–74.

Chaplin, D. Back to the Cave or Playing Away? Gender Roles in Home-from-Home Environments. *J.Consumer Stud. Home Econ.* **1999,** *23,* 181–189.

Charmaz, K. Grounded Theory: Objectivist and Constructivist Methods. In *Handbook of Qualitative Research;* 2nd ed.; Denzin, N. K., Lincoln, Y. S., Eds.; Sage: Thousand Oaks, CA, 2000; pp 509–535.

Craig, L. Does Father Care Mean Father Share? A Comparison of how Mothers and Fathers in Intact Families Spend Time with Children. *Gender Soci.* **2006,** *20,* 259–281.

Crawford, J.; Kippax, S.; Onyx, J.; Gault, U.; Benton, P. *Emotion and Gender: Constructing Meaning from Memory;* Sage: London, 1992.

Davidson, P. The Holiday and Work Experiences of Women with Young Children. *Leis. Stud.* **1996,** *15,* 89–103.

Deem, R. Women, the City and Holidays. *Leis. Stud.* **1996,** *15,* 105–119.

Denzin, N. K.; Lincoln, Y. S. *Handbook of Qualitative Research;* 2nd ed.; Sage: Thousand Oaks, CA, 2000.

Figueroa-Domecq, C.; Pritchard, A.; Segovia-Pérez, M.; Morgan, N.; Villacé-Molinero, T. Tourism Gender Research: A Critical Accounting. *Ann. Tour. Res.* **2015,** *52,* 87–103.

Fountain, J.; Schänzel, H.; Stewart, E.; Körner, N. Family Experiences of Visitor Attractions in New Zealand: Differing Opportunities for 'Family Time' and 'Own Time'. *Ann. Leis. Res.* **2015,** *18,* 3.

Freysinger, V. J.; Ray, R. O. The Activity Involvement of Women and Men in Young and Middle Adulthood: A Panel Study. *Leis. Sci.* **1994,** *16,* 193–217.

Fullagar, S. Narratives of Travel: Desire and The Movement of Feminine Subjectivity. *Leis. Stud.* **2002,** *21,* 57–74.

Gilligan, C. *In a Different Voice: Psychological Theory and Women's Development;* Harvard University Press: Cambridge, 1982.

Hall, D.; Swain, M. B.; Kinnard, V. Tourism and Gender: An Evolving Agenda. *Tour. Recreat. Res.* **2003,** *28*(2), 7–11.

Handel, G. Case Study in Family Research. In *A Case for the Case Study;* Feagin, J. R., Orum, A. M., Sjoberg, G., Eds.; The University of North Carolina Press: Chapel Hill, NC 1991; pp 244–268.

Handel, G. Family Worlds and Qualitative Family Research: Emergence and Prospects of Whole-Family Methodology. *Marriage Fam. Rev.* **1996,** *24,* 335–348.

Harrington, M. Families, Gender, Social Class, and Leisure. In *Leisure, Women, and Gender;* Freysinger, V. J., Shaw, S. M., Henderson, K. A., Bialeschki, M. D., Eds.; Venture Publishing: State College, PA, 2013; pp 325–341.

Harris, C.; Wilson, E. Travelling Beyond the Boundaries of Constraint: Women, Travel and Empowerment. In *Tourism and Gender: Embodiment, Sensuality and Experience;* Pritchard, A., Morgan, N., Ateljevic, I., Harris, C., Eds.; CABI: Wallingford, 2007; pp 235–250.

Helms, H. M.; Demo, D. H. Everyday Hassles and Family Stress. In *Families & Change;* McKenry, P. C., Price, S. J., Eds.; Sage: Thousand Oaks, CA, 2005; pp 355–378.

Henderson, K. A.; Allen, K. R. The Ethic of Care: Leisure Possibilities and Constraints for Women. *Soc. Leis.* **1991,** *14,* 97–113.

Henderson, K. A.; Hickerson, B. Women and Leisure: Premises and Performances Uncovered in an Integrative Review. *J. Leis. Res.* **2007,** *29,* 591–610.

Hilbrecht, M. Time Use in Daily Life: Women, Families, and Leisure. In *Leisure, Women, and Gender;* Freysinger, V. J., Shaw, S. M., Henderson, K. A., Bialscheki, M. D., Eds.; Venture Publishing: State College, PA, 2013; pp 177–191.

Kay, T. Where's Dad? Fatherhood in Leisure Studies. *Leis. Stud.* **2006,** *25,* 133–152.

Khoo-Lattimore, C.; Prayag, G.; Cheah, B. L. Kids on Board: Exploring the Choice Process and Vacation Needs of Asian Parents with Young Children in Resort Hotels. *J. Hosp. Mark. Manage.* [Online] **2015,** *24*(5), 511–531. http://dx.doi.org/10.1080/19368623.2014.914862

Kinnaird, V.; Hall, D., Eds. *Tourism: A Gendered Analysis;* John Wiley & Sons: Chichester, 1994.

LaRossa, R.; Bennett, L. A.; Gelles, R. J. Ethical Dilemmas in Qualitative Family Research. In *The Psychosocial Interior of the Family;* 4th ed.; Handel, G., Whitchurch, G. G., Eds.; Aldine de Gruyter: New York, 1994; pp 109–126.

Lin, Y. C.; Lehto, X. Y. A Study of Female Travelers' Needs Trajectory and Family Life Cycle. *J. Hosp. Leis. Mark.* **2006,** *15,* 65–88.

McCormack, C. Memories Bridge the Gap between Theory and Practice in Women's Leisure Research. *Ann. Leis. Res.* **1998,** *1,* 37–49.

Morse, J. M. The Significance of Saturation. *Qual. Health Res.* **1995,** *5,* 147–149.

Mottiar, Z.; Quinn, D. Is a Self-Catering Holiday with the Family Really a Holiday for Mothers? Examining the Balance of Household Responsibilities while on Holiday from a Female Perspective. *Hosp. Soc.* **2012,** *2,* 197–214.

Pritchard, A.; Morgan, N. J. Privileging the Male Gaze: Gendered Tourism Landscapes. *Ann. Tour. Res.* **2000,** *27,* 884–905.

Schänzel, H. A. Whole-Family Research: Towards a Methodology in Tourism for Encompassing Generation, Gender, and Group Dynamic Perspectives. *Tour. Anal.* **2010,** *15,* 555–569.

Schänzel, H. A.; Smith, K. A. The Absence of Fatherhood: Achieving True Gender Scholarship in Family Tourism Research. *Ann. Leis. Res.* **2011,** *14,* 129–140.

Schänzel, H. A.; Smith, K. A. The Socialization of Families away from Home: Group Dynamics and Family Functioning on Holiday. *Leis. Sci.* **2014,** *36,* 126–143.

Selänniemi, T. Couples on Holiday: (En)gendered or Endangered Experiences? In *Gender/Tourism/Fun(?);* Swain, M. B., Momsen, J. H., Eds.; Cognizant Communication Corporation: New York, 2002; pp 15–23.

Seymour, J.; McNamee, S. Being Parented: Children and Young People's Engagement with Parenting Activities. In *Learning from the Children: Culture and Identity in a Changing World;* Walden, J., Kaminski, I. M., Eds.; Berghahn: Oxford, 2012; pp 92–106.

Shaw, S. M. Conceptualizing Resistance: Women's Leisure as Political Practice. *J. Leis. Res.* **2001,** *33,* 186–201.

Shaw, S. M.; Dawson, D. Purposive Leisure: Examining Parental Discourses on Family Activities. *Leis. Sci.* **2001,** *23,* 217–231.

Shaw, S. M.; Havitz, M. E.; Delemere, F. M. I Decided to Invest in my Kids' Memories: Family Vacations, Memories, and the Social Construction of the Family. *Tour. Culture Commun.* **2008,** *8,* 13–26.

Small, J. Women's Holidays: Disruption of the Motherhood Myth. *Tour. Rev. Int.* **2005,** *9,* 139–154.

Spowart, L.; Burrows, L.; Shaw, S. 'I Just Eat, Sleep and Dream of Surfing': When Surfing Meets Motherhood. *Sport Soci.* **2010,** *13,* 1186–1203.

Spowart, L.; Hughson, J.; Shaw, S. Snowboarding Mums Carve out Fresh Tracks: Resisting Traditional Motherhood Discourse? *Ann. Leis. Res.* **2008,** *11,* 187–204.

Stevens, L.; Maclaran, P.; Catterall, M. A Space of One's Own: Women's Magazine Consumption within Family Life. *J. Consum. Behav.* **2007,** *6,* 236–252.

Swain, M. B. Gender in Tourism. *Ann. Tour. Res.* **1995,** *22,* 247–266.

Uriely, N. The Tourist Experience: Conceptual Developments. *Ann. Tour. Res.* **2005,** *32,* 199–216.

Wearing, S.; Wearing, B. Conceptualising the Selves of Tourism. *Leis. Stud.* **2001,** *20,* 143–159.

Wood, J. *Gendered Lives: Communication, Gender, and Culture;* Wadsworth: Belmont, CA, 1994.

CHAPTER 5

CITIZENS OF THE WORLD: BRAZILIAN WOMEN'S PERFORMANCES IN INDEPENDENT TRAVEL

GISELE CARVALHO[1*], CARLOS COSTA[2],
MARIA MANUEL BAPTISTA[3], and FIONA EVA BAKAS[2]

[1]Department of Economics, Management, Industrial Engineering and Tourism, University of Aveiro, Portugal / Federal Institute of Education, Science and Technology of Pará State, IFPA, Brazil

[2]Department of Economics, Management, Industrial Engineering and Tourism, University of Aveiro, Portugal

[3]Department of Languages and Cultures, Aveiro University, Portugal

*Corresponding author. E-mail:gisele.maria@ua.pt

CONTENTS

5.1   INTRODUCTION

To travel is to essentially discover ourselves and the "other," in situations outside of our daily life. Even though this premise from Serrano may sound commonplace, it is meaningful to research as there has been an increase in the number of Western women who travel alone, since they become more independent financially and emotionally (Serrano, 2014). In the kind of travel wherein women do not depend on a travel-partner, they experience moments of (self) discovery, self-confidence, and autonomy to make their own decisions (Heimtun, 2012; McNamara & Prideaux, 2010). On the other hand, the dynamic of independent travel results in intrapersonal and interpersonal interactions which provide insights into understanding the new type of tourist, who is more conscious about their part as a citizen of the globalized world. This type of tourism can also, introspectively, contribute to a better intercultural comprehension.

In the 21st century, women have been key players in social, political, cultural, and economic transformations, which justifies the importance of trying to identify how, in turn, those transformations may affect women's individual travel choices and performances during independent leisure travel. In this chapter, we seek to highlight how this new behavior may contribute to the deconstruction of stereotypes and instituted social models in relation to the performance, meanings and perceptions of women who travel independently. In this study we perceive independent travel as having characteristics of slow travel and being a leisure experience which benefits woman in fundamental aspects, such as self-development and social exchange, among others. In addition to these themes, we pose question about the needs, experiences and challenges of these women in their journeys.

5.2   REDISCOVERING THE VALUE OF LEISURE IN TRAVEL

Historically, the displacement from one place to another and the search for the novel has been occurring in different forms for centuries. However, when revisiting history, a question arises: Was the anxiety to conquer and pave the way to unknown territories the only latent searching for material treasure of that era? Or is such will inherent to a human being? Metaphorically speaking, does "pave the way for the world" mean "pave the way for the self?" In historical literature, the motivations for travels had a predominantly commercial and political character in order to dominate territories (Serrano, 2014), but was this just a manifestation of discourses surrounding travel at the time, preferring accounts of conquering material goods to personal journeys of discovery?

The act of traveling, apart from being connected to a way in which to expand frontiers, is also connected to the leisure activity that, in a capitalist society, may be understood as a dominant way of appropriation of free time. Since the industrial revolution, work has been perceived as the ultimate embodiment of being human, a thought that prevails until today, and leisure as a concept with its origin in modernity, has an increasing interconnection with work (Rhoden, 2014). In this case, a leisure experience is presented as a possibility for the individual to leave the alienating work circle, enlarge one's visual horizons and experience the profound perception of a subjective dimension while traveling.

Nowadays, the benefits of practicing leisure are known and encouraged, especially in the tourist market, because leisure is of personal, economic, and social value (Brasileiro, 2014). In that sense, traveling may be an invitation to the deconstruction of paradigms, of consolidated views and of stereotyped stigmas, to become a call to openness of the self and of the other and, therefore, to a socialization of personal and cultural different realities.

With that understanding, travel follows the same lines as the elements that characterize leisure and has similar benefits (social, personal and economic). The concept of leisure used in this study comprises of a non-working time, associated to the practice of countless leisure activities, among which, travel itself. Moreover, leisure is understood here as an organic perspective contrary to work and a great opportunity for self-fulfillment and self-enrichment (Costa, 2011; Martins, 2014). Thereby, a leisure experience can promote human and social development (Rhoden, 2014).

The quality of the leisure experience connected to travel has been a subject of study for several researchers who reflect on how independent travel may play a role in self-development, by increasing an awareness of who we are, our history, our possibilities and limitations, and our beliefs and illusions (Cuenca Cabeza, 2006; Trigo, 2010). However, in order to make ourselves receptive for all this to occur, we need courage. Leisure experience is essentially subjective and, therefore, acquires countless expressions, meanings and intensity, which makes it rich. Leisure experience also "imprints the sense to life through its capability to makes us feel alive, people of value, in state of permanent progress," that is to say that the leisure experience contributes to the construction of satisfying, positive and happy experiences, capable of favoring personal development (Monteagudo et al., 2014, p. 139).

5.2.1 SUBJECTIVITY IN INDEPENDENT TRAVEL

The traveling experience is personal and non-transferable and has its basis in the subjective experience that emotion is the most real expression of the human being. Emotion is linked to an individual's life choices, the quality of interpersonal relationships, the development of spirituality, values and beliefs, which all contribute to bring meaning to the traveling experience. In fact, we can infer that travel allows the individual to enjoy a leisure experience, from the connection between the subjective experience and the actual experience, and that the individual can intensely live the aspirations and idealizations (Serrano, 2014).

In effect, when a person experiences a full leisure experience, the self tends to continue pursuing other similar experiences, transforming, meaningful and notable, in a way that shallowness is rejected (Martins, 2014). Therefore, travel as a meaningful, profound and essential experience consists of discovering the self, in a subjective pursuit. This is achieved through recognition of one's personal history, so that choices can become more consciously in pursuit of the meanings of life and the time spent traveling results in countless benefits (Trigo, 2010; Wilson & Harris, 2006).

In that sense, a leisure experience can be observed as something mainly subjective, which gathers singularities that compose the individual as a human being, as an example of otherness, of empathy and of the comprehension of the different. In this view, travel gains a perspective of comparison to the enjoyment of life itself, that is, by traveling it is possible to live and enjoy the present moment integrally. Hence, a leisure experience is the opportunity that the subject has to spend listening to their inner thoughts and thus becoming more self-aware (Baptista, 2014). Spending idle time is a lifestyle, an existential challenge, which requires preparing, effort, dedication, and courage and an ability to qualify our time relationship, precisely because of our attention to temporality (Baptista, 2014). Therefore, we can infer that independent travel can become an idle experience that contributes to human development.

5.2.2   GENDER PERFORMANCES

For centuries, "woman" has been characterized with a single identity. Deprived of autonomy and submitted to rigid rules, women did not have access to all the rights that men had as full citizens, a right which was at the core of the claims of the female movements (Camps, 1998). The autonomy of Western women in the context of socio-cultural changes is at the center of contemporary discussions. This is because there is the trend in developed countries, for women to match or overcome men's social status, which, inevitably, affects women's socio-economic status, self-esteem, and visions of the world (Pritchard & Morgan, 2000; Wilson, 2004).

As a result, among all the ways and possibilities of emancipation that the contemporary woman has, independent travel presents itself as a subtle way to exercise autonomy and to review consolidated habits and traditions. In this scenario, in line with a worldwide tourism development trend, this study highlights women as key players of experiences in independent travels. The reasoning is that the increased demand for this kind of travel brings several singularities and new demands, and so should be better served as a market segment (Buhalis, 2001; McNamara & Prideaux, 2010).

The revelations and experiences lived by women undertaking independent travels favor several possibilities regarding their performances. This is exhibited in the form of freedom regarding the interaction between the individual and the society. In other words, women's independent travel experiences are related to the speech that is found in the body, that makes that body and for that reason mixes up with it (Butler, 2004). So, to perform is to cross geographical, emotional, ideological, political, and personal boundaries; it is to become someone more than the self at the same time; it is to have empathy, to react; to grow and to change (Schechner, 2014).

In this sense, during the traveling experience, the interviewed women update and deconstruct the role women play in independent travel and the meaning of the woman in contemporary society, through their behaviors and performances. It is observed, that in independent travel, there is a space that invites the liberation, infringement and transposition of norms that repress who we are, or who we may become, exactly because this happens out of the everyday life environment, out of the ordinary. In other words, there may be other roads to go down and different ways to be and to act in society and as Schechner says: "we must imagine, invent and perform alternative ways of becoming ourselves" (Schechner, 2014, p. 725).

Another field that can be expanded on in independent travel is that of spirituality. In this study, spirituality is perceived within the modernity context, as being a way through which new ways to experience the sacred as a misplacement of religion to the subjective sphere, arise. The practice of yoga and of meditation is perceived as integral to spirituality (Guerriero, 2014). So, those subjective experiences emerge under the aegis of traditional religions, through which the subjects give a new meaning to their connection with the sacred that, in its turn, assumes different manifestations, for example the cult of nature, energy-flows and the beliefs of past lives, among others. Furthermore, the New Era phenomenon articulates several religious expressions and cultural traditions, which allow the individual to live the sacred in a more flexible, fluid, and plural way (Oliveira, 2010).

5.3   THE PATH TAKEN: A METHODOLOGICAL APPROACH

The study is located within the interpretative phenomenological paradigm context, that is, it is a systematic study that considers the wholeness of the subjective experiences lived by an individual. Questioning everyday life allows for reflection about the meaning that events have to people in a certain context, for instance when traveling (Giorgi, 2008; Lessard-Hébert et al., 1990; Pernecky, 2010). This work is the result of an investigation carried out at the University of Aveiro, Portugal, and aims to contribute to qualitative studies on travel and gender, taking a critical approach. This study investigates the individual experiences of Brazilian women who independently travel abroad, in order to better understand the personal and emotional character of these travels. In order to do this, qualitative methodology is used, in which the researcher creates knowledge together with the participants through interviews conducted in the field (Deslauriers & Kérisit, 2008). Moreover, we choose a feminist approach that endeavors to contribute to the study's emancipatory and critical character as well as opening the intellectual and emotional space for women in society (Goldenberg, 2004; Hesse-Biber, 2012).

Actually, this type of research may assume several directions. One of the possible perspectives would be to approach the subject from an economics and management lens, through which we can understand the relative weight of the motivations and their impact on the tourism economy. However, we opt for a sociological, anthropological, and emotional approach, in order to examine the dimensions of the human subjectivity by searching to better understand what motivates women in solo travels.

5.3.1   DATA COLLECTION

The information collected was a result of 15 intensive, in-depth interviews conducted with Brazilian women that, through guiding questions, exposed their traveling experiences. The interview script developed on Erica Wilson's study of solo female travelers was used as a reference, with interview questions being formulated about female independent traveler's travel paths; the benefits and challenges of this kind of trip; self and others' perceptions; and planning of the journey (Wilson, 2004). In addition, other questions were adapted to the specific objectives of this study, such as the spirituality, performances and constraints connected with being a Brazilian woman. The interviews were conducted in the period from January to November 2014.

The inclusion criterion chosen was that participants had traveled at least once abroad, where they experienced being alone in a country other than their own, in this case, Brazil. These criteria excluded women that went alone to meet another person in a destination, besides those that had their permanent residence abroad with no intention of returning to Brazil. Sampling was completed by using multiple cases, and non-probabilistic or "snow ball" techniques. The women who participated have high academic qualifications, ranging from an undergraduate degree to a PhD. Most of them are single, do not have children and are from the south, southeast, and central-west parts of Brazil. Regarding their professional status, participants are predominantly from the human and social sciences fields. Most have visited from one to five countries independently and three of the interviewed women had already traveled to more than 20 countries by themselves.

In order to process the empirical data, we used a content analysis approach, to investigate the active role of the subject in producing knowledge. The personal and objective meaning which is implemented in social practice, is expressed through the social, cognitive, subjective, valuation, and emotional representations which are revealed during interviews (Bardin, 1977; Franco, 2008).

5.4   CITIZENS OF THE WORLD: BRAZILIAN WOMEN'S PERFORMANCES IN INDEPENDENT TRAVELS

In this study we chose the age range variable, in which the interviewees were grouped in three levels, namely: Group A—"*Young* Women," includes two women aged between 18 and 30 years; Group B—"*Adult* Women," composed by seven women aged between 31 and 40 years; Group C—"*Mature* Women," composed by six women over 41 years old. Interview analysis reveals four dimensions in the independent traveler's speech, namely: (1) Benefits, (2) Performances, (3) Constraints, and (4) Spirituality. Several similarities and some divergent points were observed in their narratives.

5.4.1   BENEFITS

"Benefits" are conceptualized as the actions of learning that have a general and specific character, for example cultural interaction and maturity, which independent travel bestows on those who are enjoying it. However, there are different characteristics among the studied age groups. The *Young* women are more flexible and seem to try to live the travel experience more intensely, valuing the lesson in self-conviviality and the challenges this kind of experience brings, which collectively may result in an expansion of their visions of the world. Therefore, it is mainly personal gains due to changes in inner growth, self-transformation, autonomy and self-confidence that stand out. Although the *Adult* and the *Mature* women share the same gains as the *Young*, it is noticeable that the older groups have an additional benefit that is translated into intellectual growth as a result from cultural exchange. This group transfers their learning to the professional field, maybe because they are more aware of cultural differences, as exposed by one of them who states that: "At work it is amazing, because I always come back with a bunch of ideas" (C.O., 36 years old).

In general, the *Mature* women feel a need to transmit the knowledge acquired in travels, as a way of contributing to the intellectual growth of those who they relate with. Moreover, the main difference among the researched groups is that the *Mature* women, in trying to become better people, consider that they sharpen their sensibility, their personal balance, and their self-consciousness, which results in them valuing family and friends more. Unlike the *Young* interviewees' group, the *Mature* group are more centered on their experiences' immaterial dimensions, recognizing independent travel as a space to overcome and face fears: "I overcame the fear that I had of several things.... I broke frontiers...you feel like a more capable person, you break barriers, prejudices, a bunch of things" (E.R., 59 years old). To them, independent travel takes on the role of a renewal and recycling agent, because independent travel: "revitalizes the soul, rejuvenates, gives joy of living (laughs)" (F.T., 41 years old). On the other hand, the *Adult* group show a more affective independence, since this group is more adventurous and more accentuated in its search for personal fulfillment. Therefore, reinforcement of self-esteem, personal growth and self-expansion are the main gains of the *Adult* group of women.

In fact, one of the greatest benefits of this kind of travel, according to several interviewees from the *Adult* and the *Mature* group of women, has to do with independent travel being a milestone in their lives, a turning point in their life. We underline that the introspection lived by these women at certain moments of their experiences as independent travelers, reflects on their future personal choices, on the way of seeing and understanding different realities and, consequently, tends to reverberate on uncountable dimensions of their existences. As one participant reflected, "It may be *clichéd* but it is true...you start giving value for what really matters, what is important, with no exceptions. Learning that, you begin applying it when you come back home...in your everyday life...you feel you have too much things...so you start taking the excess off...and learn the customs, the education change so much, the creativity. I think there are only positive aspects" (D.B., 38 years old). The influence of independent travels on participants' future personal choices is, confirmed by the testimony of another participant, who says that her travel experience: "reverberates in my work, reverberates in our relationships...you can exchange and acquire knowledge as well. I think it's a mix of things.... It does not have only one benefit...it is an expansion of who you are and who you will be" (A.S.J., 51 years old).

This means that the gains are directly related to the women's personal histories, as well as to the structures of these women's lives and to what they value and reject. From this perspective, we can infer that by being conscious of their subjectivity and by accepting themselves as different, they act contrary to the rhythm that the contemporary society uses to create uncountable strategies that forbid the individual to think, to self-interiorize and to be incessantly invited to be "out of the self." According to this understanding, that is a denial to join the alienation proposal, emerges a humanist leisure experience. A deepening of intra-personal relationships through independent travel allows greater self-reflection and connection with self.

5.4.2   PERFORMANCES

Performances are seen in the countless ways in which female independent travelers have to modify their attitudes and behaviors due to lived situations. When referring to their performances during traveling, the women's words, actions, and behaviors influence gender performances (Butler, 2004). In this respect, gender is a construction and should be seen as a dynamic process, which makes us believe that we are not fully-finished human beings but rather capable of giving a new meaning to our behavior in society within several interaction spaces, even if we must meet the present social norms.

By analyzing several behavioral traits of the studied groups, we observe that the aspiration of "being myself" is a lot more obvious in the *Adult* and *Mature*, if compared to the *Young* group. So, to the *Young* group, the freedom given by independent travel has much less strength and meaning, than it has to the groups of *Adult* and *Mature* women. This is precisely because the latter are capable of seeing several other ways and possibilities of life choices. These, as a rule of thumb, assume the risk of not "fitting" in with the established norms of the society, as for instance one woman mentions: "here I am always being watched, doing poses, and when I travel I don't. I am myself, truly" (C.O., 36 years old). In this statement, we see a clear manifestation of "breaking-through," of a transgression from the commonplace with a certain tension between a person's will and what is being demanded of them during their daily routine while performing their various roles in life. In this way participants exhibit their definition of what it is to be a "real" woman, complete and authentic, without the masks that society calls them to wear. The *Adult* and the *Mature* group realize they are powerful women, independent, free and brave, which can directly contribute to strengthening their self-esteem. As one woman says: "I have a feeling of power...that I can be in charge of my own life.... I am very proud of myself, to do these travels and to feel good...to leave the woman powerful" (F.T., 41 years old). This realization of power gained through independent travel also distinguishes the *Adult* and *Mature* groups from the *Young* group, which does not express this kind of behavior.

In general, independent travel allows for the living of a reality different from daily life, away from repressive and critical looks from the ones who surround them, as well as expanding behavioral patterns by ensuring individual anonymity. Therefore, independent travel may be an invitation to act in a spontaneous way, maybe daring, to undress or to put on "masks," time to dissimulate and/or to authenticate; situations to unveil and/or to cover attitudes, behaviors, and fantasies. All the options are possible and not necessarily self-excluding. On the other hand, the differences among groups increase when we examine the levels of self-confidence felt by the various women's groups when they are interrogated about their independent solo travel conditions. We see that the *Young* group assumes shyer behaviors and postures than the *Adult* or *Mature* groups, even elaborating fictitious situations to face or to get out of embarrassing situations: "Once I was afraid.... I said 'I'm going to meet my boyfriend who is in the hotel... my friends'. You start to come up with a bunch of things" (J.B., 27 years old). The *Adult* group shows more tranquility when dealing with this kind of situation: "Every time they asked me if I was alone, if I was married...at first I made up...but then I stopped to talk" (H.C., 33 years old). However, the *Mature* group reveals strategies to avoid it: "I am not a woman who tries to draw too much attention to me. I try to walk with discreet clothing... without drawing attention. I do not use much makeup, or wearing tight clothes, showing my body. So I think it discourages some flirting" (M.C.T., 55 years old). Along this line of thought, instances can occur during the trip that stimulate and/or favor certain personal performances according to the challenge experienced, resulting in different methods of defense or liberation, as exposed in the women's narratives. Equally, we can see some common points among the groups under analysis such as: the capacity of "finding a way around" complex situations, an experience that stimulates the creativity of these women regarding the need to come up with self-protection scenarios, to adopt a positive attitude, encouraging them to believe that they are citizens of the world.

5.4.3 CONSTRAINTS

When we examine the constraints faced by a woman during her independent journey, several aspects emerge, among which the gender and nationality aspects, relating to the condition of the "Brazilian woman on her own." Looking at this topic, the *Young* women are harassed more by men and have already lived humiliating situations due to physical and cultural differences. In these situations, the feelings of anger and indignation are more accentuated, because the *Young* group feels disrespected as people and as women. In contemporary society, men are at the top of the hierarchical structure both as aggressors and as superiors to women, as idea that supports the concept that gender roles play an important role in travel experience perception (Butler, 2004). Therefore, silence and inability to face these gendered constraints by the *Young* group result in a persistence of this behavioral pattern between men and young independent female travelers.

The *Young* and *Adult* groups were harassed by men in different situations, for example, when walking in the street or in a bar, as one woman stated: "On the street...a man approached me and asked if I speak French if I speak English.... I thought he wanted some information...because I was with a map in hand...and he said 'I need a company for dinner'" (A.F., 26 years old). Another participant also reported a similar experience, as she says: "In London I went to a pub that has music to dance.... I started dancing...there were several boys and each time one approached me in a very aggressive way...because they saw that I was alone...I know they did not want to hurt me...but this made me angry. Pissed me off! I cannot have peace? I just want to dance!" (T.G., 31 years old). Even the *Mature* group of women is harassed by men, however it happens with a lower intensity, and the majority of the testimonials of these women do not mention sexual harassment as being part of their travel experience, except one testimonial which we highlight here: "In Portugal, only a taxi driver approached me, took my hand, ran a hand over my face...he embarrassed me...and I said 'I think you're wrong, I'm a woman, but I am not prostitute, you respect me I'm not here for that'"(E.R., 55 years old).

Another point of difference among groups is that *Adult* women have fears and melancholy resulting from solitude, in addition to the restrictions connected to social norms that limit women travelers' freedom to travel independently. So, the *Adult* group of women feels a limitation in their ability to react and contest cultural stereotypes. As stated in the narrative of one woman in this group: "Something is changing. The Brazilian woman unfortunately has a stereotype...of the happy woman, the pretty woman, the fiery woman...just for being a woman...for being alone and...

for being Brazilian, all that influences.... I think that all Brazilian women alone in Europe will say the same thing" (T.G., 31 years old). They also differ from the *Young* group in creating strategies that protect from possible disturbances, for example, by dressing modestly and not wearing as much make-up as they would at home. In fact, historically, the stereotype of Brazilian women as friendly, cheerful and caring on the one hand, and erotic, exotic, and sexualized on the other hand, has been influenced by countless factors. The propagation of images of Brazilian women as having a strong sex appeal, an image which is strengthened by the high number of Brazilian women is working in international prostitution networks and associated with the sex trade (Leal & Leal, 2002; Padilla, 2008).

In terms of commonality across age groups, the women have lived with prejudices of color and/or nationality. They all confirm the sensation of vulnerability and insecurity, as well as being constantly susceptible to events and situations of threat and risk against their physical integrity, outcomes that are similar to the study of Wilson and Little (2005). Overall, being perceived as available for sex just because they travel solo, bothers all groups the most.

5.4.4 SPIRITUALITY

Regarding spirituality, the *Adult* and the *Mature* women, unlike the *Young*, share, among other experiences, the *Déjà vu* experience, an incongruent and illogical familiar sensation perceived before a situation that is odd or new to the person. Higher instances of experiencing the *Déjà vu* experience among older female travelers can be justified by a higher personal maturity resulting from their life experiences. As one woman in the *Adult* group says: "It is something that you are seeing for the first time, but it seems a bit familiar, it is that feeling of having lived this...as a past memory" (M.A., 38 years old).

However, this study finds that when a woman is inserted into a situation of vulnerability, she tends to pay more attention to the facts that surround her and surrenders to the experience, that is, she gives in to that experience and starts to interact with the others. This is in order to adapt herself to reality, which is an objective that she understands as an end in itself (Serrano, 2014). In this way, we understand that independent travel benefits moments of inner intimacy and connection with the exterior environment by observing nature and people. Introspection is also seen in the interaction between man and nature and with several forms of expression of beauty. This is because it is common that contact with nature benefits the contemplative and reflexive states, and these states are very much present in the *Mature* group of women, maybe because they have already achieved emotional maturity. As one *Mature* woman says: "The nature has invaded my body in such a big way and I started to cry, I couldn't hold, the force of the nature, the force of the place. And it messed with my spirituality, it messed with my emotions" (A.S.J., 51 years old). In this perspective, by appreciating the beauty identified in art or in nature, the individual can enjoy a deep leisure experience, since she builds a moment capable of awakening the sense of vision and hearing and is also an invitation to contemplate without taking ownership of nature's beauty (Rhoden, 2014).

All interviewees share experiences of introspection during their journeys and, overall, all believe in something transcendent that they call god, spirit, energy, nature, and human force, besides a sense of sharing and intense feeling of gratitude, that result in emotional maturity. All interviewed women report that they had at least one special and particular experience in which they got deeply emotional during their independent travels. This occurred when they were in contact with people, during meditation, by contemplating nature or by overcoming their physical and emotional limits. There is a very present wish among them to continue the learning experience and to uncover the world, alone or accompanied, with the purpose of fully developing themselves as a human beings. In relation to the introspective moments experienced by the women interviewed, there is a fundamental difference among the studied groups. While the *Young* group prefer to travel alone; the *Adults* group appreciate to travel alone or accompanied whereas the *Mature* group choose mainly to travel accompanied in order to exchange and share experiences.

5.5 CONCLUSION

The increasing demand of people searching for deeper and more meaningful traveling experiences stimulates the creation of detailed studies of those perceptions, as these are yet to be explored in detail. The complex relationships that permeate gender and travel provide the opportunity, especially through research of a qualitative nature, to better comprehend the subjective aspects of human life. Furthermore, we can say that gender roles influence contemporary society's behavior directly and globally and therefore, to reflect on this subject may contribute to the development of a collective thinking that nourishes respect and values the differences and the similarities, whatever they are. The Brazilian woman's stereotype is a recurrent aspect in participants' transcripts, which illustrate how this stereotype constrains them, especially when they are traveling alone, as it is connected to a disrespectful image. However, we believe that this reality is slowly changing, aided by access to information in the globalized world; the work of the Brazilian Tourism Ministry on promoting Brazil as a tourist destination; and the growth of Brazilian tourist flux to the exterior, particularly to the European continent.

The study revealed that, in their solo journeys, the interviewed women are judged as deficient, which is manifested in them experiencing gendered constraints and prejudice. However, we observe that independent travel provides the individual with a better comprehension of the self, as well as deepen the sense of self and of life due to the decontextualization that independent travel implies. In the group studied, a feminist perspective confirms the recovery of the self, and provides the women with the opportunity to turn to themselves and pursue their own interests, which, we understand, most women still do not. This change in attitude can be seen as a form of resistance to the current context in which they are situated and helps to promote changes in order to construct a more gender equal society (Henderson, 2002). The behavior of these women during the independent journey is influenced by existing social structures. As a result, they accept challenges and take on the responsibilities and risks that result from this freedom of choice, although that may expose their physical and emotional integrity, as is reported in their speeches.

The women protagonists of this study corroborate with the idea that the subjectivity of leisure experiences favors a personal development, which results in self-knowledge and connection to self. In addition, there are many personal benefits availed by all of the participants. In many cases, independent travel is a milestone in their lives, from which they draw lessons and reflections that may or may not transform their realities. This kind of travel provides opportunities for different performances in which women exceed emotional and intellectual boundaries. This occurs because the women are authentic and free of the judgment of their social environment of origin (Schechner, 2014).

Knowing more about the impact of women's behavior in independent travel on society as a whole, as well as on themselves, can contribute to the construction of a more equitable society. In other words, the internal and external mobility that these women experienced by traveling independently, enabled them to exchange information and feelings with the world, which could potentially gradually minimize prejudice about gendered stereotypes of independent female travelers.

KEYWORDS

- **independent travel**
- **stereotype**
- **leisure**
- **identity**
- **constraints**
- **performance**
- **spirituality**

REFERENCES

Baptista, M. Ócio, Temporalidade e Existência: Uma Leitura a Luz da Fenomenologia e Hermenêutica Heideggerreanas. In *Do Ócio – Debates no Contexto Cultural Contemporâneo;* Baptista, M., Ventura, A., Coords., Eds.; Grácio Editor: Coimbra, 2014; pp 95–102.

Bardin, L. *Análise de Conteúdo;* Edições 70: Lisboa, 1977.

Brasileiro, M. O Lazer e as Transformações Socioculturais Contemporâneas. In *Do Ócio – Debates no Contexto Cultural Contemporâneo;* Baptista, M., Ventura, A., Coords., Eds.; Grácio Editor: Coimbra, 2014; pp 33–48.

Buhalis, D. The Tourism Phenomenon: The New Tourist and Consumer. In *Tourism in the Age of Globalization;* Wahab, S., Cooper, C., Eds.; Routledge: London, 2001; pp 69–96.

Butler, J. *Undoing Gender;* Routledge: New York, 2004.

Camps, V. *El Siglo de Las Mujeres;* Cátedra: Madrid, 1998.

Costa, C.; Carvalho, I.; Breda, Z. Gender Inequalities in Tourism Employment: The Portuguese Case. *Revista Turismo Desenvolvimento.* **2011,** *15,* 37–52.

Cuenca Cabeza, M. *Aproximación Multidisciplinar a los Estudios de Ocio;* Universidade de Deusto: Bilbao, 2006.

Deslauriers, J.; Kérisit, M. O Delineamento de Pesquisa Qualitativa. In *A Pesquisa Qualitativa: Enfoques Epistemológicos e Metodológicos;* Poupart, J., Deslauriers, J., Groulx, L., Laperrière, A., Mayer, R., Pires, A., Eds.; Vozes: Petrópolis, 2008; pp 127–153.

Franco, M. *Análise de Conteúdo;* Liber Livro Editora: Brasília, 2008.

Giorgi, A. Sobre o Método Fenomenológico Utilizado Como Modo de Pesquisa Qualitativa nas Ciências Humanas: Teoria, Prática e Avaliação. In *A Pesquisa Qualitativa: Enfoques Epistemológicos e Metodológicos;* Poupart, J., Deslauriers, J., Groulx, L., Laperrière, A., Mayer, R., Pires, A., Eds.; Vozes: Petrópolis, 2008; pp 386–409.

Goldenberg, M. *A Arte de Pesquisar: Como Fazer Pesquisa Qualitativa em Ciências Sociais;* Record: Rio de Janeiro, 2004.

Guerriero, S. Até Onde Vai a Religião: Um Estudo do Religioso nos Movimentos da Nova Era. *Horizonte.* **2014,** *12*(35), 902–931.

Heimtun, B. The Friend, the Loner and the Independent Traveler: Norwegian Midlife Single Women's Social Identities when on Holiday: Gender, Place Culture. *J. Feminist Geogr.* **2012,** *19*(1), 83–101.

Henderson, K. Ocio y Género: ¿Un Concepto Global? In *Mujeres y Ocio: Nuevas Redes de Espacios y Tempos;* Setién, L., Marugán, A., Eds.; Documentos de Estudios de Ocio, 2002; Vol. 19, pp 21–38.

Hesse-Biber, S. *Handbook of Feminist Research Theory and Praxis, 2nd ed.;* Sage: Thousand Oaks, CA, **2012.**

Lafargue, P. *O Direito à Preguiça;* Editorial Teorema: Lisboa, 1977.

Leal, M. L.; Leal, M. F. *Pesquisa sobre Tráfico de Mulheres, Crianças e Adolescentes Para Fins de Exploração Sexual Comercial; PESTRAF, Relatório Nacional;* CECRIA: Brasília, 2002.

Lessard-Hébert, M.; Goyette, G.; Boutin, G. *Investigação Qualitativa: Fundamentos e Práticas;* Instituto Piaget: Lisboa, 1990.

Martins, J. Tempo livre, Ócio e Lazer: Sobre Palavras, Conceitos e Experiências. In *Do Ócio – Debates no Contexto Cultural Contemporâneo;* Baptista, M., Ventura, A., Coords., Eds.; Grácio Editor: Coimbra, 2014; pp 103–114.

McNamara, K. E.; Prideaux, B. A Typology of Solo Independent Women Travelers. *Int. J. Tour. Res.* **2010,** *12,* 253–264.

Monteagudo, M.; Cuenca, J.; Bayón, F.; Kleiber, D. Ócio ao Longo da Vida: As Potencialidades dos Itinerários de Ócio para a Promoção do Desenvolvimento Humano. In *Do ócio – Debates no Contexto Cultural Contemporâneo;* Baptista, M., Ventura A., Coords., Eds.; Grácio Editor: Coimbra, 2014; pp 135–149.

Oliveira, A. Religião e Sociedade Pós-Tradicional: O Caso da New Age Popular do Vale do Amanhecer. Revista Brasileira de História das Religiões. Ed. [Online] 2010, *2,* 277–290. www.dhi.uem.br/gtreligiao/pdf5/texto11.pdf (accessed Feb 11, 2015).

Padilla, B. O Empreendedorismo na Perspectiva de Género: Uma Primeira Aproximação ao Caso das Brasileiras em Portugal. *Revista Migrações: Número Temático Empreendedorismo Imigrante.* **2008,** *3,* 191–215.

Pernecky, T.; Jamal, T. (Hermeneutic) Phenomenology in Tourism Studies. *Ann. Tour. Res.* **2010,** *37*(4), 1055–1075.

Pritchard, A.; Morgan, N. Constructing Tourism Landscapes: Gender, Sexuality and Space. *Tour. Geogr.* **2000,** *2*(2), 115–139.

Rhoden, I. Atributos das Experiências de Ócio e Implicações Contraditórias Decorrentes do Estilo de Vida Contemporâneo. In *Do Ócio – Debates no Contexto Cultural Contemporâneo;* Baptista, M., Ventura, A., Coords., Eds.; Grácio Editor: Coimbra, 2014; pp 63–74.

Schechner, R. Podemos Ser o (Novo) Terceiro Mundo? *Revista Sociedade e Estado.* **2014,** *29*(3), 711–726.

Serrano, S. *Mulheres Viajantes;* Edições Tinta-da-China: Lisboa, 2014.

Trigo, L. A Viagem Como Experiência Significativa. In *Turismo de Experiência;* Panosso Netto, A., Gaeta, A., Orgs., Eds.; Editora Senac: São Paulo, 2010.

Wilson, E. A 'Journey of Her Own'?: The impact of Constraints on Women's Solo Travel. Ph.D. Thesis, Griffith University, Brisbane, QLD, 2004.

Wilson, E.; Harris, C. Meaningful Travel: Women, Independent Travel and Search for Self-Meaning. *Tourism.* **2006,** *542,* 161–172.

Wilson, E.; Little, D. E. A 'Relative Escape'? The Impact of Constraints on Women who Travel Solo. *Tour. Rev. Int.* **2005,** *9*(2), 155–174.

CHAPTER 6

IRANIAN WOMEN TRAVELING: EXPLORING AN UNKNOWN UNIVERSE

ROKHSHAD TAVAKOLI[1*] and PAOLO MURA[2]

[1]School of Hospitality, Tourism and Culinary Arts,
Taylor's University, Malaysia

[2]School of Hospitality, Tourism and Culinary Arts,
Taylor's University, Malaysia

*Corresponding author. E-mail: rokhshad.tavakoli@taylors.edu.my

CONTENTS

6.1   INTRODUCTION

The current identities and positions of women in Iran are the product of several historical events that have shaped Iranian society throughout the centuries. Since pre-historical times, women in Iran have contributed to form the myriad of social laws, conventions, and practices that characterize what constitutes present-day Iran. As Grishman pointed out in his seminal book, *Iran: From the Earliest Times to the Islamic Conquest*, during the Neolithic period women usually controlled tribal groups as they were regarded as individuals more powerful and innovative than men (Ghirshman, 1954). This was due mainly to women's highly developed engineering skills in agricultural techniques. In tribal societies, multiple marriages and partnerships were common for women, who were perceived as those carrying the "strongest genes." Further, as women were often highly respected spiritual and religious leaders, they often played an influential role in both private and public realms (Ghirshman, 1954). By reviewing the history of Iran, one may see that women have long attempted to negotiate and enhance their roles in society. After the 1979 Islamic Revolution, Iranian women have experienced decreasing levels of freedom in the micro (family), meso (relatives and neighbors), and macro (national and international) spheres. However, the Islamic Feminism Movement tried to rejuvenate this freedom. This branch of feminism focuses on issues concerning men's and women's equality within Islamic cultures, although Moghadam believes that these two words (Islam and Feminism) "are subjects of controversy and disagreement" (Moghadam, 2002, p. 1135).

As many historical documents and historical sources have been destroyed during the different attacks and wars of Iranian history, there exists a relative paucity of information concerning the history of Iranian women before the Islamic Revolution. Moreover, empirical material concerning women's political, socio-cultural, and economic lives after the Islamic Revolution is lacking due to the attempts of the actual regime to silence women's forms of resistance as well as academic freedom. Consequently, within the context of leisure and tourism studies, little has been written about the existing constraints influencing Iranian women's freedom of movement. As such, Iranian women's patterns of behavior on holiday have been relatively neglected by tourism scholars, especially within the context of Anglo-Saxon academic circles.

As an attempt to fill these gaps in knowledge, this chapter provides an overview of Iranian women's patterns of behavior on holiday. This work is based on an analysis of the available historical documents about Iranian women's roles in society throughout the ages and their implications for tourism. To partially overcome the lack of academic sources on Iranian women's traveling behavior, this study employs an interpretivist approach to research, whereby epistemological assumptions allow for researchers' involvement in the creation and representation of knowledge. As such, this work also engages with a reflexive approach, drawing on the observations, reflections, and experiences of the lead author. Reflexivity has been embraced by other tourism scholars to unveil the researcher's powerful role in the process of knowledge/realities production (Tucker, 2009), to encourage more honest and ethical ways of *doing* and representing research (Mura, 2015), and to analyze critically the complex structures of power underpinning the creation and diffusion of knowledge in tourism (Hall, 2004). The lead author of this chapter is an Iranian Muslim woman who was born in 1979, directly after the advent of the Islamic Revolution in Iran. She was raised in an educated family belonging to the Iranian upper middle class and experienced the dogmatic restrictions that Iranian women have had to face in leisure and tourism settings. By employing historical sources, reflexivity and personal observations, this chapter attempts to cast more light on Iranian women's patterns of behavior in leisure and tourism contexts.

6.2   THE ROLE OF WOMEN IN IRANIAN PRE-HISTORY AND MODERN ERA

The history of the land known today as Iran can be traced back to 3200 B.C. In pre-historical times, the peoples who originally inhabited the area called Mesopotamia, namely a region that historians regard as "the cradle of civilization" (Kramer, 1967; Maisels, 1993), initiated relatively advanced forms of social, political, and governmental organization (Foster, 1995). Mesopotamian civilizations included several peoples and empires, such as Sumerians, Babylonians, Assyrians, Elamites, Medes, and Akkadians. Royal inscriptions and documents found in this area allow researchers to understand how social life (including gendered relations) was organized in these cultures. More specifically, scholars have reported significant cultural differences among these civilizations about women's roles and rights in society (Lahiji & Kar, 1993). In this respect, historical sources seem to support the idea that Sumerian religious and secular routines were grounded on "matriarchal" principles, including "the feminine principle of existence" (Lahiji & Kar, 1993, p. 100).

Although archaeologists' and historians' assumptions are not always well documented, they reveal that the Sumerians worshipped *Nanshe*, the goddess of social justice, prophecy, fertility, and fishing. Besides worshipping both male and female Gods, Sumerian kings created and implemented criminal codes that included laws privileging women and orphans over men (Lahiji & Kar, 1993). One of the codes, for example, mentioned that: "rich people should not and could not get the possession of widows" (Lahiji & Kar, 1993, p. 195). The *Lipit-Ishtar* Code is the oldest legal code found in Sumerian language. *Lipit-Ishtar* was the fifth King of *Isin* (1870–1860 B.C.E), and "himself has been suggested as an early codifier of law" (Steele, 1948, p. 4). The articles in this code were continuously amended to protect women and children.

Among the several legal codes adopted in ancient Mesopotamia, the Code of *Hammurabi* (1754 B.C.) is one of the most well preserved ones. This code is renowned for his "eye for an eye law" or "law of retaliation," which is regarded by many as very authoritarian due to the harsh penalties it contemplates. Despite this, the code took a more progressive and democratic approach about commercial law, civil law and women's rights. Indeed, the code's section on family law is very protective of women's and children's rights in several aspects. For instance, the code's family section indicates that men should only marry one woman and have one wife. Exceptions were allowed only if the married woman was sterile. In one of the articles, unregistered marriage is labeled as illegal. Moreover, the marriage settlement or dowry was considered of women's possession strictly and men were allowed to use it only partially (Lahiji & Kar, 1993). The Code of *Hammurabi* also clarifies that a man does not inherit anything from his wife while a woman is entitled to inherit part of her husband's belongings (besides the dowry). Despite this, there are parts of the code that seem to privilege men over women as the latter are required to pay a higher penalty than the former if accused of infidelity.

The Elamite civilization (an ancient group of peoples who inhabited the western and south-western regions of present-time Iran) has been influenced by the practices of their neighbors, namely Babylonians, Assyrians, and Sumerians. Yet, it also developed its own cultural and social practices independently. *Susa*, one of the major commercial nodes in the world at the time, was the prosperous capital of this kingdom. Interestingly, the Elamites allowed women to hold leadership roles in politics as female rulers were quite common (Lahiji & Kar, 1993). Elamite culture has deeply influenced Iranian culture throughout the ages. "The feminine principle of existence" was the center of their religious thought and they represented goddesses and gods next to each other most of the time. In some cases, goddesses were given higher positions than gods. For example, *Išmekarab* was a goddess who had unlimited power to control people's relationships and punish those who infringed relationships' commitments and roles. In Elamite's beliefs, women were the symbol of fertility. Women and men had equal positions in juristic courts without any limitations. Their system was grounded on matriarchy but at the same time women's rights were not equal to those of men. In the case when property had to be transferred from father to children, Elamite women were protected financially. As *Ashurbanipal* conquered *Susa* in 633 B.C., the Assyrians took control of the city and many Elamites were deported. Lahiji and Kar (1993) believe that the glory of Iranian women reached its peak during the Achaemenid period. At that time, women occupied high-level positions, including ruling countries or regions (Lahiji & Kar, 1993).

6.3 HISTORY AND RELIGION: IRANIAN WOMEN FALLING FROM GRACE

As discussed in the previous paragraph, historical sources discuss the significance and agency of Iranian women in pre-historical and historical times, especially if the pre-Islamic era is referred to. Before the advent of Islam in Iran, women held key positions in society, such as judges in courts, officers in military organizations, ministers, and other governmental roles. The image of female officers leading their commandos and armies in fighting the foreign oppressors during the first Arab attack in 633 A.D (Afshar, 2009) is perhaps the most emblematic example of women's power and status in Iranian society at that time. However, with the advent of Islam, new religious and cultural values re-shaped Iranian women's lives and influenced gender relations until the current times (Afshar, 2009). A patriarchal system, which became more firmly established after Islam was embraced as the main religion, affected women's roles considerably,

especially within the context of specific professions. Islamic rules postu-
lated that women's nature is not assumedly "appropriate" for legal careers
(Inhorn, 2011). As such, becoming a judge was almost impossible for
a woman due to misconceived and socially constructed perceptions of
women as being "more emotional" and "less logical" than men. Only
recently have women been re-allowed to become judges, although only
for family matters in civil courts.

After the Islamic Revolution in 1979, many rules and regulations
prevented women from having social interactions, especially with men.
Some activists (both men and women) organized forms of resistance to
support women's rights and fought for equal opportunities. However,
many of them were forced to leave the country by the newly established
oppressive regime. Others were sentenced to imprisonment and silenced
forcefully. Among the representatives of this last cohort, activists, artists,
and poets became only apparently silent as their poems and story books
kept speaking up stridently (Moghadam, 2002). In recent decades, the
internet has become pivotal for these "dissidents" to voice their causes,
yet the employment of filtering and surveillance systems partially prevent
open debates about women's rights. The use of the internet for voicing
concerns about human/women's rights is popular among the urbanized
youngsters of Iranian major cities although freedom of speech and thought
remains a mirage in discussions related to religious and legal issues.

Considering the actual political and social scenario in Iran, it is not
surprising that forms of feminist activism are more common among women
who migrated to Western countries in search of higher levels of freedom.
These campaigns represent an attempt of resisting governmental positions
about stoning, harassment, family laws, and some social rights, which
jeopardize women's rights and lives. One of the most representative voices
of Iranian feminist activism is Shirin Ebadi (born 1947), who was a judge
before the Islamic Revolution and later a human rights activist. Since she
made significant contributions in promoting human rights (especially for
women, children, and refugees) she was awarded the Noble Peace Prize
in 2003. Recently, modernization, globalization, and political changes
have relatively expanded women's rights in Iran. However, women's
lives and identities are still hampered by several restrictions, which play a
role in shaping women's leisure activities. Importantly, issues concerning
wearing hijab and pre-marital sex do affect women's selves in both public
and private spheres.

6.4   THE IRANIAN LEGISLATIVE SYSTEM AND WOMEN

The current Iranian Civil Code, which was written before the 1979 revolution, is the result of *Reza Shah Pahlavi*'s reformist attempts of restructuring the legislative system of the country in 1926. Other countries' legislative systems were reviewed to craft this code, including French public and private law (Pirhaji et al., 2014). Although in this newly established secular legal system religious courts were abolished in 1936, matters concerning family law and inheritance were still regulated by sharia courts (Mottahedeh, 2001). Moreover, religious dogma still played an influential role in regulating criminal matters. However, it is with the advent of the Islamic Revolution in 1979 and the official constitution of the Islamic Republic of Iran that religious dogmas became the backbone of the Iranian legal system.

Within this system, limitations on the lives of women were officially legalized. The code prohibited (and still prohibits) women to run for the presidency of the country, assume leadership roles, become judges, and pursue certain educational fields. Firmly rooted in the principle of *vali-e-faqih*, the Iranian Constitution controls both public and private lives of women. Among the various restrictions, the concepts of "male surrogate" and "guardianship" represent the main pillars of Iranian Islamic Fundamentalism. As such, Iranian women are not free to choose or control various aspects of their lives. Evidence of such state-sponsored violence against women is well documented in the various articles of the constitution.

Women cannot occupy high-level political positions, such as that of President (Article 115 of Iran's Constitution). However, they can be a parliament member if they are eligible candidates based on Islamic criteria. Moreover, women are not allowed to be in high-level justice positions (Article 162 of Iran's Constitution), although more recently they have been allowed to be judges in family matters and civil courts. These codes may not influence the majority of women, but there are some codes which affect all women and in some cases both women and men. For example, according to the Article 83 of the Penal Code, known as the Law of Hodoud, the penalty for fornication is flogging, that is, 100 strokes of the lash, for unmarried male and female offenders.

The Article 21 of Iran's Constitution gives clergymen ample power to interpret the laws against women by claiming that "the government must ensure the rights of women in all respects, in conformity with Islamic criteria..." In Islamic culture, men are responsible for the family (Article 105 of the Civil Code) and "a woman cannot leave her home without her husband's permission, even to attend her father's funeral" according to the Council of Guardians. Furthermore, referring to passport-related matters, the Article 18 of passport law clearly states that married women require their husband's permission to apply for a passport. Although single women can apply for a passport without their guardians' official permission, their guardians still have the right to stop them at any stage of traveling.

The hijab is perceived an issue for women as the Article 102 of Iran's Constitution declares: "Women who appear on the street and in public without the prescribed "Islamic Hijab" will be condemned to 74 strokes of the lash." While this is not the case nowadays in everyday life practices, women could be arrested for not wearing the hijab properly.

6.5   IRANIAN WOMEN AND FREEDOM OF MOVEMENT

The Universal Declaration of Human Rights clearly refers to freedom of movement as one of the basic human rights. According to the Article 13 part 1 "everyone has the right to freedom of movement and residence within the borders of each state." Also, in accordance with Part 2 of this article "everyone has the right to leave any country, including his own, and to return to his country." Part 1 of the Article 12 of the International Covenant on Civil and Political Rights also states that "Everyone lawfully within the territory of a State shall, within that territory, have the right to liberty of movement and freedom to choose his residence." In accordance with the second part of this article "everyone shall be free to leave any country, including his own." Moreover, the fourth clause of this article stipulates that "No one shall be arbitrarily deprived of the right to enter his own country" (Universal Declaration of Human Rights, 1948). In addition to the above-mentioned declarations, which recognize freedom of movement as a general right for all human beings, there are other documents that identify and highlight the basic human rights of specific vulnerable groups (Kar, 2014). Some of these documents include the International Convention on the Elimination of All Forms of Racial Discrimination (Article 5), the Convention on the Rights of the Child (Article 10), the Convention on the Elimination of Discrimination against Women (Article 15), and the International Convention on the Protection of the Rights of All Migrant Workers and their family members (Article 39).

There are special cases in which the right of free movement can be restrained by the governments (e.g., people involved in criminal activities); yet, gender should never be conceived as one of these limiting factors. Unfortunately this does not seem to be the case in Iran. To have a better understanding of the freedom of movement in Iran's law, the legal status of women and their legal obligations to their husbands need to be taken into consideration (Kar, 2014). According to Article 1105 of Iran's Civil Code, "in the marriage, being the head of the family is the characteristic of a husband." As such, husbands have financial obligations toward their wives, including the responsibility of paying "alimony." Indeed, the Article 1106 of the civil code states that "In permanent marriage the wife's alimony is the husband's responsibility." The husband's financial obligation is considered as a right for women, but "A woman shall not be entitled to alimony whenever she refuses the marriage duties without a legitimate excuse" (Article 1108 of the Civil Code). In other words, women are granted the right to alimony as far as they respect the leading role of men and obey all his commands.

Husbands can control any aspects of women's lives, including travel and tourism experiences. According to the Article 18 of the Issuing Passport Act, adopted on March 1, 1973, "A passport is issued for persons under the conditions set forth in this Article:

> …Three-married women, even under 18 years, required a written consent of the husband – and in emergencies, the city prosecutor – to apply for a passport Women living with their husbands abroad and women married to foreign men keeping their citizenship are exempted from the requirements of this part.

The Article 19 also states that "If the obstacles of issuing the passports occur after the issuance or who by virtue of Article 18 is subject to the consent that allows the issuance of passports is dismissed, passport holder is prevented from leaving and passport will be confiscation until the impediment stops."

The Passport Act violates one of the basic human rights of women, namely the freedom of movement. Even when the husband's consent is given, there exists the possibility for him to change his decision at any moment and prevent his wife from leaving the country (Kar, 2014). Part 3 of the Article 18 allows women to appeal the husband's decision in case of "emergencies." Yet the question arises as to what constitutes an emergency. Indeed, the ambiguity of this term makes its recognition subjective.

6.6   IRANIAN WOMEN, IDENTITIES, AND TOURISM

6.6.1   HIJAB AND IDENTITIES

The social practice of covering body and hair in Iran is not grounded on Islamic traditions as Iranian women used to wear veils since the times of the Achaemenid dynasty (ca. 700–330 B.C.). However, it is not clear if this practice was driven by religious or cultural reasons (or both) (Javadi Faraz, 2008). Although during the Qajar Period Iranian women wore *burqa*, Reza Shah, the founder of Pahlavi dynasty, in January 1936 forced women to "unveil" and follow western clothing (Amir-Ebrahimi, 2006). However, before the Islamic Revolution wearing hijab was a personal choice. It is after the Islamic Revolution that wearing hijab became mandatory for all women by the age of nine. According to the Islamic Republic of Iran's law, women must cover their bodies and hair in public but how to cover them is a matter of personal preferences. Although women are somehow free to choose how to cover themselves, the government promotes *chador* as the "best hijab" for Iranians.

Post-modern and globalizing forces play an important role in the process of changing individual and social identities among women (Heisey, 2011), who often need to navigate among multiple (and contrasting) selves in their routines (Tavakoli & Mura, 2015). Women have to fully cover their body and hair in governmental places, either as employees or as customers. Some of them maintain this dress code in both public and private realms, although they rarely cover themselves if they are in private spaces with their *Mahrams*. Yet, the number of women who challenge this dress code in non-governmental and private places is increasing. Indeed, wearing tight dresses (not approved by the Islamic police) and heavy make-ups in public are becoming "normal" and resemble a social practice quite common before the Islamic Revolution (Farmanfarmaian, 2008). Using different masks during one day is not something unusual for Iranian girls. These masks can be facial makeup, clothes, or behavioral masks (Goffman, 1959). Dress and makeup masks do change in relation to the family members with whom the women interact, and the specific context in which women "perform." There are many cases of modern girls who would put on make-up outside the house and then remove it before returning home to avoid generational conflicts in the family.

Issues concerning hijab and negotiation of identities are not limited to the daily routines. There are two main different patterns of behavior that characterize Iranian female tourists during their journeys. These models of behaviors are shaped by the destination chosen, namely if that destination is domestic or international. In the case of domestic tourism, due to the Islamic rules and restrictions imposed by the government, women are forced to cover themselves and refrain from any sort of hedonistic behavior during the trip, although some female travelers challenge these rules and manage to escape the Islamic police eye. Wearing hijab is compulsory even on the beach and also swimming is forbidden in public, unless in protected areas specifically designated for women. These protected areas cater for the needs of some religious women who do not like to swim in public and mixed beaches. For example, during a family trip, women have to wear hijab and watch their kids and men swimming in the sea or they have to go to female-only beaches. In both cases they may not enjoy the feeling of "togetherness" with their family members. Either they observe the family members' enjoyment or they may enjoy their time without them but in different way. It needs to be noted that within domestic destinations definitions of (and ways of wearing) hijab and dress codes for women change from city to city. The dress code in Tehran (the cosmopolitan capital of Iran), for example, is very different from that practiced in small towns and cities in the mountainous regions of central Iran (e.g., Yazd). This difference would be obvious for women traveling from big cities to smaller towns. Moreover, not only the dress code but also the patterns of behavior of female tourists coming from other regions of Iran may increase the possibility of cultural clashes. This issue has created anti-tourism movements in some small religious cities as some of the religious leaders perceive tourism as a catalyst for immorality and fornication. As such, Iranian female travelers are forced to respect the locals' cultural values and control their behaviors in order to avoid verbal and visual forms of harassment, as well as corporeal punishment.

Based on women's comments received in the lead author's previous research and her observations of their behaviors outside Iran (Tavakoli, 2016), it is perhaps not surprising to claim that many young Iranian women prefer to travel abroad to escape from some of these restrictions. However, even in foreign countries religious and societal rules are not entirely forgotten (Tavakoli & Mura, 2015). Indeed, some women may decide to wear the hijab and avoid patterns of behavior perceived as "not appropriate" by Islamic rules for many reasons. They may have internalized these practices over the years or they may feel intimidated as certain patterns of behavior may have negative implications once they return to Iran. However, others also take advantage of higher levels of actual and perceived freedom by wearing bikinis in beach-oriented destinations. It is worth mentioning that in many families, women's dress codes and patterns of behaviors are controlled by their guardians, even outside the country's borders.

6.6.2 FREEDOM OF TRAVELING

According to the Civil Code, which is influenced by Islamic law, women cannot travel overseas without their guardian's official permission if they are single and under aged (18 years old). Logically, women may have freedom of traveling from the time they turn 18 until they get married. Due to women's increased economic and social independence, the age at which women get married has dramatically expanded, creating a quite long interval between adult age (18 years old) and marriage. As a result, Iranian women have been capable of traveling more often abroad. However, this trend was criticized by the religious authorities, who have requested the parliament to amend the law and change the minimum age for traveling from 18 to 40. Due to feminist activists' resistances, the law was not approved by the parliament.

Choosing a destination is one of the many limitations that many Iranian female travelers have to face as this decision needs family members' approval. To obtain guardians' approval for traveling to certain destinations is far from easy and very unusual as "others" (both males and females) play an influential role in the issuance of this permit. After marriage, the husband's permission is required for female travelers, namely an unofficial permission for inbound tourism and an official one for outbound travel. Furthermore, if women travel inside the country they are required to carry a letter from the organization they belong to, which should indicate the purpose of the trip. Without this letter, women would not be accepted by hotels or other accommodation providers.

The other major issue in inbound traveling is sharing a room with "non-*mahrams,*" which is not allowed for anyone. Although young tourists often travel with non-*mahrams*, they risk being arrested and punished based on Islamic rules. The issue concerning non-*mahrams* applies not only to young tourists who travel with strangers or friends but also to family members traveling together. For example, a single girl cannot be accommodated in the same room with her sister and brother in law. This problem can influence women's travel decision-making processes as it may lead to higher travel expenses and thus discourage women to travel. This issue contributes to strengthen women's preferences for foreign destinations.

Despite these limitations, certain hedonistic patterns of behavior common among the young tourists on holiday, such as drinking alcohol and having sexual intercourse (Mura, 2010), are not allowed in Islam and consequently forbidden in Iran, despite being sought after by many young female domestic tourists (Hafezi, 2014). According to the Islamic law, drinking alcohol is forbidden for all Muslims. After the Islamic Revolution, young people have consumed alcohol even more than the time before the revolution. Today, many homemade alcohol-based beverages are available in Iranian houses (Hafezi, 2014). As mentioned previously, the penalty for drinking alcohol in Iran is 80 lashes. Interestingly, Iran scored 166 in the world ranking of alcohol consumption, while by calculating the number of alcoholic beverages consumed per capita, Iran would be placed on the 19th place. This puts Iran ahead of Russia and Germany in terms of alcohol consumption (Namazi, 2014). As drinking alcohol is part of youngsters' leisure activities during holidays, foreign countries are preferred by Iranian women.

Pre-marital sexual relationships are also forbidden in Islamic cultures. Unlike Western societies, Iranian culture has always banned the possibility for women to have multiple relationships before marriage. Indeed, being a virgin is one of the main requirements for women to marry and a proof of it needs to be given the day after the wedding. On the contrary, society accepts the idea of men having pre-marital relationships with different women. These limitations contribute to women's desires of traveling overseas in search of higher levels of freedom.

The idea of a girl having sexual relationships before marriage is not accepted by Iranian society, yet there are forms of resistance that challenge this taboo. Recently, a new term came to the attention of the media, which refers to a phenomenon called "White marriage or Ezdevaj-e-Sefid." This new phenomenon explains new types of relationships between young boys and girls, who decide to live together despite not being legally married. In the past few years this phenomenon has been prominent in the capital of Iran, Tehran, and other major cities. It seems that increasing numbers of young people are living together without any legal license in main Iranian cities (Rahimpour, 2014) and have no intention of getting married. The main belief of this group is that living together without getting married is crucial to avoid the legal and financial complications of traditional marriages. In this way they can also avoid legal commitments. This phenomenon has propelled an illegal domestic market concerning types of accommodation (especially for travelers). As non-married couples are not allowed to stay in hotels or other registered lodgings, there are many unregistered homestays that provide accommodation for these "unofficial" couples. These unofficial homestays are the best places for some young tourists to perform hedonistic patterns of behavior in private. For example, tourists can enjoy swimming together with family members or partners of opposite gender in these spaces. They can also dance and drink alcoholic beverages, behaviors which are not allowed in public. However, these spaces are not risk free, as they also represent places in which young women could put themselves at risk of being harassed or sexually assaulted.

6.7 CONCLUSION

This chapter is an exploratory chapter on Iranian female travelers, which can be furthered and expanded through additional empirical research. This chapter is an attempt to open a discussion on some of the limitations and restrictions faced by Iranian female travelers. It has also explored how these women may learn how to negotiate and present their multiple identities in different contexts. Importantly, Iranian women have consistently begun challenging patriarchal views of femininity (both in private and public spheres) and resisted existing gendered structures of power. *My Stealthy Freedom*, an online movement initiated by Masih Alinejad, is perhaps one of the most representative examples of Iranian women's desire to contest and voice their lack of freedom. More specifically, this movement employs Facebook to encourage Iranian women to promote their rights.

The work presented in this chapter has emphasized that freedom represents an important aspect of Iranian women's lives. As such, women have taken a more conscious and proactive approach about their rights. Indeed, in the last years Iranian women have worked hard to achieve higher levels of freedom by improving their level of education, working in public spaces, and participating more actively in social activities. What can be referred to as a "silent revolution" has given women more visibility and independence, especially within the context of virtual realities. Importantly, this revolution has permeated all the aspects of women's lives, including tourism experiences. Indeed, the travel patterns of Iranian women have been shaped by freedom campaigns like "My Stealthy Freedom." Many Iranian women have become independent travelers by breaking free from the financial and social constraints of their guardians. However, while some women are still struggling to achieve their desired levels of freedom in leisure and tourism contexts, many others are not even aware of their rights. Forms of tourist behavior perceived as hedonistic and not aligned to religious and cultural beliefs are closely scrutinized and curbed by the Iranian government (both inside and outside the country). Yet, Iranian women's "silent revolution" keeps resonating loudly.

KEYWORDS

- **pre-historical time**
- **Iranian women**
- **Islamic Revolution**
- **freedom of movement**
- **identities**
- **Islamic laws**

REFERENCES

Afshar, H. Islam, Women, and the Politics of Violence: Illustration from the Middle East. In *Religion and the Politics of Peace and Conflict;* Hogan, L., Lehrke, D., Eds.; Pickwick: Eugene, OR, 2009; p 202.

Amir-Ebrahimi, M. Conquering Enclosed Public Spaces. *Cities.* **2006,** *23*(6), 455–461.

Farmanfarmaian, R. *War and Peace in Qajar Persia: Implications Past and Present;* Routledge: New York, 2008.

Foster, B. R. Social Reform in Ancient Mesopotamia. In *Social Justice in the Ancient World;* Irani, K. D., Silver, M., Eds.; Greenwood Press: Westport, CT, 1995; Vol. 354, p 165.

Ghirshman, R. *Iran from the Earliest Times to the Islamic Conquest;* Penguin Books: London, 1954; Vol. 239.

Goffman, E. *The Presentation of Self in Everyday Life Garden City;* Doubleday: New York, 1959.

Hafezi, P. Moonshine is Just a Phone Call Away in Islamic Iran. Reuters. [Online] 2014, http://www.Reuters.com/article/2014/03/26/iran-alcohol-idUSL5N0LF1GK20140326 (accessed Jul 7, 2015).

Hall, M. Reflexivity and Tourism Research. In *Qualitative Research in Tourism: Ontologies, Epistemologies and Methodologies;* Phillimore, J., Goodson, L., Eds.; Routledge: New York, 2004; p 137.

Heisey, D. R. Iranian Perspectives on Communication in an Age of Globalization. *Intercult. Comm. Stud.* **2011,** *20*(1), 36–48.

Inhorn, M. C. Globalization and Gametes: Reproductive 'Tourism,' Islamic Bioethics, and Middle Eastern Modernity. *Anthropol. Med.* **2011,** *18*(1), 87–103.

Javadi Faraz, S. *The Iranian Government's Approach Towards the Use of Hijab;* Master Dissertation, Universiti Putra Malaysia, 2008.

Kar, M. The Right of Freedom of Movement. E-Collaborative for Civic Education. [Online] 2014, https://tavaana.org/sites/default/files/main reading-third session_0.pdf (accessed May 10, 2015).

Kramer, S. N. *Cradle of Civilization;* Time-Life: New York, 1967.

Lahiji, S.; Kar, M. *The Quest for Identity: The Image of Iranian Women in Prehistory and History;* Roshangraran Publishers: Tehran, 1993.

Maisels, C. K. *Near East: Archaeology in the 'Cradle of Civilization';* Routledge: London, 1993.

Moghadam, V. M. Islamic Feminism and Its Discontents: Toward a Resolution of the Debate. *J. Women Cul. Soc.* **2002,** *27*(4), 1135–1171.

Mottahedeh, R. *Loyalty and Leadership in an Early Islamic Society, 2nd ed.;* I. B.Tauris & Co: New York, 2001.

Mura, P. 'Scary…but I like it!' Young Tourists' Perceptions of Fear on Holiday. *JTCC.* **2010,** *8*(1–2), 30–49.

Mura, P. 'To Participate or not to Participate?' a Reflective Account. *Curr. Issues Tour.* **2015,** *18*(1), 83–98.

Namazi, M. Iran's Drinking Problem. IranWire. [Online] 2014, http://www.thedailybeast.com/articles /2014/08/16/iran-s-drinking-problem.html (accessed May 10, 2015).

Pirhaji, M.; Ahmad Yusoff, S. S.; Mohamed Isa, S.; Jalali, M. Investigation of Defects of Article 264 of Iranian Civil Code. Asian Soc. Sci. **2014,** *10,* 7.

Rahimpour, R. Can Iran 'Control' Its Cohabiting Couples? BBC News. [Online] 2014 http://www.bbc.com/news/world-middle-east-30391593 (accessed May 10, 2015).

Steele, F. R. The Code Lipit-Ishtar. *AJA.* **1948,** *52,* 3.

Tavakoli, R. (2016). My journeys in Second Life: An authoethnography. In Khoo-Lattimore, C and Mura, P. Gneder and Tourism in Asia. Channel View: Bristol

Tavakoli, R.; Mura, P. 'Journeys in Second Life'– Iranian Muslim Women's Behaviour in Virtual Tourist Destinations. *Tour. Manage.* **2015,** *46,* 398–407.

Tucker, H. Recognizing Emotion and its Postcolonial Potentialities: Discomfort and Shame in a Tourism Encounter in Turkey. *Tour. Geogr.* **2009,** *11*(4), 444–461.

Universal Declaration of Human Rights. General Assembly, Palais de Chaillot, Paris. Adopted December 10, 1948.

SECTION III
Gendered Approaches to Studying Women's Travel

CHAPTER 7

EXPANDING UNDERSTANDING: USING THE *'CHORASTER'* TO PROVIDE A VOICE FOR THE FEMALE TRAVELER

JENNIE SMALL[1*] and STEPHEN WEARING[2]

[1]*UTS Business School, University of Technology Sydney, Australia*

[2]*Newcastle Business School, The University of Newcastle, Australia*

Corresponding author. E-mail: jennifer.small@uts.edu.au

CONTENTS

7.1   FROM *FLÂNEUR* TO *CHORASTER*

This chapter takes as its starting point the proposition that an understanding of tourist experiences and interactions requires a shift in our thinking of the tourist as a gazing *flâneur* to imagining the tourist as an interacting *choraster* (Wearing & Wearing, 1996). While much of the thinking within tourism studies has moved on considerably since Wearing and Wearing's paper was published, the central arguments, nevertheless, provide a touch-stone for many of the ideas we present here in exploring the experiences of women travelers (Wearing & Wearing, 1996).

Wearing and Wearing suggest that in the early tourism literature some of the initial sociological works were concerned with the tourist *himself* and the part that holidays played in establishing an identity and sense of self that was essentially male. Holidays were seen as a culturally sanctioned escape route for Western *men* from the large anomic forces that compose a technological world. Cohen and Taylor argued that the tourist uses all aspects of *his* holiday for the manipulation of *his* well-being (Cohen & Taylor, 1976). At this point in the tourism literature, these arguments soon became diverted into a debate about the authenticity or otherwise of the tourist experience and the tourist destination (MacCannell, 1976). In many ways, these developments focused attention on the attractions of the tourist destination and away from tourism as experience (although MacCannell did draw attention to the tourist experience as a means of authenticating the self). Ultimately, however, such a shift objectified the destination—it became a specific geographical site which was presented to the tourist for "his" gaze (Urry, 2002). Thus, the manner of presentation became all-important and its authenticity, or otherwise, became the focus of analysis, with the objects of the gaze categorized in terms of a set of dualisms—romantic/collective, historical/modern, and authentic/unauthentic (Urry, 2002). At the same time, the tourist came to be regarded as something of a *flâneur*. Indeed, according to Urry (2002) the nineteenth century literary construction of the *flâneur* can perhaps be regarded as a forerunner of the twentieth century tourist in that both were generally seen to be escaping the everyday world for an ephemeral, fugitive, and contingent leisure experience (Stevenson, 2003; Wearing et al., 2010).

Wearing et al. (2010) suggest that the original *flâneur* was regarded as a new kind of urban dweller who had the time to wander, watch, and browse in the public spaces of the emerging modern city (Benjamin, 1973).

The *flâneur* was a poet, an artist, and a "stroller". He has been described as an amateur "street detective" (Morawski, 1994; Shields, 1994) who moved effortlessly and, seemingly, invisibly through the shopping arcades of Paris. The *flâneur* spent his day simply watching the urban spectacle; observing people and window-shopping (Stevenson, 2003). But in the act of strolling, the *flâneur* did not just observe life but was seemingly engaged in an "archaeological" process of unearthing the myths and "collective dreams" of modernity (Frisby, 1986, p. 224). The *flâneur* was a gentleman who stood wholly outside the production process (Wilson, 1995). He was also away from home and in search of the unfamiliar (Lechte, 1995). All of these characteristics, it has been argued, seem to fit the contemporary tourist—or, rather, established conceptions of the tourist (Urry, 2002).

The *flâneur* was unquestionably male, and *flânerie* was a way of experiencing and occupying space that was available (if not only, then surely predominantly) to men.

> It is this *flâneur*, the *flâneur* as a man of pleasure, as a man who takes visual possession of the city, who has emerged in postmodern feminist discourse as the embodiment of the 'male gaze'. He represents men's visual and voyeuristic mastery over women. According to this view, the *flâneur's* freedom to wander at will through the city is essentially a masculine freedom. Thus the very idea of the *flâneur* reveals it to be a gendered concept (Wilson, 1995, p. 65).

However, while the signs and symbols for which he searched (through his use and observations of space) may have been those of the collective, the *flâneur* remained detached from what he observed. He chose not to engage with either the people or the places he visited, thus his way of seeing and being in space was highly idiosyncratic and individualistic—it was not interactive (Wearing & Wearing, 1996).

When applied to tourism, the *flâneur*-tourist is conceptualized as being at the center of the phenomenon observing on "his" terms. As a result, we are left with very little scope to understand the female traveler whose travel experiences seem to occur in what might be seen as a more interactive, experiential space (Wearing et al., 2010). Such an observation leads us to suggest that women tourists will gain no more than fleeting satisfaction from destinations dressed up to capture the gaze of the *flâneur*. It is necessary to move away from considering tourism solely in terms of the figure of the *flâneur* to recognize the lived complexity of modern life and to develop a framework for investigating the ways in which the female travelers' cultural identities and histories are constituted and inscribed both in space and on the self. As with other poststructuralist feminist writers striving for women-centered knowledges, Grosz (1986, 1995a) suggests a number of strategies in reconceptualizing women's public space. While we must be careful not to replace one form of essentialism with another, Grosz's work provides a useful starting point for developing a way of thinking about tourist cultures in terms of interaction and experience, rather than as objectified activities or sights. Grosz's notion of *chora* is useful here in that it may give tourism studies the scope to consider the tourism experience as involving both guests and hosts and the places within which encounters between them occur. Grosz argues that *chora*, Plato's space between being and becoming or the "space in which place is made possible," contains many of the characteristics which masculinist knowledge has expelled (Grosz, 1995b, p. 51). Rather than being the object of the stroller's gaze, the concept of *chora* suggests a space which is occupied and given meaning by the people who use and interact within that space and, as such, is open to possibilities.

> Chora then is the space in which place is made possible.... It is the space that engenders without possessing, that nurtures without requirements of its own, that receives without giving, and that gives without receiving, a space that evades all characterization including the disconcerting logic of identity, of hierarchy of being, the regulation of order... (Grosz, 1995b, p. 51).

Wearing and Wearing (1996) propose that, in reappropriating the implied maternal dimensions of space, as Grosz suggests, it is possible to orient the ways in which spatiality is imagined, lived and used and thus make way for the silenced/marginalized to reoccupy the places from which they (discursively) have been constrained, re/displaced or expelled. It may also expose men's appropriation of the whole of space. The challenge, then, is to envision a more nuanced version of the tourist and the tourist experience, to conceptualize the tourist space not as one-dimensional and monolithic, but as many places which are constructed through use, visual consumption, imagination and experience (Stevenson, 2003; Wearing et al., 2010). With regard to tourism, Wearing and Wearing suggest that the concept of *chora* helps us understand the tourist experience and opens the way for tourist destinations to be seen and understood as spaces in which people interact with places, peoples and cultures and where, in turn, the spaces (destinations) as they are lived and experienced take their meaning from the people who occupy them (Wearing & Wearing, 1996). To this end, Wearing and Wearing argue that the idea of the *choraster* is potentially more fruitful than that of the *flâneur* (Wearing & Wearing, 1996). Studies which report the interactive focus of women's holiday spaces support this view.

7.2 WOMEN TOURISTS AS *CHORASTERS*

A theory of women's and girls' holidays must acknowledge the significance of social interactions and interconnectedness with people, a theme well documented in other types of women's leisure (Green, 1998). At all ages, women's lives are interwoven with others through the circulating discourses but, for women, the discourse of social connectedness links them directly with others. Chodorow claimed that it is this socially constructed embeddedness in social interaction and personal relationships which differentiates women's lives from those of men (Chodorow, 1989). In tourism, these relationships can give meaning to the holiday space and the holiday in general. As Wearing and Wearing explain, "Tourist destinations as *chora* allow tourism…to be seen as a process rather than as an activity in which a specific place as the object of the tourist gaze defines the specific experience open to the tourist" (Wearing & Wearing, 1996, p. 235). Although it is the tourist–host interaction which interests Wearing and Wearing, the concept of *chora* as interactive space is also useful for explaining tourist–tourist interactions at the destination.

Tourism scholars writing on tourist motivation (such as Crompton, 1979; Dann, 1977; Krippendorf, 1987; Pearce, 2005) identify social interaction as a reason for travel. Pearce cites relationships as one of three core travel motives for leisure travel while most traditional malestream tourist motivation theories view the social motive as one of many travel motives (Pearce, 2005). All fail to appreciate the *totality* of the social for most women. Feminist researchers (such as, Berdychevsky et al., 2013; Davidson, 1996; Gibson et al., 2012; Heimtun & Jordan, 2011; Small, 2003, 2005a, 2005b, 2008), taking a social constructionist approach, reveal the centrality of social interaction to women's experience. Small's study of women's and girls' holiday memories at different ages of their life course found that social connectedness and interaction, while most prominent as a memory of young adulthood holidays, was an enduring memory of women's "good" and "bad" holidays at all ages and a defining feature of holidays and women's subjectivities (Small, 2005a). At most ages, holidays were a time to escape certain social interactions and to enhance other relationships. Significant social interaction was primarily with the women's and girls' travel companions, other tourists, or family with whom they were staying. Social interaction was experienced differently at different ages but was a core component to the success (or not) of a holiday. For holidays in girlhood (age 12), having a girlfriend with whom to share the holiday activities was recalled as essential to the enjoyment of a holiday. In young adulthood, social relations were *the point* of the holiday and the holiday as a public arena (Reimer, 1995) allowed the young women to explore social relations. By middle age when the women were mothers, a holiday was recalled positively if it constituted a change in social relations from caring for others to sharing with others. Even in older age where the destination itself had grown in significance to the holiday experience, relationships remained a focus of the holiday experience. Throughout the women's lives, valued holiday experiences did not entail "gazing" on the destination. Even among the older women, the relationship between the women and the destination was not so much one of subject/object as interactive. The women were a part of the environment, appreciating "the world in which I belong."

While there are many practical reasons for traveling with another, such as security and financial benefits, the pleasure of another's company is a key consideration for many women. Indeed, among Small's sample of nearly one hundred women and girls, few expressed any desire to travel solo (Small, 2005a). Traveling solo would not be pleasurable and, if not pleasurable, then such travel would, "*not* be a holiday." Although solo women's holidays are increasing in popularity, contributing to new subjectivities and empowerment (Jordan & Gibson, 2005; Wilson & Little, 2005), Wilson and Little found that there was still "a strong desire for social interaction along the way" (Wilson & Little, 2005, p. 165). For many women, other people (traveling companions, other tourists, and local hosts) do more than *enhance* the experience; they *are* the experience, the *essence* of the holiday.

As Davidson says, "The holiday is a space to nurture and develop the relationships that are significant to women by providing time and activities that are not available in the normal routine" (Davidson, 1996, p. 99). Those relationships contribute to women's identity and affirm who they are in relation to others. The holiday space, as different from home space, allows for new subjectivities to emerge through social interactions. Wearing and Wearing referred to the new subjectivity as "the socially constructed self that comes with and goes home with the tourist" (Davidson, 1996, p. 230). As Ganetz says, "These free spaces are absolutely essential if the individual, together with others in similar situations, is to be able to seek, experiment and shape his or her own identity and subjectivity" (Ganetz, 1995, p. 87). Davidson, in her study of mothers with pre-school children, found that a holiday was a time to develop/indulge an identity.

> The value that women place on relationships implies that the role they fill within these relationships is important and valuable to themselves. To value being with children, partner, or friends is to value the role as mother, partner and friend respectively. There are different 'selves' able to be nurtured in a holiday and, to a limited extent, the holiday provides choice over which particular self or selves will be engaged – the mother, partner, social or individual self (Davidson, 1996, p. 97).

Inherent in social connectedness is awareness of and attentiveness to others. Women are not only gazing on the destination but gazing on others and gazing on themselves in their interactions. As Small found, the emotions the women recalled in holiday experiences (such as, joy, excitement, embarrassment, shame, guilt, and fear) were born out of sensitivity to their relations with others (Small, 2005a). They were alert to societal rules for engagement. Similarly, in a study examining young women's attitudes to their physical appearance on holiday (Small, 2016), social comparison and feedback from others were significant to body-appearance dis/satisfaction. The women were, both affecting and affected, gazing on others' bodies and gazing on themselves. Related to attentiveness to others is concern and caring for others, a dominant feature of many women's holidays. As Lesko explains, "caring assumes a fundamental relation among people and their actions and is grounded upon a relational and interpretive form of thinking" (Lesko, 1988, p. 139). On holiday, caring may be for one's family/children or emotional support for friends experiencing life crises (Gibson et al., 2012).

The significance of social interaction to women's holidays is reflected not only in their positive experiences but also in their negative experiences. As Davidson found, "relationships had a significant effect on whether the holiday was considered to be good or bad…relationships were significant in constructing the experience as a holiday or not" (Davidson, 1996, p. 96). In other words, other people can "make or break" a holiday confirming that "the meaning lies not in the activity itself…but in the context of relationship and responsibility" (Bella, 1989, p. 168). The holiday space can be spoiled by stressful, unpleasant interactions with others, such as, family arguments, incompatibility among travel companions or when caring is too much like "work" (Small, 2005a, 2005b).

7.2.1 SOCIABILITY AND FUN

A theory of women's holidays needs to acknowledge relationality and the importance of caring but also recognize women's need at times to escape obligations to others. For many women, holidays provide a space for women to expand their sense of identity beyond that of carer of others (Gibson et al., 2012; Small, 2005b). Holidays can be a liminoid period (Turner, 1977) where,

> The content of the social relations is no longer normative, hierarchical and distant, but close and egalitarian, a state that he [Turner] calls communitas…people feel they are communicating with each other as individual persons rather than as performers of roles (Graburn, 1983, p. 14).

Sociability, the inherent pleasure of being with others, is significant for women and continues throughout women's lives (Arber & Evandrou, 1993; Bernard & Meade, 1993; Sizoo, 1997; Small, 2005a). Wearing (1998) refers to Simmel (1950) in explaining sociability:

> Sociability is the pure play form of sociation where individuals meet together purely for the sake of meeting with others, with no serious motive or goal in mind – 'sociability has no objective purpose, no content, no extrinsic results, it entirely depends upon the personalities among whom it occurs. Its aim is nothing but the success of the sociable moment and, at most, a memory of it' (1950, p.45) (Wearing, 1998, p. 116).

"Pure play" can be "fun." Simmel's (1910) work on sociability, provided Podilchak (1985) the theoretical basis for an exploration on the social organization of fun. Leisure and tourism can provide spaces for this important kind of qualitative life experience. As Green, Hebron, and Woodward claim, " 'Real leisure' should offer the opportunity for having fun in company, usually outside the home environment" (Green et al., 1990, p. 6). Women's holidays which focus on the pleasure of being with others, thus, have the potential for the holiday to be experienced as fun. Interestingly, the scholarly tourism literature has little to say about the matter. An explanation for the silence might be found in the gap between the cultural code of leisure which "emphasizes individualistic, self-referential enjoyment models" (Podilchak, 1991, p. 137) and the defining features of fun: "a social emotional interactive process which deconstructs the social and historical biographical inequalities of lived experience to create a with-equal other social-human bond" (Podilchak, 1991, p. 134). The assertion that for men the incentive for leisure is competition and for women the incentive is social (Colley cited in Henderson et al., 1996) suggests that the cultural code of leisure is a masculine code which has no room for the non-hierarchical social dimension which can result in fun. Certainly, interpersonal relationships in leisure have been considered more "casual" leisure than "serious" leisure and thus inferior with less durable outcome. However, as Shen and Yarnal contend, we should view serious and casual leisure, not as a dichotomy but as a continuum on various dimensions of leisure experience (Shen & Yarnal, 2010). Traditionally, fun and the social have been seen as unrelated to self-development and a constraint to the concept of flow (Podilchak, 1991). Yet such distinctions might not be appropriate for women. The establishment of fun as a relationship construction indicates its relevance for women. The importance of the social in leisure for women's identity suggests that for women, fun contributes to subjectivity. When fun is experienced, there is a "fusion of emotional intersubjectivity" (Podilchak, 1991, p. 145). Rather than viewing fun passively, a more appropriate view, at least for women, is to see fun as resulting from the active engagement and the reframing of ("a growing out of") an activity with others (Podilchak, 1991, p. 140).

7.2.2 THE OTHERS IN THE HOLIDAY SPACE

Women–women friendships appear to be closer and more intimate than those of men (Fehr, 1996); they also tend to be more communal and less agentic (Rawlin cited in Davidson, 1996). Playfulness can assist in a sense of communitas, as Berdychevsky et al. (2013) found in their study of women-only holidays or, as they are popularly called, "girlfriend getaways". If traveling in a non-hierarchical space, fun and laughter become possible. Small found that among her participants, the middle-aged and older women rarely referred to their relationship with their male spouse in their holiday memories (Small, 2005). On the other hand, when these women traveled with female friends, these experiences were recalled and remembered favorably, demonstrating the fun and "the sheer pleasure women can experience from the company of other women" (Green et al., 1990, p. 143). Here patriarchal controls were diminished and responsibility for others lessened.

Leisure study writers claim that women's relationships with other women in leisure activities can be significant in identity construction, empowerment, and resistance (Woodward & Green, 1991; Ganetz, 1995; Hamson, 1995; Green, 1998). Crawford, Kippax, Onyx, Gault, and Benton found in women-only travel "there was a sense of shared adventure, shared satisfaction, mutual support … nobody was RESPONSIBLE" (Crawford et al., 1992, p. 144). Similarly, Berdychevsky et al. (2013) reported the therapeutic nature of the relationships involved in "girlfriend getaways" (GGAs) and the women's increased sense of empowerment, achieved through (a) escape from routine (including a break from family and significant other), (b) altered gender dynamics (diminished power differentials, absence of sexual tension, and sharing a holiday with those who have similar ways of thinking and interacting), and (c) existential authenticity (whereby the women engaged in self-making and bodily aspects and reinforced family ties and communitas). The authors concluded: "the different styles of interaction noted on GGA and the feelings of freedom and entitlement that enabled the women to (re)construct their subjectivities, including relationships with self and others, support the suggestion that GGA might be understood as *chora* (Wearing & Wearing, 1996)" (Berdychevsky et al., 2013, p. 618). Nonetheless, they and others have found that women-only holidays are not immune to conflict. Berdychevsky et al. (2013) reported spats between some of their women participants. Certainly Heimtun and Jordan's research provides evidence of interpersonal conflict among women travel companions (Heimtun & Jordan, 2011). However, they concluded that the many strategies adopted to deal with conflict to protect friendships and holiday experiences were testament to the value the women placed on maintaining their relationships.

Women's experience of ongoing social connectedness is not accounted for in developmental theories which view separation from others as leading to attachment and adulthood. The idea that intimacy and identity are connected runs counter to Erikson's (1963) androcentric life span development model which posits identity as a stage before intimacy and generativity. For women, the two appear to be merged and to develop throughout life. The interactive nature of women's tourist spaces explains why women cannot be considered *flâneurs* who simply gaze on the destination with a disassociated "gaze" (Wearing & Wearing, 1996). That women do not wander the world unobserved, as suggested by the traditional understanding of *flâneurie*, is another reason for their dissociation from the male *flâneur*. Further, women's gaze is often directed at themselves rather than exercising their gaze on sexualized others. In reference to solo women travelers, Jordan and Aitchison report that, when alone in public spaces, solo female tourists engage in self-surveillance "as a result of believing themselves to be gazed upon in a sexualized way" (Jordan & Aitchison, 2008, p. 339).

7.3   CONCLUSION

This chapter contributes to an understanding of the female traveler that is subject-centered, dynamic, and capable of dealing with the complexity of contemporary tourism and tourist interactive cultures experienced by women. A key guiding assumption is that a one-dimensional approach to the study of tourism is unsatisfying and unsatisfactory. Understanding women's experiences takes us beyond the male theorization that has traditionally been used to understand tourists' experiences. Urry's influential work on the tourist gaze pointed to the centrality of the sensory, in particular sight, to travel and tourist experiences (Urry, 2002). Significantly, Urry made reference to the evocative figure of the *flâneur*—a nineteenth century literary construction who seemingly walked the arcades of Paris unobserved, consuming its spaces through the processes of looking and walking but never engaging. We used this as a starting point from which to develop a framework for situating women's tourist experiences within the context of the destination. To this end, we followed Wearing and Wearing (1996) in suggesting that the notion of the *choraster* is more useful than the *flâneur* in providing the conceptual space for imagining the female traveler. For women, the tourist experience is not simply a matter of a detached gazing on a destination but rather an engaging, socially interactive experience. Nor is the experience one in which they remain unobserved. They are often highly visible, especially in those tourist spaces which are masculine and sexualized. Further, the gaze of women is often an inward gaze as they survey the self in terms of appearance and behavior. That women's experience is not individualistic but interactive implies that social interaction should not be treated as one of many tourist motives but valued for its centrality in women's lives and travel experiences. It is clear that tourist spaces are not one-dimensional and monolithic but have many meanings. Destinations take their meaning from the people who occupy them thus they cannot be understood without reference to the interactions of people in that space. The significance of social interactions to women's holidays suggests the usefulness of the notions of *chora* and *choraster* as a way to expand our understanding of the experience of female tourists.

KEYWORDS

- **tourist**
- **social interactions**
- **women's holidays**
- **chora and choraster**
- **leisure**

REFERENCES

Arber, S.; Evandrou, M. Mapping the Territory: Ageing, Independence and the Life Course. In *Ageing, Independence and the Life Course;* Arber, S., Evandrou, M., Eds; Jessica Kingsley Publishers: London, 1993; pp 9–26.

Bella, L. Women and Leisure: Beyond Androcentrism. In *Understanding Leisure and Recreation: Mapping the Past, Charting the Future;* Jackson, E., Burton, T., Eds.; Venture Publishing: State College, PA, 1989; pp 151–179.

Benjamin, W. *Charles Baudelaire: A Lyric Poet in the Era of High Capitalism;* New Left Books: London, 1973.

Berdychevsky, L.; Gibson, H.; Bell, H. Girlfriend Getaways and Women's Well-Being. *J. Leis. Res.* **2013,** *45,* 602–623.

Bernard, M.; Meade, K. A Third Age Lifestyle for Older Women? In *Women Come of Age: Perspectives on the Lives of Older Women;* Bernard, M., Meade, K., Eds.; Edward Arnold: London, 1993; pp 146–166.

Chodorow, N. *Feminism and Psychoanalytic Theory;* Yale University Press: New Haven, CT, 1989.

Cohen, S.; Taylor, L. *Escape Attempts;* Penguin: Harmondsworth, UK, 1976.

Crawford, J.; Kippax, S.; Onyx, J.; Gault, U.; Benton, P. *Emotion and Gender: Constructing Meaning from Memory;* Sage: London, 1992.

Crompton, J. Motivations for Pleasure Travel. *Ann. Tour. Res.* **1979,** *6,* 408–424.

Dann, G. Anomie, Ego-Enhancement and Tourism. *Ann. Tour. Res.* **1977,** *4*(4), 184–194.

Davidson, P. The Holiday and Work Experiences of Women with Young Children. *Leis. Stud.* **1996,** *15*(2), 89–103.

Erikson, E. *Childhood and Society;* W.W. Norton & Co.: New York, 1963.

Fehr, B. *Friendship Processes;* Sage: Thousand Oaks, CA, 1996.

Frisby, D. *Fragments of Modernity: Theories of Modernity in the Work of Simmel, Kracauer and Benjamin;* MIT Press: Cambridge, UK, 1986.

Ganetz, H. The Shop, the Home and Femininity as a Masquerade. In *Youth Culture in Late Modernity;* Fornäs, J., Bolin, G., Eds.; Sage: London, 1995; pp 72–99.

Gibson, H.; Berdychevsky, L.; Bell, H. Girlfriend Getaways over the Life Course: Change and Continuity. *Ann. Leis. Res.* **2012,** *15*(1), 38–54.

Graburn, N. The Anthropology of Tourism. *Ann. Tour. Res.* **1983,** *10,* 9–33.

Green, E. Flexible Work, Disappearing Leisure? Feminist Perspectives on Women's Leisure as Spaces for Resistance to Gender Stereotypes. In *Gender, Space and Identity: Leisure Culture and Commerce;* Aitchison, C., Jordan, F., Eds.; Leisure Studies Association: Eastbourne, UK, 1998; pp 111–126.

Green, E.; Hebron, S.; Woodward, D. *Women's Leisure, What Leisure?* Macmillan Education: Basingstoke, UK, 1990.

Grosz, E. Conclusion. What is Feminist Theory? In *Feminist Challenges;* Pateman, C., Grosz, E., Eds.; Allen & Unwin: Sydney, New South Wales, 1986; pp 190–204.

Grosz, E. *Space, Time and Perversion: Essays on the Politics of Body;* Routledge: London, 1995a.

Grosz, E. Women, Chora, Dwelling. In *Postmodern Cities and Spaces;* Watson, S., Gibson, K., Eds.; Blackwell: Oxford, UK, 1995b; pp 47–58.

Hamson, R. Writing Women's Friendship: An Intimate Experience? In *(Hetero) Sexual Politics;* Maynard, M., Purvis, J., Eds .; Taylor & Francis: London, 1995; pp 125–138.

Heimtun, B.; Jordon, F. 'Wish YOU weren't here!' Interpersonal Conflicts and the Touristic Experiences of Norwegian and British Women Travelling with Friends. *Tour. Stud.* **2011,** *11,* 271–290.

Henderson, K.; Bialeschki, M.; Shaw, S.; Freysinger, V. *Both Gains and Gaps: Feminist Perspectives on Women's Leisure;* Venture Publishing: State College, PA, 1996.

Jordan, F.; Aitchison, C. Tourism and the Sexualisation of the Gaze. Solo Female Tourists' Experiences of Gendered Power, Surveillance and Embodiment. *Leis. Stud.* **2008,** *27*(3), 329–349.

Jordan, F.; Gibson, H. 'We're not Stupid…but we'll not Stay Home either': Experiences of Solo Women Travelers. *Tour. Rev. Int.* **2005,** *9,* 195–211.

Krippendorf, J. *The Holiday Makers: Understanding the Impact of Leisure and Travel;* Heinemann: London, 1987.

Lechte, J. (Not) Belonging in Postmodern Space. In *Postmodern Cities and Spaces;* Watson, S., Gibson, K., Eds.; Blackwell: Oxford, UK, 1995; pp 97–111.

Lesko, N. *Symbolizing Society: Stories, Rites and Structure in a Catholic High School;* The Falmer Press: Philadelphia, PA, 1988.

MacCannell, D. *The Tourist: A New Theory of the Leisure Class;* The Macmillan Press: London, 1976.

Morawski, S. The Hopeless Game of *Flânerie.* In *The Flâneur;* Tester, K., Ed.; Routledge: London, 1994; pp 181–97.

Pearce, P. *Tourist Behaviour: Themes and Conceptual Schemes;* Channel View Publications: Clevedon, UK, 2005.

Podilchak, W. The Social Organization of Fun. *Loisir et Société / Soci. Leis.* 1985, *8,* 685–691.

Podilchak, W. Distinctions of Fun, Enjoyment and Leisure. *Leis. Stud.* **1991,** *10*(2), 133–148.

Reimer, B. Youth and Modern Lifestyles. In *Youth Culture in Late Modernity;* Fornäs, J., Bolin, G., Eds.; Sage: London, 1995; pp 120–144.

Shen, X.; Yarnal, C. Blowing Open the Serious Leisure-Casual Leisure Dichotomy: What's in there? *Leis. Sci.* **2010,** *32,* 162–179.

Shields, R. Fancy Footwork: Walter Benjamin's Notes on Flânerie. In *The Flâneur;* Tester, K., Ed.; Routledge: London, 1994; pp 61–80.

Sizoo, E. How Women Change Places and Places Change Women. In *Women's Lifeworlds: Women's Narratives on Shaping their Realities;* Sizoo, E., Ed.; Routledge: London, 1997; pp 221–248.

Small, J. The Voice of Older Women Tourists. *Tour. Recre. Res.* **2003,** *28*(2), 31–39.

Small, J. Holiday Experiences of Women and Girls over the Life-Course. Ph.D. Dissertation, University of Technology Sydney, Sydney, New South Wales, 2005a.

Small, J. Women's Holidays: The Disruption of the Motherhood Myth. *Tour. Rev. Int.* **2005b,** *9*(2), 139–154.

Small, J. The Absence of Childhood in Tourism Studies. *Ann. Tour. Res.* **2008,** *35,* 772–789.

Small, J. Holiday Bodies: Young Women and their Appearance. Annals of Tourism Research. 2016,58, 18-32.

Stevenson, D. *Cities and Urban Cultures;* Open University Press: Maidenhead, UK, 2003.

Urry, J. *The Tourist Gaze, 2nd ed.;* Sage: London, 2002.

Wearing, B. *Leisure and Feminist Theory;* Sage: London, 1998.

Wearing , S. L.; Stevenson, D.; Young, T. *Tourist Cultures: Identity, Place and the Traveler;* Sage: London, 2010.

Wearing, B.; Wearing, S. Refocussing the Tourist Experience: The *Flâneur* and the *Choraster. Leis. Stud.* **1996,** *15,* 229–243.

Wilson, E. The Invisible *Flâneur.* In *Postmodern Cities and Spaces;* Watson, S., Gibson, K., Eds.; Blackwell: Oxford, UK, 1995; pp 59–79.

Wilson, E.; Little, D. A 'Relative Escape'? The Impact of Constraints on Women who Travel Solo. *Tour. Rev Int.* **2005,** *9,* 155–175.

Woodward, D.; Green, E. In Celebration of Women's Friendships: Collusion, Catharsis or Challenge? In *Ideology, Leisure Policy and Practice;* Botterill, D., Tomlinson, A., Eds.; Leisure Studies Association: Eastbourne, UK, 1991; pp 49–60.

CHAPTER 8

WOMEN'S TRAVEL NARRATIVES OF PARIS AND THE EMOTIONAL GEOGRAPHIES OF PLACE

KELLEY A. MCCLINCHEY

Department of Geography and Environmental Studies,
Wilfrid Laurier University, Canada

E-mail: kelleymcclinchey@yahoo.ca

CONTENTS

8.1   INTRODUCTION

"So, in Paris, I will relearn how to live." (Marton, 2012, p. 33)

Paris has been the subject of dozens of travel memoirs. From Ernest Hemingway's *A Moveable Feast* and Gertrude Stein's *Paris, France*, writers have documented their adventures, challenges, and sensuous experiences in the City of Light. Both men and women have documented descriptive, thorough and eloquent accounts of their Paris pursuits. However, women's travel to Paris is distinct and has been expressed both explicitly and implicitly through non-fiction travel books. Although many of these texts are referred to as travel memoirs, the travel book resembles or is a subspecies of a memoir, an autobiographical narrative (Dann, 1999). A travel book is also much like a quest romance, based on the idea of a hero setting out, experiencing trials and adventure, and returning home victorious and changed (Dann, 1999).

While Laing and Frost considered how books, including non-fiction narratives, as cultural phenomena affect our conceptualization of travel, attention in academia of the impact or influence of literature on tourism is still lacking (Laing &Frost, 2012). Dann asked, "why do bookstores continue to devote considerable space to these and similarly popular titles, while scholarly considerations for their appeal are so correspondingly scarce and conspicuously absent?" (Dann, 1999, p. 161). The examination of tourism centered texts still awaits serious critical interest (Osagie & Buzinde, 2011). Ryan et al. concluded that tourism studies of the role of novels must be contextualized within disciplines of literary criticism (Ryan et al., 2009). Furthermore, Laing and Frost argue that the book is a powerful agent for cultural change (Laing & Frost, 2012). The text as discourse is an important product of social relations, and "we need to explore and understand how their meanings have been constructed and used across the totality of human experience and that includes tourism experiences" (Jaworski & Pritchard, 2005, p. 2 cited in Osagie & Buzinde, 2011).

There is an overwhelming number of contemporary women's travel narratives of Paris and there is no shortage of recent publications in the past 10 years. Therefore, this chapter seeks to answer why there is such an abundance of women's travel books about Paris and what over-arching themes might exist in these texts? What do these themes say about women's travel and how place, in this case Paris, affects women specifically? Furthermore, we need to understand the influence of this literary genre on women's travel within the context of emotional geographies of place.

8.2 CONCEPTUAL APPROACH

8.2.1 LITERARY TRAVEL

Literary travel is not simply a function of "literary influences" but a medium through which a range of cultural meanings and values may be communicated (Squire, 1994). It has grasped the attention of tourism scholars as a form of niche tourism (Herbert, 2001) and garnered the attention of researchers exploring the Grand Tour, the English Lake District, and Prince Edward Island, Canada (Fawcett & Cormack, 2001; Squire, 1994; Towner, 1985). These examples earlier on in the literary tourism research illustrated the strength of literary tourism in specific regions and the complexities in dealing with heritage, nostalgia, authenticity, reality, and imagination for distinct tourist experiences. Recently, the literary tourism discussion has returned because of the way in which media has altered how we record, document and share our travel realities and imaginaries, both through time and space (Salazar, 2012). Notable research has explored travel literature and/or travel writing more recently. Enoch and Grossman examined travel diaries of tourists in India by processing their experience through writing a diary the tourists deconstruct and reconstruct "India" and "Home" as well as the relationship between them (Enoch & Grossman, 2010). Reijinders investigated why people feel the need to connect to fictional stories about places that bridge reality and imagination (Reijinders, 2011). Furthermore, tourism scholars, through interdisciplinary approaches, are applying more complex theoretical analyzes to various forms of travel writing and with women specifically. For example, Osagie and Buzinde applied postcolonial literary theory to analyze Jamaica Kincaid's quasi-autobiographical book, *A Small Place*, a critique of tourism in Antigua (Osagie & Buzinde, 2011).

8.2.2 WOMEN'S TRAVEL AND TRAVEL WRITING

Women's travel has been a subject of study in tourism for quite some time (Bartos, 1982). Previous research has described women's travel patterns and feelings, such as enjoyment and social interaction, associated with them (Ohlenschlager, 1990). More specific examples include studies on segmenting women pleasure travelers on traveler typologies as well as decision-making roles (Kerstetter & Pennington-Gray, 1999; Pennington-Gray & Kerstetter, 2001). Socio-cultural, practical, and spatial categories emerged as women's travel constraints relating to social and gendered location as females (Wilson & Little, 2005). Other research has focused on women's motivation to travel for leisure such as experience, escape, relaxation, social ties, and self-esteem (Chiang & Jogaratnam, 2006). Rojek argued that motivation for women's travel in the nineteenth and twentieth centuries was as an escape from modern life (Rojek, 1993). Small found that women want freedom in their travels; freedom from their unpaid positions as care-givers of house, pets, husband, children, and others (Small, 2005). Women yearned for a space of their own, to experience the freedom of travel and holidays.

Although travelers have documented their experiences through writing for centuries, only recently have scholars taken a special interest with regard to women travel writers (Richards & Wilson, 2004). Researchers in literature and in tourism have studied women travel writers of the 18th and 19th centuries as part of the Grand Tour (Bohls, 1995; Lawrence, 1994; Robinson, 1990) and women's travel writing in the 20th century has been examined by literature, media, and tourism scholars focusing on post-colonial women's travel (Kelley, 2005; Mulligan, 2000; Osagie & Buzinde, 2011). However, less is known about women travelers and travel writers in the 21st century and during the feminist or post-feminist eras (Genz & Brabon, 2012; Rojek, 1993).

Some recent notable examples demonstrate a growing trend in this direction. Laing explored the Italian fantasy for women through books and films, examining the way in which this narrative has entered popular culture through a feminist analysis of the representation of Italy through media (Laing, 2010). Wilson et al. found that travel provides a mechanism for life-changing experiences for women through guidebooks (Wilson et al., 2009). Laing and Frost argued that these life-changing experiences are also present in autobiographical texts such Corinne Hofmann's *The White Masai* (Hofmann, 1999) and Elizabeth Gilbert's *Eat, Pray, Love* (Gilbert, 2006, 2012). Women's travel has interested researchers focusing on sensuality, embodiment, and experience (e.g., Pritchard, 2007). Yet little attention has been paid to the emotional aspects of women's travel, especially in relation to place. The concept of emotional geographies has yet to be applied to the context of women's travel, travel writing in general, and women's travel books of Paris more specifically.

8.2.3 EMOTIONAL GEOGRAPHIES

Emotions are universal throughout human cultures. Psychologists have determined that some of these basic emotions include happiness, sadness, fear, disgust, anger, surprise, satisfaction, pride, contempt, embarrassment, and amusement (Ekman, 1999). Emotions are not easily defined, measured, or singled out and are often combined together in various degrees (Plutchik & Kellerman, 1980). They are also highly subjective, related to each individual's experience and multi-dimensional which is likely why they have only been recently empirically studied in human geography (Hockenbury & Hockenbury, 2007). What little talk of emotion there is occurs squarely in the cultural (and often feminist) corners of the discipline (Anderson & Smith, 2001; Nash, 2000). Anderson and Smith argued that "this marginalization of emotion has been part of a gender politics of research in which detachment, objectivity and rationality have been valued, and implicitly masculinized, while engaged engagement, subjectivity, passion and desire have been devalued, and frequently feminized" (Anderson & Smith, 2001, p. 7).

The recent "emotional turn" in geography results as much from positive recognition that emotions already have an important place in our own and others' work (Bondi et al., 2005). Bondi et al. compiled researchers' accounts of emotions through bodies, places, and environments (Bondi et al., 2005). Wide ranging studies in this volume explored emotional responses of the body to loss, aging, eating, dying, memory as well as relating emotion to places such as the Scottish Highlands, going out at night, fast-food restaurants and meaningful natural landscapes. Collis discovered that, for women, the connection between emotion and identity is very strong (Collis, 2005). Furthermore, the way men and women display and manage their emotional selves differs greatly even with regard to place and environment (Williams, 2000). While much of the present work explores emotions and place in natural and rural areas, Hubbard explored the emotional geographies of "going-out" in the city (Hubbard, 2005). Furthermore, Conradson argued that components of places that are influential emotionally are not only the people or events, but may also include the various non-human life forms and inanimate things that comprise a place or landscape (Conradson, 2005).

Emotions have been discussed specifically relating to women's travel narratives. Falcone focused on female backpackers whose narratives fluctuated between promoting a strong, resilient character who embraces risk taking behavior as part of an enriched travel experience and feelings of anger, fear, vulnerability, and loss of control (Falcone, 2011). Other examples of female travel and emotions focused on solo international travel and the perceived travel fears relating to others' perceptions, vulnerability, sense of restricted access, and a feeling of conspicuousness. Focusing on independent women's travel, Wilson and Harris argued for the concept of meaningful travel finding three key themes: search for self and identity, self-empowerment and connectedness with others (Wilson & Harris, 2006). Wilson, Holdsworth and Witsel argued that there is a conflicting discourse in women's travel guidebooks around empowerment versus fear (Wilson et al., 2009).

While much work has been explored in terms of the emotional in bodies and space, there is still a lack of understanding as to the feelings places inspire in us such as passion, awe, dread, worry, loss, love, and connection. An emotional geography, then, attempts to understand emotion—experientially and conceptually—in terms of its socio-spatial mediation and articulation rather than as entirely interiorized mental status (Bondi et al., 2005). For example, Urry focused directly on the way emotions are located within the consumption of tourist places (Urry, 2005). Urry showed how specific sites are constructed in ways saturated with emotion, sometimes wild and frightening, and sometimes aesthetically pleasing and relaxing and sometimes dependent on ideas of rootedness. This can be specifically applied to the way in which women travelers embody Paris and communicate it through their narratives.

8.3 METHOD

Over the past 10 years, the number of Paris travel memoirs written by women has greatly increased. While some of the memoirs originated as novels others are compilations of what began as web-based blogs that morphed into published volumes. Regardless of how they commenced, not only are more women traveling Paris independently, with a partner, or with family, but they are finding a voice and sharing it with a wider community. As such, it is an important time to understand how women travelers, and travel writers, perceive Paris and what this means for their needs and desires for travel experiences as a whole. Moreover, the emotional and sensuous components of travel experiences especially for women experiencing urban tourism are missing in current academic literature.

The travel books chosen were categorized as contemporary travel literature in that they were published after 1990. Contemporary travel literature differentiated from other travel literature about Paris published in the 20th century (e.g., Gertrude Stein's "Paris, France," 1940). These texts have had a profound impact on how Paris is represented in literature, however, their form as modernist memoirs differ from those published during/after the "postmodern turn." For this research, 16 English language travel books authored by women were selected by the author (see Table 8.1). A comprehensive list was created from local bookstores and web searches of Amazon.ca and Indigo.ca as well as travel websites/blogs about Paris or France. While this may not be the total number of contemporary travel texts about Paris authored by women, it represents a sample that is indicative of the authorship, style of writing, content, form, and locations experienced by the authors.

TABLE 8.1   Contemporary Women's Travel Narratives of Paris.

Title	Author	Date Published/ publisher	Type of experience	Pg.
Lunch in Paris: A love story with recipes	Elizabeth Bard	2010, Back Bay Books, NY	Single, American short trip to Paris, but never left	314
we'll always have Paris	Jennifer Coburn	2014, Sourcebooks, Naperville, Illinois	Married mother takes young daughter on tour of Europe American	372
C'est la vie	Suzie Gershman	2004, Penguin, NY	Widowed, American new life experience	263
True pPleasures: A memoir of women in Paris	Lucinda Holdforth	2005, Greystone Books, Vancouver, British Columbia	single, Australian, new life experience, walking Paris discovering strong Parisian Women of the past	226
An extraordinary theory of objects	Stephanie LaCava	2012, Harper Perennial, NY	adolescent, American year in Paris	180

TABLE 8.1   *(Continued)*

Title	Author	Date Published/ publisher	Type of experience	Pg.
Paris: Times eight	Deirdre Kelly	2009, D&M Publishers, Vancouver, BC	Single then married, Canadian, eight visits to Paris for various purposes	304
French milk	Lucy Knisley	2007, Simon and Shuster, NY	Single, new experience, American, traveled with mother	193
Mastering the art of French eating	Ann Mah	2013, Penguin Group, NY	married, American Husband transferred employment	273
Paris: A love story	Katie Marton	2012, Simon and Schuster, NY	widowed, American several trips to Paris with husband	199
Breathless: An American girl in Paris	Nancy K. Miller	2013, Seal Press, Berkeley, California	Single, american, new life experience	238
Paris: Extraordinary moments	Adrienne Michel Sager	2014, Silver Pen Press, South Carolina	Married, American, frequently travels to Paris conducting art/culture tours	222
Paris letters	Janice MacLeod	2014, Sourcebooks Naperville, Illinois	Single, Canadian two-year trip to Europe – ends in desire to stay in Paris (love and new life experience)	249
Paris, my sweet	Amy Thomas	2012, Sourcebooks, Illinois	Single, American new employment	280
Almost french	Sarah Turnbull	2002, Gotham Books, NY	Single, Australian new life experience	304
Seven letters from Paris	Samantha Verant	2014, Sourcebooks Naperville, Illinois	Separated, American, new life experience, re-kindling romance	251
French toast	Harriet Welty-Rochefort	1997, St. Martin's Press, NY	Single then married, American, new life experience	205

To be human is to operate in a world of meaning, thus the travel book is comprised of meaningful accounts of travelers' experiences, ones from which the researcher cannot be distanced through a superior vista (Pernecky,

2010). Phenomenology does not merely call for an account of things we see in our world but shifts the focus to our "seeing" of objects and the world and the meaning they hold (e.g., the experience of reading a book on travel writing) (Pernecky & Jamal, 2010). Hermeneutic philosophers such as Heidegger (1962) and Gadamer (1989) rethink interpretation as underpinning all forms of understanding and they see it as ontological, as fundamental to being human (Ablett & Dyer, 2009). Thus the central idea behind hermeneutics is that the analyst of the text must seek to bring out the meanings of a text from the perspective of its author (Bryman, 2001). Hermeneutics emphasizes a detailed reading or examination of text. A researcher conducts "a reading" to discover meaning embedded in the text (Neuman, 2000). Qualitative content analysis can be hermeneutic when it is sensitive to the context within which the texts were produced (Bryman, 2001). Latent content analysis is an interpretive reading of the symbolism underlying the physical data and a search for themes and concepts (Berg, 2008). Concepts involve words grouped together into conceptual clusters that form around a particular theme or idea (Berg, 2008).

8.4   WOMEN'S STRENGTHS AND STRUGGLES WITH PARIS

Authors of the books examined in this study were indeed motivated by their desire to share their emotional experiences of their travels in Paris. These narratives were by no means rose-colored. There were descriptive accounts of zinc-barred cafes, calm-quiet moments of reflection, and exquisite relationships with food, historical stone-wall inscriptions, and the most beautiful walks in the world. However, authors were sure to record raw accounts of their struggles, the instances of depression, questions regarding their identity, and concerns about their future. They were also surprised at the strength they had to persevere when, especially for some, there was no direction in their life past "today." There were some interesting themes that emerged from these narratives relating to transformation, freedom and self-identity, and sensuous and emotional place experiences.

8.4.1   TRANSFORMATION

Frost characterized transformation in tourism as a life-changing experience, or as an epiphany (Frost, 2010). In a similar sense, travel experiences in Paris brought about life-changes not only by the actions/behaviors of the authors but by how they perceived themselves. Transformation related, in some instances, to motivation for travel. Some of the authors left for Paris as part of an escape, to take a break from a hectic life too focused on building a career and thus needed a change of pace. Janice MacLeod stated, "Before I arrived in Paris, I was living in California, working as a copywriter in an advertising agency. I was thirty-four, single, lonely, feeling unfulfilled by my job, and on the brink of burnout. Something had to change" (MacLeod, 2014, p.1). Holdforth came to Paris because her life was in transition, she did not like the job she was doing anymore so she decided to take a personal tour "contemplating a life change" (Holdforth, 2005, p. 7). She wanted to investigate the lives, loves, and losses of Paris' celebrated women of the past; Gertrude Stein, Nancy Mitford, George Sand, Madame de Pompadour, and others,

> Another phase in my life was coming to an end, which simply meant I had to prepare myself for more change, more new beginnings. This was not a cause for exhilaration, but, at thirty-five, for weary deflation. More of the same old quest – if only I could put my finger on what the quest was all about (p. 7).

White and White explored travel as transition with long-term travelers in the Australian Outback and found that the significance of place played a role in how the travelers imposed endings and new beginnings in their life journey (White & White, 2004). Similar notions can be extended to the significance of Paris in the transformations and transitions of these women travelers.

Rojek argued that motivation for women's travel in the nineteenth and twentieth centuries has been as an escape from modern life (Rojek, 1993). Other research has focused on women's motivation to travel for leisure such as discovering experience, escape, relax, social ties, and self-esteem (Chiang & Jogaratnam, 2006). For Deirdre Kelly escape meant something different (Kelly, 2009). Life for her growing up was not great, "I hated having a single mom, hated being left alone at home while she was sleeping around, going out dancing, and staying out without calling home. I waited and read and worried" (p. 5).

Other women's initial reason for traveling to Paris was for short-term employment. Thomas was asked to work in Paris as a copywriter for the Louis Vuitton advertising account (Thomas, 2012). She had been to Paris before, so her company figured she would be a good candidate for the position. On the other hand, Mah lived in Washington, DC but moved all the time because of her husband's position in the U.S. Foreign Service (Mah, 2013). After they got to Paris her husband was stationed in Baghdad and she was left to explore Paris on her own (Mah, 2013). While both of these women end up in Paris because of fates of employment, their emotions are vastly different. Thomas is ecstatic, elated, and looking forward to exploring all the boulangeries and patisseries on the Velib. But Mah is despondent, apprehensive, and nervous about exploring the city alone:

> At first I wasn't sure how to maneuver myself *toute seule*. I missed my husband like an internal organ, and the city, which seemed so quaintly formal when we were together – with its *bonjours* and *bonsoirs*, and four-course-dinner parties, and cheek kisses instead of hugs – felt a little cold now that I was alone (p. 3).

For others, transformation meant a physical move and a deeply emotional motivation for leaving. Gershman's husband passed away suddenly and all she could think about was that her life had to change somehow (2004). Having traveled to Paris frequently as a couple, they had made plans to go again and stay longer. But with his passing, she was even more determined to continue their dream, even if it were alone. Similarly, Kati Marton first knew Paris as the daughter of political refugees from Hungary but she returned often as a college student, and with her first husband Peter Jennings as well as with her second husband Richard Holbrooke (who worked in the U.S. Foreign Service) (Marton, 2012). As Richard passes away and Marton is overcome with grief in a restaurant ladies room, she decides she needs to leave: "I need to get away. Paris seems the right place....It is where I became who I am. In a life of multiple uprooting, Paris has been my one fixed point" (p. 32).

There were other examples where women simply used the trip to Paris as a way to re-evaluate their own feelings about life choices and relationships with others. Jennifer Coburn whose own father died when quite young, had a deep-seated fear for her own mortality. As a result, she wanted her daughter to see the magic of Paris "before it was too late" (2014) For Nancy Miller she used her Paris travels to escape her Jewish upbringing yet she became more attached to her parents (Miller, 2013). If anything, Miller's transformation was that she had to emotionally and cognitively accept herself for who she was. Although Paris held strong memories for Miller as a motivational tool in understanding herself, she returned to the United States, needing more time to figure out her life. On the lighter side of things, Knisley, a cartoonist, summarized at the end of her book what her trip meant to her emotionally (Knisley, 2007). She was able to get along better with her mother, let go and allow herself to accept love even though she was afraid of heartbreak, and she was able to embrace her changing role from teenager/young-adult to adult.

Part of the theme of transformation for authors was feeling triumphant after "surviving" challenges. Dealing with French language difficulties, bureaucracy, specific cultural traditions, and social expectations and behaviors were aspects of the authors' narratives that weaved through their journey through self-discovery and enlightenment. These narratives are a "quest for self-discovery." While many of the authors experienced a transformation, whether emotional or even physical (by moving to Paris), they were not necessarily "looking" for it. It is not so much that these authors are looking for change but of spiritual development and self-actualization. The traveler gains an insight into their own capabilities and some might be characterized as a rite of passage or moving to another stage of adulthood (Laing & Frost, 2012). The process of transformation is emotional. These women were conflicted; often, the challenges and trials they experienced made them question their decisions, as well as the guilt they must have felt in "causing trouble" for those around them. However, their quest for freedom, self-identity as well as the sensuous emotional experiences in Paris outweighed the challenges, guilt and doubt they felt about their travel.

8.4.2   FREEDOM AND SELF-IDENTITY

Many of the authors' initial travels to Paris were motivated by a desire for freedom (e.g., Miller, 2013; Welty-Rochefort, 1997) and escape (e.g., Turnbull, 2002; Verant, 2014; Holdforth, 2005). Miller's motivation for traveling to Paris was escape *and* freedom,

> I went to Paris because I was enamored of the sexy nouvelle vogue movies, which, like the eighteenth century novels I had read in college, offered entry into scenarios of freedom barred to me as long as I lived at home. I wanted to be sophisticated and daring…I longed to escape….
> (p.vi).

Her time in Paris helped form an identity even if it was challenging, sometimes false and conflicted. Paris taught her through trial and error (many times over), that searching for freedom and escape may bring you closer to who you really are, what truly is who you are meant to be.

Women want freedom in their travels and a space of their own to experience this freedom (Small, 2005). On talking about why women of the past were so enraptured with Paris, Holdforth wrote, "Paris provided a space for women to free themselves, if they chose, from the tangled web of romantic and familial relationships. It was where they could be free to *be* themselves. Free even to *reinvent* themselves" (Holdforth, 2005, p. 12).

Even though these authors choose to travel alone and are aware of the risks involved in facing challenges by themselves, their desire for change, escape, and freedom is wrought with emotion. Emotions run strong when Thomas is faced with challenges with the French way of doing things and in the realization that she has changed, so much so that she no longer shares the same future dreams as her best friend (Thomas, 2012). Even though Thomas was "having a love affair – with a city," she starts to feel sorry for herself (p. 40). Thomas also felt conflicted emotions about returning home:

> I didn't know if it was the flood of emotions from seeing so many friends at once or if it was something else, but I suddenly didn't feel like myself. I was nodding my head at all the right points in the conversation, but inside I was floating away. I couldn't get close to anyone. These were friends who knew me inside and out. But they didn't feel the same. The bar and city didn't feel the same. *I* didn't feel the same (p. 101).

Interestingly, almost all of the female writers in their desire for escape and freedom often felt lost and perhaps in a transition phase of a new self-identity (Desforges, 2000). Thus, in order to calm their fears, nerves, feelings of loneliness, confusion, frustration, or embarrassment, they turned to food. Mah learns through the course of her time in Paris, that food is more than just caloric intake and consumption. There are the freshest ingredients; the quality of preparation, traditional recipes, simple ingredients, time to enjoy the meal, food is *pour fair plaisir* (p. 121). Mah was not necessarily searching for escape or freedom yet she still experienced a renewed self-identity through her connection with Paris,

It allowed me to create something unexpected: my Paris – not Calvin's Paris or our Paris but mine, one of new friends and cobblestoned street shortcuts and pastry-shop discoveries of my very own, one for me to share with my husband once he returned. For the rest of my life, I would, I knew, remember my experiences in Paris, drawing upon them like a long, cool drink of water (p. 231).

8.4.3 SENSUOUS AND EMOTIONAL EXPERIENCES OF PLACE

Rodaway explored in great detail how the use of our senses aids our understanding of place experience at individual and social levels, in different historical, cultural, and technological contexts (Rodaway, 1994). Rodaway referred to "the senses"—touch, smell, taste, sight, and hearing. Travel books about Paris are full of sensuous descriptions of physical places such as Luxembourg Gardens, the Eiffel Tower at night, streetscapes, squares, boulangeries and viennoisseries, open-air food markets and cafes. It was not only important for many of the authors to creatively describe places in Paris, but to also give detailed directions on how to get there. Thomas described the hot chocolate at Angelina, "Angelina's hot chocolate is so smooth and velvety, each sip sensuously coats your tongue and teeth it's both refined and indulgent; it's a simple recipe but a sophisticated experience…It's the perfect way to warm up on a rainy spring day" (Thomas, 2012, p. 64). Turnbull also explained the divinity of the hot chocolate at Les Deux Magots, "The liquid pours slowly like an oil slick of dark molten mousse. I take a mouthful – and nearly die of pleasure" (Turnbull, 2002, p. 40). Authors put into words their emotional and sensuous experiences with food in Paris. MacLeod described how food in Paris changed her entire outlook on eating and consumption,

> I walked down a market street lined with restaurants and tourist shops and found a crepe stand where they whipped up a crepe with egg, mushroom, and cheese. With my first bite, I almost fell over. The paper-thin warm pancake enclosed the cheese, which pulled the egg and mushroom together in a trinity of amazing (p. 57).

Adrienne Michel Sager had been to Paris numerous times giving history and art tours to visiting tour groups (Sager, 2014). She never tires of the simple little moments that combine together to make up Paris, much like the tiny brush strokes of Monet in his creation of a masterpiece. Adrienne described one moment outside her tiny hotel window:

> Waking up in Paris is always a mysterious and thrilling experience.... The sounds and environment are unique, incomparable, and consistently unpredictable. The thundering of trucks first wakes me: I sit up and wander over to the lace-curtained window and open it. I gasp as I see, once again, the rooftops with their clay pots and wrought iron balconies. I have seen this view a hundred times, but it is new every time I see it, a scene at once *cliché*, novel and strange....The bakery across the way is about to open. The owner is scrubbing the sidewalk outside her shop with a broom and a bucket fill of sudsy water. The smell of bread baking floats up to my window (p. 153–154).

Paris for these women was a sensuous and emotional place. Many of their narratives consisted of positive experiences in specific locations eloquently and colorfully described so that the reader would at least try to comprehend the pleasure they had. Positive experiences, however, were not always possible. For Bard, her ways to get through challenging times, such as trying to return a pair of shoes she later did not want, were with walks and food,

> By the time I left the shop, trailing my shopping bag behind me, I was almost in tears. I was too weak for indignation and too disgusted with myself to go back in. That was the moment things hit rock bottom. The girl who was going to set the world on fire couldn't even return a pair of shoes. There is only one antidote for a day like that: chocolate (Bard, 2014, p. 244).

Deirdre Kelly's poignant yet realistic account of eight different trips to Paris illustrated a roller coaster of emotions: "For a long while I sat by the Medici fountain in the Jardin de Luxembourg. The waters were as deep and dark as my mood. It was quickly becoming my favorite place in Paris – away from the crowds, the laughing faces, that now seemed to mock my ineptitude" (p. 29). Thomas also finds part of her travels challenging and feels sad, lonely, and misses some of the comforts of home (Thomas, 2012). A lover of sweets, even a cookie cannot comfort her in this instance,

> I had come to Paris for a new chapter, I reminded myself. For new experiences and friends. For new tastes and possibilities. For a whole new

way of learning – about the world and myself. I just hadn't expected that part of the 'new me' would feel so forlorn that even a chocolate chip cookie would fail to make me smile (p. 181).

Though many of these women were motivated by escape, freedom and independence, and also craved a change of life-direction, they still experienced personal conflict and guilt at not following through with the goals, dreams or life they (and perhaps others) expected themselves to have. Thomas, speaking about her friend AJ's wedding, "At that very moment that AJ was diving into the dream life that we had fantasized about growing up together, my heart had led me further afield. My heart had taken me to Paris" (Thomas, 2012, p. 211). After experiencing some ups and downs relating to cultural differences, Holdforth also attended a friend's wedding and wrote,

Finally Paris began to make sense to me. A city that was formal and frivolous, ancient and ageless, intensely conservative and furiously modern. That night, with the joyful newlyweds and the floating air and the music and the silly conversations in four languages, I felt a tender connection with the city. I knew that I would keep coming back (Hold-forth, 2005, p. 19).

Some authors felt angry and frustrated with how difficult it can be to function in another culture; simple everyday activities such as ordering meat or produce at the market, going to a bank, post-office, or shopping for clothes were a challenge. The emotional rollercoaster that is Paris is wrought with frustration and sometimes anger—but it is often short-lived. Usually a walk through the historic streets, a savory or sweet meal at a café, bakery or patisserie, or a trip to a local museum or favorite boutique usually turns the tides around quickly. The sensuousness of Paris's physical space reminds women with steadfast assurance that the everyday upheavals are minor blips on the radar screen of happiness.

8.5   THE EMOTIONAL GEOGRAPHIES OF PARIS

"Places do have the capacity to shape our feelings" (Conradson, 2005 p. 105). These emotions become integral to how places are imagined and portrayed, with profound implications for the embodied experiences of tourists and locals. The pleasure of such places derives from the consumption of goods and services that somehow stand for or signify that place (Urry, 2005). This can be specifically applied to the way in which women travelers embody Paris and communicate it through their narratives. Paris evokes extremely meaningful and emotional experiences for the women travel writers in this study in locations within the city well known for giving gratification. Places are emotionally pleasurable because they are sites of intense and heightened consumption (Urry, 2005). However, these emotions can also be negative. On Turnbull's relationship with Paris, "one minute it fills you with a rush of passion, the next you're full of fury.... Yes, it's a love – hate relationship. But it's charged with so much mystery, longing and the French specialty – seduction – that we can't resist coming back for more" (Turnbull, 2002).

Female backpackers also fluctuated between feelings of anger, fear, vulnerability and a loss of control to building strength and resiliency (Falcone, 2011). For the women traveling in Paris, vulnerability had more to do with their emotions; opening themselves up to new forms of identity and self-awareness. Similar to findings in Wilson and Harris, these women described extremely meaningful experiences (2006). However, for these travel writers, their search for self-identity and self-empowerment was more happenstance rather than motivational. These women needed escape, freedom, and independence, yet often times felt lost; lost in career choices, lost in love, or had lost loved ones. Thus, for them, being in Paris enabled them to find whatever it was that they were *not necessarily* looking for. Women felt empowered when "surviving" challenges or being reminded of the sensuous experiences all around them (Wilson et al., 2009). For Holdforth, there is a deep respect for the empowering ability of Paris for women,

> This was a city in which a woman might define herself, and be accepted by society at her own definition. It's a captivating idea – that you can transcend your past, your genealogy, your childhood experiences, or even the heavy weight of your own culture. But it took me some years to understand the special feminine allure of Paris (p.13) . . . And here I am in Paris, the city that attracts women who want to make themselves, from Edith Wharton to Gertrude Stein. Paris is where a woman can make – or remake – herself (2005, p. 159).

Holdforth's personal journey exploring Paris's historical women, their stories and the locations with which they frequented in the city, enabled her to fully grasp the lure of Paris for women of the past, "I found that the individual stories of these women's lives did not exist in isolation, but connected across time and space, like in the grand narrative tapestry that is the story of Paris itself" (Holdforth, 2005, p. 9).

In truth, the narratives of Paris's historic women are not much different from those of the contemporary women's travel narratives I explored in this chapter. There were over-arching themes present within these women's stories: Transformation; freedom and self-identity; and sensuous and emotional experiences of place. Subsequently, Paris is much more than a distinct destination with a unique cultural heritage. Paris has an aura, a sense of place, a *je ne sais quoi* if you will, that embraces what women desire out of life in general and their everyday experiences specifically.

The chance to make whatever one chooses with her life—that's the promise Paris offers women travelers. Though the city itself and the "romance" with the city disappointed these women at times, their relation-ship with Paris is an intimate one. There were emotional ups and downs yet these authors continued falling in love with it. On one hand, Paris can be an unrealistic love affair but, on the other, these women's passion and acceptance for Paris's imperfections as a place is much like the trials and tribulations of a real romantic relationship. Paris is an attractive destina-tion because it holds women in its highest esteem, as independent, as free to be who they want; as empowered and unapologetic. Paris embraces women and allows them to be themselves surrounded by the beauty of place; imperfections and all.

As Adrienne Michel Sager concluded in her narrative,

> Paris is like a gift-wrapped present. Unwrap it and there is always a surprise inside....Paris is full of never-ending sensory stimulation, of music and noise and people of every face, emotion and story. Around you are people with joyful faces, or perhaps tense expressions, they sip their tiny cups of coffee, wishing for a connection to other souls who are also waiting for a present. Do they know? Paris is the present (2014, p. 222).

8.6 CONCLUSION

There are countless examples of how women travelers have emotional experiences in, and with, place. Paris is but one example as shown through these travel books that evokes such strong sentiment from women both recently as well as historically for over two centuries. As acceptable perceptions toward women travelers increase at a global scale, women are venturing into territory previously not traveled to often, if at all, by women. Women are also being recognized now as the prominent decision makers and consumers of major travel experiences. As a result of the increasing "acceptability" of women travelers and their motivations, there has been an increase in travel books published by women exploring more obscure urban, rural, and wilderness destinations. Because of this, it is important, now more than ever, to understand how women think and feel about the places they visit. Women have in the past been claimed as the more emotional sex (Bondi et al., 2005). However, it is time that as women, and as critical geographers and tourism researchers, we embrace these emotions that may in fact lead us to significant relationships and connections with place; dynamics that we previously have not been in tune with as a result of objective, masculinized forms of investigation and inquiry.

KEYWORDS

- Paris
- literary genre
- travel writing
- narratives
- hermeneutics
- transformation
- freedom
- identity

REFERENCES

Ablett, P. G.; Dyer, P. K. Heritage and Hermeneutics: Towards a Broader Interpretation of Interpretation. *Curr. Issues Tour.* **2009,** *12*(3), 209–233.
Anderson, K.; Smith, S. Editorial: Emotional Geographies. *Trans. Inst. Br. Geogr.* **2001,** *26,* 7–10.

Bartos, R. Women and Travel. *J. Travel Res.* **1982,** *20*(4), 3–9.

Berg, B. C. *Qualitative Research Methods for the Social Sciences;* Allyn & Bacon: Boston, MA, 2008.

Bohls, E. A. *Women Travel Writers and the Language of Aesthetics, 1716–1817;* Cambridge University Press: Cambridge, 1995.

Bondi, L.; Davidson, J.; Smith, M. Introduction: Geography's 'Emotional Turn'. In *Emotional Geographies;* Bondi, L., Davidson, J., Smith, M., Eds.; Ashgate Publishing: Surrey, 2005; pp 1–16.

Bryman, A. *Social Research Methods;* Oxford University Press: Oxford, 2001.

Chiang, C.; Jogaratnam, G. Why do Women Travel Solo for Purposes of Leisure? *J. Vacat. Market.* **2006,** *12*(1), 59–70.

Collis, M. 'Mourning the Loss' or 'No Regrets': Exploring Women's Emotional Response to Hysterectomy. In *Emotional Geographies;* Bondi, L., Davidson, J., Smith, M., Eds.; Ashgate Publishing: Surrey, 2005; pp 33–48.

Conradson, D. Freedom, Space and Perspective: Moving Encounters with Other Ecologies. In *Emotional Geographies;* Bondi, L., Davidson, J., Smith, M., Eds.; Ashgate Publishing: Surrey, 2005; pp 103–116.

Dann, G. Writing Out the Tourist in Space and Time. *Ann. Tour. Res.* **1999,** *26*(1), 159–187.

Desforges, L. Traveling the World: Identity and Travel Biography. *Ann. Tour. Res.* **2000,** *27*(4), 926–945.

Ekman, P. Basic Emotions. In *Handbook of Cognition and Emotion;* Dalgleish, T., Power, M., Eds.; John Wiley & Sons: Sussex, 1999, 45–60.

Enoch, Y.; Grossman, R. Blogs of Israeli and Danish Backpackers to India. *Ann. Tour. Res.* **2010,** *37*(2), 520–536.

Falcone, E. Risk, Excitement and Emotional Conflict in Women's Travel Narratives. Recreation and Society in Africa, Asia and Latin America: Special Issue on Leisure. *Tour. Risk.* [Online] **2011,** *1,* 2. https://journal.lib.uoguelph.ca/index.php/rasaala/article/view/1511/2107 (Accessed: May 10, 2015).

Fawcett, C.; Cormack, P. Guarding Authenticity at Literary Tourism Sites. *Ann. Tour. Res.* **2001,** *28*(3), 686–704.

Frost, W. Life Changing Experiences: Film and Tourists in the Australian Outback. *Ann. Tour. Res.* **2010,** *37*(3), 707–726.

Gadamer, H. *Truth and Method, 2nd ed.;* Sheed & Ward: London, 1989.

Genz, S.; Brabon, B. A. *Postfeminism: Cultural Texts and Theories;* Edinburgh University Press: Edinburgh, 2012.

Heidegger, M. *Being and Time.* Harper & Row: New York, 1962.

Herbert, D. Literary Places, Tourism and the Heritage Experience. *Ann. Tour. Res.* **2001,** *28*(2), 312–333.

Hockenbury, D. H.; Hockenbury, S. E. *Discovering Psychology;* Worth Publishers: New York, 2007.

Holdforth, L. *True Pleasures: A Memoir of Women in Paris;* Greystone Books: Vancouver, Canada, 2005.

Hubbard, P. The Geographies of 'going out': Emotion and Embodiment in the Evening Economy. In *Emotional Geographies;* Bondi, L., Davidson, J., Smith, M., Eds.; Ashgate Publishing: Surrey, 2005; pp 117–134.

Kelley, J. Increasingly 'Imaginative Geographies': Excursions into Otherness, Fantasy, and Modernism in Early Twentieth Century Women's Travel Writing. *J. Narrat. Theory.* **2005,** *35*(3), 357–372.

Kerstetter, D.; Pennington-Gray, L. Decision-Making Roles Adopted by University-Educated Women who Travel for Pleasure. *J. Hospit. Leisure Market.* **1999,** *6*(3), 23–39.

Knisley, L. *French Milk;* Simon & Shuster: New York, 2007.

Laing, J. In *Women, the Media and the Italian Dream,* Proceedings of the International Tourism and Media Conference, Tourism Research Unit, Monash University and School of Management, La Trobe University: Prato, 2010.

Laing, J.; Frost, W. *Books and Travel: Inspirations, Quests and Transformations;* Channel View Publications: Bristol, 2012.

Lawrence, K. *Penelope Voyages: Women and Travel in the British Literary Tradition;* Cornell University Press: New York, 1994.

Mah, A. *Mastering the Art of French Eating;* Penguin Group: New York, 2013.

MacLeod, J. *Paris Letters;* Sourcebooks: Naperville, IL, 2014.

Marton, K. *Paris: A Love Story;* Simon & Schuster: New York, 2012.

Miller, N. K. *Breathless: An American Girl in Paris;* Seal Press: Berkeley, CA, 2013.

Mulligan, M. New Directions or the End of the Road? Women's Travel Writing at the Millennium. *J. English Stud.* **2000,** *2,* 61–78.

Nash, C. Performity in Practice: Some Recent Work in Cultural Geography. *Prog. Hum. Geogr.* **2000,** *24*(4), 653–664.

Neuman, W. L. *Social Research Methods: Qualitative and Quantitative Approaches;* Allyn & Bacon: Boston, MA, 2000.

Ohlenschlager, S. Women also Travel. In *Current Issues in Planning;* Trench, S., Oc, T., Eds.; Gower publishing: Aldershot, 1990; pp 26–32.

Osagie, I.; Buzinde, C. Culture and Post-Colonial Resistance: Antigua in Kincaid's a Small Place. *Ann. Tour. Res.* **2011,** *38*(1), 210–230.

Pan, S.; Ryan, C. Gender, Framing, and Travelogues. *J. Travel Res.* **2007,** *45,* 464–474.

Pennington-Gray, L. A.; Kerstetter, D. L. What do University-Educated Women Want from their Pleasure Travel Experiences? *J. Travel Res.* **2001,** *40*(1), 49–56.

Pernecky, T. The being of Tourism. *J. Tour. Peace Res.* **2010,** *1*(1), 1–15.

Pernecky, T.; Jamal, T. (Hermeneutic) Phenomenology in Tourism Studies. *Ann. Tour. Res.* **2010,** *37*(4), 1055–1075.

Plutchik, R.; Kellman, H. *Emotion: Theory, Research, and Experience: Theories of Emotion;* Academic Press: New York, 1980; *Vol. 1.*

Pritchard, A. *Tourism and Gender: Embodiment, Sensuality and Experience;* CABI International: Oxfordshire, 2007.

Reijinders, S. Stalking the Count: Dracula, Fandom and Tourism. *Ann. Tour. Res.* **2011,** *38*(1), 231–248.

Richards, G.; Wilson, J. Travel Writers and Writers who Travel: Nomadic Icons for the Backpacker Subculture? *J. Tour. Cult.Change.* **2004,** *2*(1), 46–68.

Robinson, J. *Wayward Women: A Guide to Women Travelers;* Oxford University Press: Oxford, 1990.

Rodaway, P. *Sensuous Geographies: Body, Sense and Place;* Routledge: Abingdon, UK, 1994.

Rojek, C. *Ways of Escape: Modern Transformations in Leisure and Travel;* MacMillan: London, 1993.

Ryan, C.; Yanning, Z.; Huimin, G.; Song, L. Tourism, a Classic Novel and Television: The Case of Cao Xueqin's Dream of the Red Mansions and Grand View Gardens, Beijing. *J. Travel Res.* **2009,** *48*(1), 14–28.

Salazar, N. B. Tourism Imaginaries: A Conceptual Approach. *Ann. Tour. Res.* **2012,** *39*(2), 863–882.

Santos, C. A. Framing Portugal: Representational Dynamics. *Ann. Tour. Res.* **2004,** *31*(1), 122–138.

Small, J. Women's Holidays: Disruption of the Motherhood Myth. *Tour. Rev. Int.* **2005,** *9*(2), 139–154.

Squire, S. The Cultural Values of Literary Tourism. *Ann. Tour. Res.* **1994,** *21,* 103–120.

Thomas, A. *Paris, my Sweet;* Sourcebooks: Naperville, IL, 2012.

Towner, J. The Grand Tour: A Key Phase in the History of Tourism. *Ann. Tour. Res.* **1985,** *12,* 297–333.

Turnbull, S. *Almost French;* Gotham Books: New York, 2002.

Urry, J. The Place of Emotions within Place. In *Emotional Geographies;* Bondi, L., Davidson, J., Smith, M., Eds.; Ashgate Publishing: Farnham, , 2005; pp 77–86.

Verant, S. *Seven Letters from Paris;* Sourcebooks: Naperville, IL, 2014.

Welty-Rochefort, H. *French Toast;* St. Martin's Press: New York, 1997.

White, N. R.; White, P. B. Travel as Transition: Identity and Place. *Ann. Tour. Res.* **2004,** *31*(1), 200–218.

Williams, S. *Emotion and Social Theory: Corporeal Reflections on the (Ir)rational;* Routledge: Abingdon, 2000.

Wilson, E.; Little, D. E. A 'Relative Escape'? The Impact of Constraints on Women who Travel Solo. *Tour. Rev. Int.* **2005,** *9*(2), 155–175.

Wilson, E.; Harris, C. Meaningful Travel: Women, Independent Travel and the Search for Self and Meaning. *Tourism.* **2006,** *54*(2), 161–172.

Wilson, E.; Little, D. E. The Solo Female Travel Experience: Exploring the 'Geography of Women's Fear'. *Curr. Issues Tour.* **2008,** *11*(2), 167–186.

Wilson, E.; Holdsworth, L.; Witsel, M. Gutsy Women? Conflicting Discourses in Women's Travel Guidebooks. *Tour. Recre. Res.* **2009,** *34*(1), 3–11.

Yan, G.; Santos, C. A. 'China Forever': Tourism Discourse and Self-Orientalism. *Ann. Tour. Res.* **2009,** *36*(2), 295–315.

CHAPTER 9

RISK PERCEPTION OF ASIAN SOLO FEMALE TRAVELERS: AN AUTOETHNOGRAPHIC APPROACH

ELAINE CHIAO LING YANG

Griffith Institute for Tourism, Griffith Business School, Griffith University, Australia

E-mail: elaine.yang@griffithuni.edu.au

CONTENTS

9.1   INTRODUCTION

Traveling alone can be a pleasant and often life-changing experience for women. As Freya Stark, a British female explorer and travel writer during the 1930s, commented, "to awaken alone in a strange town is one of the pleasantest sensations in the world" (Lewis, 2014, p. 40). While Stark's observation certainly still applies today, compared to women traveling in Stark's time, contemporary female travelers have gained more freedom in mobility and economic independence. The emerging solo female travel market is essentially a manifestation of the advancement of gender equality in recent decades (Bond, 1997; Jordan & Gibson, 2005; Wilson & Little, 2008). This is especially the case in the West where 72% of American women are interested in solo holidays (Kim, 2014). Although tourism has arisen much later in Asia, a similar trend is observed in the region. The growth of tourism is further spurred by the Chinese market since China opened its door to the world and other emerging developing nations (Winter et al., 2009).

The presence of Asian solo female travelers has become increasingly noticeable, though there is limited statistical information and in-depth understanding concerning this group of travelers. What others know about us (i.e., Asian solo female travelers) is rather contradictory. On the one hand, a Trip Advisor's survey suggests that one in three women from Southeast Asia opts to travel alone (The Star, 2014). On the other hand, the common stereotype suggests that Asian women are not inclined to embark on a solo holiday (Cai & Combrink, 2000; Zhang & Hitchcock, 2014), because they are apparently perceived to be more vulnerable by virtue of the Asian social expectation of what it is to be a respectable (Asian) woman. In light of this disparity, this chapter explores the risk perception of Asian solo female travelers, with an aim to contribute an in-depth understanding of how social structure and culture intersect with gender norms in constructing the perception of risk. In particular, an auto-ethnographic approach was utilized to provide a voiced, embodied, and reflexive understanding. I have conducted interviews with actual travelers but I realize that my conscious experience in the field allows me to better interpret my participants' accounts and to contextualize the subtle gender performance in the face of the constructed risk. Thus, this study is based on my own autoethnographic accounts supported with testimonies from my fellow travelers.

9.2   RISK AND SOLO FEMALE TRAVELERS

Risk in itself is a problematized concept, especially when it is examined through a gendered/feminist lens. There are many ways to define risk, depending on one's epistemological position. For example, positivists regard risk as an objective and measurable danger. Critical realists still consider risk as an objective danger, but see that the concept of risk is mediated by social and cultural processes (Beck, 1992; Douglas & Wildavsky, 1982; Giddens, 1991). In contrast, social constructionists perceive risk as a social and cultural construction which is informed by the underlying power relations of a society (Foucault, 1990; Gustafson, 1998; Lupton, 2013). For the purposes of this chapter and the work I am carrying out in the area of women's travel, risk is construed as a social construction shaped by unequal power relations underlying the patriarchal social structure and gendered tourism space (Gustafson, 1998).

The recent body of literature concerning solo female travelers has specifically addressed issues of constraint (Wilson, 2004; Wilson & Little, 2003, 2005), fear (Wilson & Little, 2008), adventure (Elsrud, 2005; Little & Wilson, 2005; McNamara & Prideaux, 2010), and the unwanted (male) gaze (Jordan & Aitchison, 2008; Jordan & Gibson, 2005). Despite this body of work, there seems to be little attempt to interrogate how solo female travelers perceive and negotiate risk. This chapter contends that it is significant to explore risk as an independent subject of inquiry based on four rationales. First, previous studies suggest that safety and security are the main concerns and constraints for solo female travelers in using the gendered tourism space (Jordan & Gibson, 2005; Wilson et al., 2009; Wilson & Little, 2005). Feelings of vulnerability (Jordan & Gibson, 2005) and insecurity (Tseng & Li, 2004) are commonly documented in the accounts of solo female travelers as the feminine body is frequently subjected to unwanted objectified gaze, and at times, sexual harassment (Jordan & Aitchison, 2008; Jordan & Gibson, 2005; Wilson & Little, 2005, 2008). Second, risk is often constructed to be part and parcel of the solo female travel experience. Risk contributes to the adventurousness of solo female travel (Elsrud, 2001, 2005) and the excitement of travel in general (Cater, 2006; Quintal et al., 2010). It is by resisting the gendered risks and constraints that solo female travelers gain the self-transformation experience and the sense of empowerment (Wilson & Little, 2005). Third, risk can be perceived differently between men and women. This gendered risk perception is a reflection of the unequal power relations underlying the patriarchal social structure (Gustafson, 1998). By challenging risk, solo female travelers are able to re-examine and re-construct their self- and gender-identity. Last but not least, how individuals perceive risk is further mediated by culture, race, and ethnicity (Lupton, 2013). Different societies and cultural groups may hold different impressions of men and women participating in risky activities. This understanding echoes with Henderson and Gibson's call for intersectional research in which tourism and leisure researchers are urged to investigate gender in relation to other social and cultural dimensions (Henderson & Gibson, 2013).

This chapter is devoted to unpacking the risk perception of solo female travelers, focusing on the experience and self-perception of Asian women. Although, to my knowledge, no study has conducted in-depth exploration of the risk perception of Asian women who travel alone, the fragmentary accounts of Asian solo female travelers are traceable in existing literature concerning backpackers. It is noted that the effects of risk are amplified in Asian female backpackers due to the societal and cultural expectations (Muzaini, 2006; Teo & Leong, 2006). For instance, Asian women in (post)Confucian and Islamic societies are socialized into, though not exclusively, a similar set of gender norms, which include being submissive, domesticated, and family-oriented (Tang & Tang, 2001; Zhang & Hitchcock, 2014).

This circumstance is becomes more complicated when Asian women travel in Asian developing countries where sex tourism prevails (Muzaini, 2006; Teo & Leong, 2006). Asian female backpackers are portrayed as the exotic (Asian) and erotic (women) others because their ethnicity and gender do not fit into the typical image of backpackers which are mostly white males (Teo & Leong, 2006). Their non-white solo presence often put them at risk of being sexually objectified and at times misperceived as local sex workers (Muzaini, 2006). In addition to this, tourism providers in Asia and Asian male travelers were reported to hold biased impressions against Western and Asian female travelers: The former is regarded as brave and independent while the latter is vulnerable and reliant (Teo & Leong, 2006). How other males observe Asian women could also be conceptualized as a source of risk for Asian solo female travelers as their singleness is examined under the collective gaze, or in a Foucauldian term, the social surveillance (Jordan & Aitchison, 2008). The vulnerable image of Asian women that preoccupies local men and other male travelers could render Asian solo female travelers "easy targets" for sexual attempts and male violence which eventually shape the perceived risk of these women.

9.3 METHODOLOGY: AN AUTOETHNOGRAPHIC APPROACH

The main inquiry of this study is to explore how Asian solo female travelers perceive risk. In order to fully grasp the nuances of Asian women's travel experience that is highly contextualized, autoethnography is considered as an appropriate research approach. Autoethnography is an interpretive and reflexive methodology which shares grounds with feminist and poststructuralist research (Noy, 2008). It focuses on the embodied experience of the situated researcher (Fleming & Fullagar, 2007). The definition of autoethnography is evolving and subject to various interpretations. In general, autoethnography can be described as a research procedure in which "the researcher addresses herself or himself ('auto'), as a subject of a larger social, cultural or institutional group ('ethno'), by ways of revealing research and writing ('graphy')" (Noy, 2008, p. 143).

Autoethnography can be broadly divided into two camps: evocative and analytical autoethnography (Anderson & Austin, 2012). This study fits into the analytical camp as it is committed to theoretical analysis rather than aesthetical representation. One of the key features of analytical autoethnography is the study of self and its connection to the social and cultural context (Ellis, 2004). The basis of autoethnography lies in the understanding that individuals and culture are interwoven and individuals are cultural agents (Chang, 2008). As self is a socio-cultural phenomenon (Church, 1995) and "our lives and personal identities are essentially plot-driven social stories" (Wright, 2010, p. 119), self-reflection provides a window through which to observe the underlying social forces, power relations, and cultural identities that shape one's behaviors (Fleming & Fullagar, 2007). In brief, an autoethnographer gazes inward on one's personal experience and looks outward on the social and cultural forces which formed the lived experience (Ellis, 2004).

As a critical and reflexive methodology, autoethnography enables the researcher to confront the "dark side" of one's personal experience, such as risk, rather than looking at the superficial tourist performances from a distance, as normally captured in positivist and non-reflexive approaches (Noy, 2008). The current landscape of tourism research is

highly dominated by positivist perspectives which have limited explanation power of the embodied and performative tourist behaviors (Morgan
& Pritchard, 2005). To address this gap, some tourism scholars advocate
a reflexive research approach which values the researcher's subjectivity
and reflexivity to carve out a new intellectual space for tourism research
(Morgan & Pritchard, 2005; Scarles & Sanderson, 2007; Wright, 2010).
There is an increasing understanding that all researchers are biographi-
cally and culturally situated and it is impossible to exclude the self from
research (Denzin & Lincoln, 2011; Tribe, 2004). Despite this recognition, embodied, situated, and reflexive research methods such as autoethnography are still largely underused approaches in tourism (Morgan &
Pritchard, 2005; Wilson & Hollinshead, 2015; Wright, 2010). Thus, this
chapter seeks to further contribute to this body of knowledge by taking the
less traveled path to demonstrate the feasibility and values of autoethnography in tourism research.

Autoethnographic data may take many forms, including personal narrative, diary, poem, and fiction, to name but a few (Chang, 2008; Ellis, 2004).
In this study, I analyzed my travel diary based on a recent solo holiday
to Thailand which lasted for 10 days. Scholars have advised that unlike
ethnography, autoethnography does not demand extended observation in
the studied context as the researcher has access to the first-hand participation or insider's view (Scarles & Sanderson, 2007). To gain autoethnographic insights, I became *the researcher* and *the researched* at the same
time. I recorded in detail my observation, first-hand experience, conversa-
tion with other travelers, and personal reflection of traveling alone in the
form of personal narratives compiled in a travel diary. My cultural position
as a Malaysian Chinese allows to me reflect on the nuances of the experience of being an Asian solo female traveler in an Asian tourism context.
As a seasoned traveler who has embraced solo travel for around five years,
I was robbed twice, verbally harassed, tailed, and gazed at undesirably. It
is therefore important to acknowledge the influence of past travel experience on my travel behavior and risk awareness during the recent trip. For
instance, when encountering risks or uncomfortable situations, I made a
decision based on my "gut feeling" or intuition, which is a contextualized
personal knowledge accumulated from past experiences and emotions
(Alaszewski & Coxon, 2009; Slovic et al., 2005). As this study is part of
my PhD research, at time of writing this chapter I have researched this
topic for nearly nine months and have conducted 10 in-depth interviews

with Asian women who have traveled alone prior to the field trip. The literature and my participants' accounts have influenced the way I perceived solo travel and the associated risk to a certain extent.

While this is predominantly an autoethnographic study, I also drew on accounts from other travelers. I interviewed 15 fellow travelers, two tourism providers, and three locals to obtain additional information to confirm, complement or reject my self-reflection (Chang, 2008). Table 9.1 presents the profile of the travelers. Some of the conversations took the form of formal interviews which were digitally recorded and transcribed. Others were short conversations which were documented in my travel diary shortly after the encounter. The travel diary was analyzed critically, guided by existing literature on solo female travelers, risk research, and gender studies. Particularly, I drew extensively upon poststructural feminist and postcolonial feminist perspectives in reading the text, with an attempt to construct an understanding of how risk perception is constructed and mediated by cultural identity. In the interest of brevity, only selected memories or events are discussed herein below. As Wright noted, the focus of autoethnographic writing lies in the explanation and interpretation of the experience, rather than in the details of the memory (Wright, 2010).

TABLE 9.1 Profiles of Fellow Travelers/Informants.

Solo status/gender Cultural background	Solo/female	Solo/male	With friend(s)/ female	With friend(s)/ male
Asian	10* + 3	2	6	1
Western	2	1	–	–

Notes: *Off-site interviews conducted prior to the trip.

9.4 THE RISK PERCEPTION OF ASIAN SOLO FEMALE TRAVELERS

9.4.1 THE FEARFUL ASIAN WOMEN

The contextualizing discussion earlier has revealed some gendered perceptions against Asian women: They are not prone to holiday solo (Zhang & Hitchcock, 2014) and are likely to perceive a greater sense of risk (Teo & Leong, 2006). Although these studies were not devoted to tourist risk perception *per se*, they have brought up a taken-for-granted viewpoint concerning the fearful image of Asian women. As an Asian myself, I find no ground to refute these socially and culturally constructed perceptions as they are firmly entrenched in contemporary Asian social contexts. This is reflected in an excerpt from my travel diary below, in which I discuss meeting Fred, a Malaysian male traveler who I met in Bangkok:

> I met Fred (Malaysian Chinese, Solo Male Traveler) in a backpacker hostel, Bangkok. When asked about his view on Asian women traveling alone, he said, "If they are *brave* enough, why not?" He brought up an interesting point which bothers me, why must Asian women be "brave" enough to travel alone? (Diary, April 2015)

As reflected in the above excerpt, Asian women often need to be "brave" if they want to travel alone. Arguably, the nature of risk faced by solo female travelers in general can be similar. For example, my student, Tom, warned me about his hometown (Bangkok) the day before I flew there. He commented that there are some places in Bangkok where women, especially those who are alone, should watch out, signalling the effect of "the geography of women's fear" (Wilson & Little, 2008). However, I would argue that the intensity of risk is likely to be perceived and responded to differently by Asian women due to social expectation and cultural values.

I remember at the beginning of my own solo travel career that my parents were extremely worried about my personal safety because of two intrinsic differences. They believed that I am *different* from Western women who appeared to be tougher because Asians are smaller in size (I am only five feet tall) and thus weaker in strength which would render me an easy victim; and I am *different* from men because men are less likely to grapple with sexual risk. That was five years ago but this stereotype does not seem to have shifted. Many fellow travelers I met on the trip received a similar response from their family and friends. At times, they chose to lie about their solo holiday.

> Usually I don't really tell her [*mother*] the truth....I will tell her that I have friends for one or two days then I will be on my own for the rest of the trip....I will tell her in this way which I think will be better.... [*Parents*] will still think that no matter where you go, as long as you are alone then there is a possibility that you will be in danger....Solo traveling is really, really not common, at least not in my social circle (Samantha, Malaysian Chinese, Solo Female Traveler).

All my friends are worried about me. Actually my parents didn't know that I travel alone. I can't tell them. They won't allow me because of my safety. I lied to them. I said I am traveling with two of my friends.... They also think that Thailand is a dangerous place, so I can't tell them that I travel alone (Mandy, Hong Konger, Solo Female Traveler).

Others' perceptions could have an impact on the risk perception of Asian solo female travelers. First, parents could instill their own fears into the travelers. Second, filial respect is one of the core cultural values in Asia, especially in Confucian-influenced societies (Lieber et al., 2004). Out of respect for their elders, Samantha and Mandy chose not to reveal their decisions for solo holidays, so as to avoid confrontation. Yet for other Asian women, they might have simply dropped the idea of traveling alone.

I met Aliya (Malaysian Malay, travel with partner) on the plane on my way back to Australia. She traveled with her husband. We had a good long chat on religion (Aliya is a Muslim) and travel. When asked about her perception of solo travel, she described it as dangerous. She also mentioned that her husband and family members would not allow her to travel alone (Diary, April 2015).

Aliya lives up to the gendered image of an Asian Muslim woman who is expected to be an obedient wife (Schröter, 2013),thus she will not consider traveling alone because her husband does not *allow* her to do so. Besides, she believes that it is dangerous for women to travel alone which once again, implies the fearful image of Asian women.

Wilson and Little have discussed the social appropriateness for women to travel alone in their model of sociocultural constraint in which Western solo female travelers were reported to have experienced similar disapproving reactions (Wilson & Little, 2005). According to Wilson and Little, doubts that others have against solo female travelers signify the issues of social inappropriateness and safety (Wilson & Little, 2005). My lived experience and observations align with Wilson and Little's findings and further support their assumption on the effect of culture in compounding the socially constructed fear (Wilson & Little, 2005). With that said, Wilson and Little's study was published 10 years ago and their study focused predominantly on Western (white) women's experiences (Wilson & Little, 2005). My encounters with Western fellow travelers suggest a different scenario. Across all the Western women I met on the road, none of them seemed to note family members disapproving of their solo travels. Admittedly, I have limited data on which to base this argument, but virtually all of the stories I have been told suggest that Western women's attitudes toward solo travel might have changed over the years, as did the perceived constraints and risks. This is not surprising given that gender equality is an on-going movement and seems to be more advanced in the developed West compared to the developing East (World Economic Forum, 2014).

The discussion thus far suggests two emerging trends. On a macro or social level, women's attitudes toward solo travel are changing as a result of the advancement of gender equality worldwide (e.g., access to education and employment), despite the acceptance level being uneven between East and West. On a micro or cultural level, Asian women's travel behavior continues to be mediated by cultural values (e.g., the obedient gender image and filial piety). However, the existence of Asian solo female travelers implies that these women are active agents who challenge the status quo and reclaim the gendered and ethicized tourism space. One way to overcome the sociocultural barrier is to conceal their solo trip. Many of my Asian fellow travelers confessed that they lied to their family members in order to gain access to the form of travel which is perceived as risky and inappropriate by many collectivist Asian societies.

9.4.2 GUT FEELING" AND SOLO FEMALE TRAVEL

Many travel guidebooks advise solo/independent female travelers to use common sense, gut feeling, or intuition to avoid risk (Wilson et al., 2009). Similar statements were found in the accounts of solo female travelers, including those reported in prior research (Campbell, 2009), in my on-going research, and through my own travel experiences. In fact, my recent solo trip to Thailand was marked by one critical incident in which I escaped from a dubious backpacker hostel in Phuket as my gut feeling told me to do so.

> I booked the accommodation in a rush, decided to stay with *X* hostel based on Trip Advisor's reviews….I knew the hostel was right above a pub but I was thinking that I should stay at least one night near the nightlife center just to get the hang of it…. When I finally found *Y* building, I was a bit shocked and lost. There was no sign and I couldn't find the way going up into the hostel. A lady working in the store showed me the way.

It was a quiet stairway, quite hidden. My instinct told me that this was not good. It's exactly that kind of stair that I would avoid if given a choice. I climbed up to the third floor; my first impression was that the place had been abandoned.... There was a guy, not friendly looking, having lunch in the foyer with scattered tables and chairs. I was a bit anxious. I walked into the hostel. The receptionist was a young sturdy guy, not friendly, and not fluent in English. I could be wrong, but judging from his accent, he wasn't a Thai.... The room had four beds and no window. It smelled a bit weird, maybe because of the bad ventilation. There was no one in the room. My gut feeling told me, it didn't feel right. *B* hostel (in Bangkok) doesn't have a window but it felt comfy and safe. *X* was a big no no. My gut feeling told me to get out of there no matter what, even if I couldn't get a refund. I think that place may be good for young and budget party-goers. Not just any kind of backpacker. It might be unfair to judge the hostel without staying there, but when I'm alone, my instinct is an impor-tant indicator. Besides, there was no locker in the room. It's the people, the atmosphere, and the location that freaked me out. Within one minute, I retreated from the room with my big backpack (Diary, April 2015).

Prior research suggests that gut feeling or intuition is highly relevant in risk decision making (Ball & Watt, 2013). Intuition is a non-analytical, experiential, and nonverbal way to apprehend the external world and to evaluate risk in this case (Slovic et al., 2007). I was unable to articulate why I felt unsafe during the event, especially when I was aware of the highly positive rating and reviews of the hostel on Trip Advisor[1]. From a rational way of thinking, the risk of staying in that hostel is low. However, there was a voice from within that urged me to leave right away. Intuition, as described by prior researchers, is a form of contextualized knowledge shaped by feelings and past experiences (Alaszewski & Coxon, 2009), and constructed by the society. As a woman, I was taught to be fearful, espe-cially when being alone in isolated places. Fear of this nature is cultivated in women by family and peers, and through many forms of cultural repre-sentations (Wilson & Little, 2008), such as media, books, and movies. It provides a reference point for intuition. At that moment, I felt very anxious and I was sweating. My heartbeat accelerated. So I retreated. In retro-spect, I was able to identify a number of factors which could have influ-enced my risk judgment, which included the hidden entrance, deserted surroundings, unwelcoming male staff, absence of locker, just to name a

---

[1]To ensure anonymity of the hostel, the reference for this comment is precluded.

few. Nevertheless, the focus of the discussion here is not to identify the determining factors but to reveal the social and cultural construction of gut feeling, risk perception, and women's travel experience.

As mentioned in the excerpt, "when I'm alone, my instinct is an important indicator," solo female travelers are taught or socialized to use gut feeling in the face of danger. This is reflected in Wilson et al. critical discourse analysis of women's travel guidebooks, which reveal "common sense and intuition" as a prevalent theme (Wilson et al., 2009). The fact that solo female travelers are advised to rely on gut feeling substantiates the risk of solo female travel and reinforces the notion of gendered tourism space which is dominated by men (Wilson et al., 2009). At another level, intuition is built on contextualized *personal* knowledge (Alaszewski & Coxon, 2009). Person or self is an extension of the community, a cultural agent (Chang, 2008), and a socio-cultural phenomenon (Church, 1995). Based on this understanding, personal knowledge is essentially shaped by the shared experience of a social and cultural group (Alaszewski & Coxon, 2009). For instance, I found that *X* hostel is not for any kind of traveler, at least not for me who is an Asian solo female traveler in my late 20s. Located right in the middle of the night life center of Phuket, and directly above a bar, the hostel appears to be appealing predominantly to Western youth and budget partygoers, with a focus on drinking and socializing (Bui et al., 2013). Based on the experience of all Asian solo female travelers I interviewed before and during the trip, only one informant was prone to drinking and partying. The rest of the Asian women generally commented that they would not drink when traveling alone to avoid danger, or because drinking as a form of socializing was not part of their culture. When I ventured into *X* hostel, my solo status and travel behavior (as mediated by cultural norms) were unable to fit into the context. The feeling of uneasiness raised my risk awareness and activated my gut feeling.

9.4.3 THE MEANINGS OF RISK-TAKING

It (solo travel) brings the ultimate independence (Kaew, Thai, Asian solo female traveler).

Travel and risk are intrinsically interwoven due to their intangible nature (March & Woodside, 2005). For women who travel alone, the perceived risk would be higher as they are more sensitive to certain types of risks in the gendered tourism space, as compared to their male counterparts (Wilson & Little, 2008). This chapter argues that the perception of risk is likely to be augmented for Asian solo female travelers due to different gender norms and cultural values. By traveling alone, Asian women are taking risks consciously as we are well informed or warned about the risk and danger of solo travel, either through travel guidebooks and information posted on online travel forums, or by people (e.g., family members and friends) around us. Thus, the last theme of this autoethnographic study explores why Asian solo female travelers take risks, in other words, the meanings of their risk-taking.

I asked myself the same question every time I traveled alone. At times I cursed myself for getting into this, especially when I was robbed, ill, ran out of cash, and was all alone. But when I returned home, I felt *different*. Borrowing my informant's words, "risk [*of solo travel*] is something that you don't want to face but you need to in order to gain something you want" (Aisha, Malaysian Malay, Asian solo female traveler).

> As I was looking for a decent foot massage parlor, I ventured into an unfamiliar street. Holding my bag tight, avoiding any eye contact with the guys passing by, I flagged another street and I am proud of myself (Diary, April 2015).
>
> I want to challenge myself...even though that route is not the favorite route.... I think I gained satisfaction. I was satisfied because I was able to do that and then I am more confident about myself. I think no matter where I go after this [*taking the less beaten route alone*], if I have a challenge I will still survive. It is important how you feel about yourself, how you think about yourself (Aisha, Malaysian Malay, Asian solo female traveler).

The experience shared by many of my informants and by me as autoethnographer lend support to Noy's argument of the transformative experience of solo/independent travel (2004). The transformative aspects of solo travel offer individuals an opportunity to construct, communicate, and transform their identities, sense of selves, worldviews, and social positions (Noy, 2004). Similar sentiments were found in literature concerning solo female travelers, in which the sense of empowerment, freedom, and confidence were some of the stated benefits (Elsrud, 1998; Gibson & Jordan, 1998; Obenour, 2005). Because of being confined to a gender role in which society has treated one unjustly for a long time, the quest for empowerment is particularly prominent for women. The need to resist gender roles and to re-define gender identities through solo travel is felt even more strongly among women in Asia where gender inequalities are particularly perpetuated (Guo, 2014). Prior to a trip, Asian women have to negotiate with the risk of social acceptance and cultural appropriateness. During the lone journey, they wrestle with sexualized risk in the gendered and ethicized tourism space. After they return home, despite feeling empowered and transformed, many of my informants (including myself) reveal that they do not fit into the conventional gender identities in their home culture.

> I don't think I'm a very typical Malaysian woman. Some of the culture or elements that they have, I don't really agree with sometimes. For example, Malaysian women are very dependent. Some things they will not do alone or they refuse to do alone or they are used to getting help from other people, especially from men. But for me, I don't really agree with that. Why can't you just get it done by yourself? (Samantha, Malaysian Chinese, solo female traveler).

Morgan and Pritchard regard identities as reflexive projects in which individuals have the agency to choose, affirm, or reconstruct their social identities (2005). Perhaps the project of risk-taking in solo female travel can be used to attest or even construct the different versions of gender identities in different cultural contexts.

9.5   CONCLUSION

Researchers advocate that by engaging in critical, interpretive and feminist research frameworks, tourism scholars can confront the "racialized, masculinist backlash to the proliferation of qualitative inquiry methods over the past two decades" (Denzin & Lincoln, 2005, p. 9). This autoethnographic study, writing from an Asian female traveler's perspective, serves this purpose. This study sets to explore the risk perception of Asian solo female travelers, which is an uncharted area of research. The study was based on my actual travel experience and stories of other female travelers which I collected before and during a recent trip to Thailand. Extensive data were yielded from that trip, but space precludes detailed discussion. Three major themes emerging from the findings were included for analysis. Discussion of "the fearful Asian women" considers the social risk faced by female travelers prior to the trip, focusing on Asian gender norms and cultural values. Based on a critical event from my solo trip, the second theme examines the role of intuition in the face of risk, highlighting its social constructive nature. The last theme explores the meanings of risk-taking based on post-trip self-reflection, emphasizing the (re)construction of self- and gender-identities.

The values of this study are twofold. First, it tapped into a meaningful research area (i.e., non-white, non-male travel experience) which has yet to receive much scholarly attention. The findings of this study, despite its brevity, have contributed an important groundwork for future postcolonial gender research in tourism. Second, this study has demonstrated the potential of autoethnography—a potentially engaging and insightful research approach which has not figured prominently in tourism studies. Tourism research has been widely criticized for being overly scientific, realist, and positivist, and thus it may fail to provide in-depth understandings of the underlying meanings and complications of tourist behavior (Morgan & Pritchard, 2005). Autoethnography provides a possible solution to address some of these criticisms. In addition to the potential analytical insights enabled by the approach, the other most valuable feature of autoethnography lies in "the exposure of self who is also a spectator" which would "take us somewhere we couldn't otherwise get to" (Behar, 1996, p. 14).

As with any research approach, autoethnography has its intrinsic limitations and challenges. Most prominently, autoethnography is a piece of art intersecting with science (Anderson & Austin, 2012). with indefinite research procedures and processes (Morgan & Pritchard, 2005). Thus, it is difficult to evaluate the quality of autoethnography using traditional evaluation criteria for qualitative research. Likewise, autoethnographers are required to be highly self-aware and are forced to reflect on their own lived experiences and write about them, which can at times lead to uncomfortable emotions (Morgan & Pritchard, 2005). Despite the aforementioned limitations, autoethnography is a highly valuable tool for tourism research because, after all, tourism is an industry and a study field that is concerned with people. Lastly, I argue that the values of autoethnography are augmented in gender research as it unveils the voices and experiences of previously silenced groups, such as Asian solo female travelers.

KEYWORDS

- autoethnography
- Asian female travelers
- Gender
- risk
- solo travel

REFERENCES

Alaszewski, A.; Coxon, K. Uncertainty in Everyday Life: Risk, Worry and Trust. *Health Risk Soci.* **2009,** *11*(3), 201–207.

Anderson, L.; Austin, M. Autoethnography in Leisure Studies. *Leis. Stud.* **2012,** *31*(2), 131–146.

Ball, D. J.; Watt, J. Further Thoughts on the Utility of Risk Matrices. *Risk Anal.* **2013,** *33*(11), 2068–2078.

Beck, U. *Risk Society: Towards a New Modernity;* SAGE: London, 1992.

Behar, R. *The Vulnerable Obserever: Anthropology that Breaks your Heart;* Beacon Press: Boston, MA, 1996.

Bond, M. Women Travelers: A New Growth Market. Hotel Online. [Online] 1997. http://www.hotel-online.com/News/PressReleases/PataWomenTravelers_Nov1997.html (accessed Aug 30, 2014).

Bui, H. T.; Wilkins, H. C.; Lee, Y. S. The 'Imagined West' of Young Independent Travelers from Asia. *Ann. Leis. Res.* **2013,** *16*(2), 130–148.

Cai, L. A.; Combrink, T. E. Japanese Female Travelers - a Unique Outbound Market. *APJTR.* **2000,** *5*(1), 16–24.

Campbell, A. The Importance of Being Valued: Solo 'Grey Nomads' as Volunteers at the National Folk Festival. *Ann. Leis. Res.* **2009,** *12*(3–4), 277–294.

Cater, C. I. Playing with Risk? Participant Perceptions of Risk and Management Implications in Adventure Tourism. *Tour. Manage.* **2006,** *27*(2), 317–325.

Chang, H. *Autoethnography as Method;* Left Coast Press: Walnut Creek, CA, 2008.

Church, K. *Forbidden Narratives;* Gordon & Breach: London, 1995.

Denzin, N. K.; Lincoln, Y. S. *The SAGE Handbook of Qualitative Research, 3rd ed.;* SAGE: Thousand Oaks, CA, 2005.

Denzin, N. K.; Lincoln, Y. S. *The SAGE Handbook of Qualitative Research, 4th ed.;* SAGE: Thousand Oaks, CA, 2011.

Douglas, M.; Wildavsky, A. *Risk and Culture: An Essay on the Selection of Technological and Environmental Dangers;* University of California Press: Berkeley, CA, 1982.

Ellis, C. *The Ethnographic I: A Methodological Novel about Autoethnography*; Altamira Press: Oxford, UK, 2004.

Elsrud, T. Time Creation in Travelling: The Taking and Making of Time among Women Backpackers. *Time Soci.* **1998,** *7*(2–3), 309–334.

Elsrud, T. Risk Creation in Traveling: Backpacker Adventure Narration. *Ann. Tour. Res.* **2001,** *28*(3), 597–617.

Elsrud, T. Recapturing the Adventuress: Narratives on Identity and Gendered Positioning in Backpacking. *Tour. Rev. Int.* **2005,** *9*(2), 123–137.

Fleming, C.; Fullagar, S. Reflexive Methodologies: An Autoethnography of the Gendered Performance of Sport/Management. *Ann. Leis. Res.* **2007,** *10*(3–4), 238–256.

Foucault, M. *The History of Sexuality;* Vintage Books: New York, 1990.

Gibson, H.; Jordan, F. In *Shirley Valentine Lives! The Experience of Solo Women Traveler,* Presented at the 5th Congress of the World Leisure and Recreation Association, Sao Paulo, Brazil, Oct 26–30, 1998.

Giddens, A. *Modernity and Self-Identity: Self and Society in the Late Modern Age;* Stanford University Press: Redwood City, CA, 1991.

Guo, Y. Chinese Women and Travel: Historical and Contemporary Experiences. *Ann. Tour. Res.* **2014,** *46,* 179–181.

Gustafson, P. E. Gender Differences in Risk Perception: Theoretical and Methodological Perspectives. *Risk Anal.* **1998,** *18*(6), 805–811.

Henderson, K. A.; Gibson, H. J. An Integrative Review of Women, Gender, and Leisure: Increasing Complexities. *J. Leis. Res.* **2013,** *45*(2), 115–135.

Jordan, F.; Aitchison, C. Tourism and the Sexualisation of the Gaze: Solo Female Tourists' Experiences of Gendered Power, Surveillance and Embodiment. *Leis. Stud.* **2008,** *27*(3), 329–349.

Jordan, F.; Gibson, H. "We're Not Stupid...But We'll Not Stay Home Either": Experiences of Solo Women Travelers. *Tour. Rev. Int.* **2005,** *9*(2), 195–211.

Kim, J. I Want to be alone! 72 Percent of American Women will Vacation Solo This Year. Yahoo! Travel 2014. https://www.yahoo.com/travel/the-rise-of-the-solo-lady-traveler-by-the-numbers-85084024117.html (accessed Jan 16, 2015).

Lewis, H. 101 Tips for Women Travelers. http://www.oattravel.com/marketing/101-tips-for-women-travelers-ebook (accessed Sep 20, 2014).

Lieber, E. L. I.; Nihira, K.; Mink, I. T. Filial Piety, Modernization, and the Challenges of Raising Children for Chinese Immigrants: Quantitative and Qualitative Evidence. *Ethos.* **2004,** *32*(3), 324–347.

Little, D. E.; Wilson, E. Adventure and the Gender Gap: Acknowledging Diversity of Experience. *Loisir et Société / Soci. Leis.* **2005,** *28*(1), 185–208.

Lupton, D. *Risk, 2nd ed.;* Routledge: Oxon, UK, 2013.

March, R.; Woodside, A. G. *Tourism Behaviour: Travelers' Decisions and Actions;* CABI: Oxon, UK, 2005.

McNamara, K. E.; Prideaux, B. A Typology of Solo Independent Women Travelers. *Int. J. Tour. Res.* **2010,** *12*(3), 253–264.

Morgan, N.; Pritchard, A. On Souvenirs and Metonymy: Narratives of Memory, Metaphor and Materiality. *Tour. Stud.* **2005,** 5(1), 29–53.

Muzaini, H. Backpacking Southeast Asia: Strategies of 'Looking Local'. *Ann. Tour. Res.* **2006,** *33*(1), 144–161.

Noy, C. This Trip Really Changed Me: Backpackers' Narratives of Self-Change. *Ann. Tour. Res.* **2004,** *31*(1), 78–102.

Noy, C. The Poetics of Tourist Experience: An Autoethnography of a Family Trip to Eilat. *J. Tour. Cult. Change.* **2008,** *5*(3), 141–157.

Obenour, W. L. The 'journey' of Independence for Female Backpackers. *Tour. Rev. Int.* **2005,** *9*(2), 213–227.

Quintal, V. A.; Lee, J. A.; Soutar, G. N. Risk, Uncertainty and the Theory of Planned Behavior: A Tourism Example. *Tour. Manage.* **2010,** *31*(6), 797–805.

Scarles, C.; Sanderson, E. Becoming Researched: The Opportunities of Autoethnography in Tourism Research. In *Beating the Odds with Tourism Research*, Proceedings of Travel and Tourism Research Association 38th Annual Conference, Las Vegas, NV, Jun 17–20, 2007; pp 253–262.

Schröter, S. *Gender and Islam in Southeast Asia: Women's Rights Movements, Religious Resurgence and Local Traditions;* Brill: Leiden, Netherlands, 2013.

Slovic, P.; Finucane, M. L.; Peters, E.; MacGregor, D. G. The Affect Heuristic. *Eur. J. Opera. Res.* **2007,** *177*(3), 1333–1352.

Slovic, P.; Peters, E.; Finucane, M. L.; MacGregor, D. G. Affect, Risk, and Decision Making. *Health Psychol.* **2005,** 24(4) (Suppl), S35–S40.

Tang, T. N.; Tang, C. S. Gender Role Internalization, Multiple Roles, and Chinese Women's Mental Health. *Psychol. Women Q.* **2001,** *25*(3), 181–196.

Teo, P.; Leong, S. A Postcolonial Analysis of Backpacking. *Ann. Tour. Res.* **2006,** *33*(1), 109–131.

The Star. People with Two X Chromosomes are Travelling Solo. The Star. [Online] May 29, 2014. http://www.thestar.com.my/Travel/Asia/2014/06/10/People-with-two-X-chromosomes-are-travelling-solo (accessed Feb 14, 2015).

Tribe, J. *Knowing About Tourism: Epistemological Issues.* In *Qualitative Research in Tourism: Ontologies, Epistemologies and Methodologies;* Phillimore, J., Goodson, L., Eds.; Routledge: London, 2004; pp 46–62.

Tseng, P. F.; Li, C. J. Bon Voyage: The Restless Insecurity Encroaching Female Backpackers. *J. Hosp. Home Eco.* **2004,** *1*(2), 127–142.

Wilson, E. A 'Journey of her Own'?: The Impact of Constraints on Women's Solo Travel. Ph.D. Dissertation, Griffith University, Brisbane, Queensland, 2004.

Wilson, E.; Holdsworth, L.; Witsel, M. Gutsy Women? Conflicting Discourses in Women's Travel Guidebooks. *Tour. Recr. Res.* **2009,** *34*(1), 3–11.

Wilson, E.; Hollinshead, K. Qualitative Tourism Research: Opportunities in the Emergent Soft Sciences. *Ann. Tour. Res.* **2015,** *54,* 30–47.

Wilson, E.; Little, D. Solo Women Travelers: What Constraints their Experience. In *CAUTHE 2003: Riding the Wave of Tourism and Hospitality Research,* Proceedings of 12th International Research Conference of the Council of Australian University Tourism and Hospitality Education, Lismore, Australia, Feb 5–8, 2003; Braithwaite, R. W., Ed.; Southern Cross University: Lismore, New South Wales, 2003; pp 1601–1606.

Wilson, E.; Little, D. E. A 'relative Escape'? the Impact of Constraints on Women Who Travel Solo. *Tour. Rev. Int.* **2005,** *9*(2), 155–175.

Wilson, E.; Little, D. E. The Solo Female Travel Experience: Exploring the 'Geography of Women's Fear'. *Curr. Issue Tour.* **2008,** *11*(2), 167–186.

Winter, T.; Teo, P.; Chang, T. C. *Asia on Tour: Exploring the Rise of Asian Tourism;* Routledge: Abingdon, UK, 2009.

World Economic Forum. The Global Gender Gap Index 2014. 2014. http://reports. weforum.org/global-gender-gap-report-2014/rankings (accessed Mar 15, 2015).

Wright, R. K. 'Been There, Done That': Embracing Our Post-Trip Experiential Recollections Through the Social Construction and Subjective Consumption of Personal Narratives. In *The Tourism and Leisure Eexperience;* Morgan, M., Lugosi, P., Ritchie, J. R. B., Eds.; Channel View: Bristol, UK, 2010; pp 99–116.

Zhang, Y.; Hitchcock, M. J. The Chinese Female Tourist Gaze: A Netnography of Young Women's Blogs on Macao. *Curr. Issues Tour.* [Online early access]. Published Online: Jun 9, 2014. http://www.tandfonline.com /doi/abs/10.1080/13683500. 2014.904845#. VdvqivmqpBc (accessed Dec 15, 2014).

SECTION IV
Contemporary Women's Travel: Trends and Experiences

CHAPTER 10

INDEPENDENT WOMEN TRAVELERS' EXPERIENCES AND IDENTITY DEVELOPMENT THROUGH MULTI-SENSUAL EXPERIENCES IN NEW ZEALAND

LINDA M. MYERS

Department of Tourism, University of Sunderland, UK

E-mail: lindammyers@hotmail.com

CONTENTS

10.1   INTRODUCTION

Contemporary women, particularly those from first world communities, are in a privileged position, with increased mobility and financial independence, enabling them to grasp travel opportunities during both their leisure and business time. Male-dominated cultural values and attitudes, which once constrained women's travel movement, have arguably weakened, allowing the latter greater freedom and personal choice. As a consequence, women are able to plan unique journeys and multi-sensual activities suited to their needs and personal ambitions. This chapter considers the literature on independent women travelers, travel and identity construction, as well as adventure and nature-based experiences in the travel context. The research employs qualitative empirical evidence collected in 60 in-depth interviews conducted in backpacker hostels and outdoor spaces in New Zealand.

Physiological, emotional, and psychological reactions during, and in reflective thought after, their travel activities resulted in a heightened awareness of the self and potential identity development for the women. The women's experiences are explored within three themes: empowering moments, emotional moments, and reflexive moments. The researcher's intention is to add in-depth knowledge to the growing body of literature about independent women's physical travel experiences specifically focusing upon the value of adventurous and nature-based activities and relating this to the women's identity development.

10.2   REVIEW OF THE LITERATURE

10.2.1   INDEPENDENT WOMEN TRAVELERS

Independent travelers, who have also been referred to as free independent travelers (FITs), tend to be environmentally aware, enthusiastic, and motivated to experience new ways of life. They are generally off-the-beaten-track explorers with a thirst for experiencing the "real thing" and avoiding mass tourism in favor of a more individualistic approach to travel. *The Tourists of Early New Zealand: "Lady Travelers"*, by Bee Dawson, compiles the stories and journeys on Victorian women regarded as New Zealand's first women adventure tourists, who were considered remarkable characters who often had to fight against social mores of that time (Dawson, 2001).

Stereotypical gender roles persisted into the 20th century whereby adventure and adventurous activities had largely been a male domain. However, things are gradually changing and according to Elsrud, women today seem to be as adventurous and bold as any male traveler she had interviewed (Elsrud, 2005). Cave and Ryan maintain that "female backpackers in New Zealand do adopt what have been traditionally regarded as adventure roles" (Cave & Ryan, 2005, p. 427). As time progresses, gendered roles in society are changing and blurring, allowing women travelers greater freedom to explore the world. Elsrud's gendered approach further asserts that women travelers adopt adventure narratives, incorporating risky experiences into their travel stories as part of their journey of independence, empowerment, and self-development (Elsrud, 2001, 2005). Increasingly women's travel experiences are being researched; one major step forward was made in the journal *Tourism Review International*, which published a Special Issue on Female Travelers in 2005 (Bowen, 2005). Following this significant publication, Harris and Wilson found that travel can be a source of empowerment for women, "positive aspects of power and agency can be experienced by the women through travel" (Harris & Wilson, 2007, p. 246). Small considered the embodiment of the tourist experience in her analysis and identified movement, sensual and emotional experiences as factors through which the holiday is remembered (2005). More recently, Myers considered women travelers' adventure experiences with a specific emphasis on overcoming fears and perceived risk which then resulted in a sense of achievement and empowerment (Myers, 2010). Falconer examines the role of risk, excitement, fear, and emotional conflict in women's travel narratives (Falconer, 2011). The aim of this research is to extend the knowledge of women travel experiences by considering the potential adventurous and nature-based travel experiences have in the re-assessment of a women's self-identity.

10.2.2   TRAVEL AND IDENTITY CONSTRUCTION

Traditionally in Western society, a woman's identity was defined in relation to others; as a wife, mother, and daughter. Green found that traditionally women's identities were constructed around domestic and caring duties in the home and local community (Green, 1998). In contrast, DesForges reported that contemporary women, from first world communities have increased mobility and financial independence, all of which increase the potential of developing more complex, fluid, and dynamic identities. Travel provides a further tool for women to use to construct their identities in addition to that of family roles (DesForges, 2000). In this study, the older women in particular, who may have performed the identity of a mother and wife for many years, suddenly find their old roles have expired, as the children grow up, or they are widowed or divorced. The independent women travelers are using the travel environment as a transitional time and space to re-adjust, re-assess, and find the "real" women or "self," who has been semi-submerged for many years. A liminal space is created through travel, where women have the time to explore their identity (Elsrud, 2001). Haldrup and Larsen discuss that the travel arena is a place where personal biographies and memories provide more understanding of social selves and social relationships (Haldrup & Lawson, 2003). This study considers the women's travel biographies and memories, in an attempt to understand how their identities may be affected.

Byrne distinguishes between a women's self-identity and her social identity; she then uses four elements to emphasis women's self-identity (Byrne, 2003). These elements are relevant to this study whose focus is upon self-identity rather than social identity, although it could be argued that both are inter-twinned. The first element is that interaction with others invokes the idea of the constant awareness of the consequences of interaction, which in turn affects the sense of self. Byrne's second element concerns knowledge and consciousness of the self, self-awareness of personal strengths and weaknesses, and knowledge of known values (Byrne, 2003). The third element focuses on caring for the self, the emotional and spiritual self as well as caring for the body. The final element according to Byrne is that of being self-reflexive (Byrne, 2003). In this chapter, stories of adventurous experiences provide the data from which to identify personal achievement, reflection, and identity development. The focus in this study is related to Byrne's second, third, and fourth elements; that of acquiring self-knowledge, attending to emotions and feelings, and being self-reflexive (Byrne, 2003). Participation in adventure and nature-based tourism activities provides an arena through which the women can explore their identity. New Zealand provides "unpredictable extremes of stimulus, where the natural elements are easily felt, visible and accessible" an ideal country to experience (Beard & Wilson, 2002, p. 221).

10.2.3   NATURE-BASED AND ADVENTURE TOURISM

Nature-based tourism comprises a number of outdoor activities undertaken by tourists in the natural environment, activities which awaken the body's senses, often making them multi-sensual experiences. They range from high impact "extreme" adventure activities such as skydiving, bungee jumping, and paragliding to more relaxing "soft" adventure activities such as bush walking, wildlife tours, and cruises (New Zealand Tourism International Visitors Survey, 2009–2013). Backpackers and independent travelers associate "extreme" and "soft" adventure activities with New Zealand, and are very keen to get involved and they appreciate the potential benefits the activities can provide. As Lightfoot acknowledges, one main benefit of participating in such activities is that it can lead to a person being able to express a strong and independent identity (Lightfoot, 1997). Adrenaline rush or "risky" activities undertaken by women travelers, such as skydiving, white water rafting, kayaking, and mountaineering, are considered in Myers and Hannam (2012). This chapter's main focus is predominantly on the "softer" adventure activities on offer such as swimming with dolphins and walking.

Adventure with nature and wildlife can involve the psychological feelings associated with fear and risk, a sense of achievement and/or fulfilling an ambition but are also about the production of memories, biographies, and photographs (Swarbrooke et al., 2003). When considering the geographies of leisure and tourism Veijola and Jokinen's work leads us toward an understanding of the bodily senses in tourism, in that the body provides a point of "affordance" between ourselves and our surroundings (Veijola & Jokinen, 1994). The human senses provide information on the surrounding world and mediate everyday experiences, according to Rodaway, allowing individuals to make sense of the world (Rodaway, 1994). Consalvo suggests these environmental sensations often tap into emotionally and spiritually uplifting memories (Consalvo, 1995). Kellert found psychological responses occurred to individuals spending time in green spaces. Being exposed to environmental stimuli, the natural elements—sounds, smells, temperatures, and textures—increased performance and creativity and helped decrease stress level (Kellert,1993). New Zealand's varied landscapes provided many opportunities for the women to awaken their senses and respond to natural stimuli.

10.3 RESEARCH METHODS

Women travelers from around the world were randomly selected, through "purposive" sampling, although a small amount of unplanned "snowballing" occurred, whereby women volunteered through friends in hostels and on notice boards. Sixty women from around the world, aged 17–75 were questioned about their travel experiences in New Zealand. Many were on a longer travel journey, incorporating New Zealand as part of their world tour. The interviews were conducted in outdoor public areas, hostels, as well as on various forms of transport. Primary data included face-to-face interviews, recorded by dictaphone, which varied in length between 36 and 60 min. Secondary data, drawn from about a third of the participants, included written reflection and photographs from their journey with specific emphasis on any personal developments and meanings of their travel journey. The data were transcribed and themes of interest were identified. The women were on the whole well educated, articulate, from Western societies, and have an awareness of their own self-development.

The findings in this chapter document the respondents' travel experiences, positive benefits, associated with identity development. The focus of this chapter is upon meaningful "moments" experienced during nature-based activities. The activities chosen included "extreme activities" such as tandem sky diving, paragliding, and bungee jumping, while tramping, whale watching, and dolphin swimming were selected from the "softer activities" menu on offer in New Zealand.

10.4 FINDINGS

The women participated in a wide range of activities, including extreme adventure, tramping (walking), and wildlife tourism. The younger women had a tendency to participate in the more physically demanding activities while the older women preferred the more sedate, relaxing pursuits New Zealand had to offer. Richards and Wilson found that "young travelers (under 26) place more emphasis on social contact and excitement, while slightly older travelers are seeking more individualized experiences and are less often in search of extreme experiences" (Richards & Wilson, 2003, p. 26). In this study, the older women in particular, who may have performed the identity of a mother and wife for many years suddenly found that old roles had expired, as the children grew up, or they were widowed or divorced. Due to rapid social change in the older women's lifetimes, the women very much appreciated the opportunity to travel and participate in a large number of tourist activities and experiences that have, opened up for them. Travel is being used by independent women travelers, as a time and space to re-adjust, re-assess, and find the "real" women or "self," who has been semi-submerged for many years (Myers, 2010). Paula, aged 37 from England: "Aspects of my identity have changed to a certain extent as a consequence of my travel experiences, I am much broader minded and more confident about myself. I felt a much stronger and independent person as a result of it."

Henderson found that women identify the outdoor environment with learning about themselves; as a place to gain spiritual completeness and overcome self-doubt (Henderson, 1992). The word use in the following quotes emphasizes the special moments experienced by the women; exploring New Zealand's countryside inducing a "warm feeling inside," "a special quiet calm," "time to reflect," triggering a physiological responses, "tears to my eyes," "hair on the back of the neck standing up," and helped achieve a state and inner feeling of "calm," and "peacefulness" and to realize "a once in a lifetime experience." The women in this study acknowledged the beauty of the New Zealand landscapes and were emotionally touched and challenged while participating in the adventure activities: skydiving, paragliding, swimming with dolphins, and tramping in the natural environment. A heightened awareness of personal self-consciousness and personal control was experienced by some women as they undertook what they referred to as "cool" experiences. Desforges (2000), and Humberstone and Collins (1998) have suggested that women more often than men are motivated by reflective and spiritual tourism experiences as opposed to being motivated by competitive and exploitative experiences. The findings in this study suggest that independent women travelers are motivated by reflective, emotional, and spiritual encounters in tourism. Overall, their choice of activities and their response afterward gave no indication that competition and exploitative experiences were motivating factors.

Skydiving, paragliding, and bungee jumping were the most popular extreme activities, while tramping, whale watching, and dolphin swimming were the softer choices. Through participation, the women gained "experience capital" which resulted in three themes being identified during the data analysis—empowering moments, emotional moments, and reflexive moments. By closely considering the women's responses to these moments, evidence is provided to extend the academic knowledge of women's travel experiences and the potential of travel to contribute to a women's self-identity development.

10.4.1 EMPOWERING MOMENTS

In the past, the gendered roles in society recognized travel and adventure as a largely male pastime. However, in resisting past constraints, women can exercise power and consequently experience these sites and activities as empowering (Shaw, 1994). Studies focusing on solo women travelers have previously indicated that travel space is of great importance in self-development, independence, and empowerment (Elsrud, 1998; Wilson & Little, 2005). This section considers examples of empowering moments, which can be achieved through the extreme activities such as skydiving and paragliding. For example, Liz, aged 61, from Canada stated that: "overcoming challenges, like skydiving helps strengthens the trust in yourself as well as a boost to your self-confidence and self-esteem, a much deeper inner learning."

Laura aged 27 from England adds:

> You just feel really insignificant it was just a vast amount of space, I could see these tiny little cows in the field down below. Amazing, it was just the whole feeling of falling as well sort of being like under control, and then when you get photos they took you're like wow, I actually jumped and you know I can think I just did that for myself wow, yeah.... I'm not an adventurous person at all, but I feel like one now, I can say I have jumped out of a plane.

As these women re-live their experience, words reveal the feeling of empowerment gained through the experience, bodily significance, and self-perspective in the surrounding space. Above all other aspects in the interviews, the physical adventure and environmental encounters were when the women's recollections and memories were more vivid, descriptive, and meaningful. They were recalled with a real sense of alertness and great enthusiasm. The benefits of participation amount to not just the physical exercise but the holistic experience. Physical activities involve body and mind synchronizing (Cater, 2007). Such empowerment can evoke feelings of achievement and success for women once a challenge has been overcome. Positive feelings of strength of body and mind can contribute to a change in identity according to McDermott (2004).

Una from Ireland, aged 35, reflected:

> I was very nervous about it coz I'd been a bit afraid of heights, so it was a real challenge for me, I didn't think I would do it, you're strapped to an instructor and you just have to run like hell off the mountain. It's fast and everything just, your mouth dries up coz of the wind and it's just unbelievably cold but, yeah, it was an incredible experience and felt like something had changed like I'd done something really dramatic and that things wouldn't be the same ever again and it's really weird it's really hard to describe, it was like I was just different somehow. I was so proud of myself I couldn't wait to tell my friends and family.

And, as Anne aged 56 from Canada reflected: "I felt proud of myself that I had done it, a sense of achievement, I realized the important things are people in my life, it was a fantastic experience. A sense of freedom to do something for me instead of others." Liberation from their normal frame of reference or gendered role, gave the women the opportunity to experience out of the ordinary activities. The many feelings and emotions described above led to a more positive self-image for these women. Little research has considered women's first-hand experiences of participation in adventure activities, specifically skydiving and paragliding and the ensuing positive personal development. Consequently these findings add to the current knowledge about women travelers and their spirit of adventure and potential benefits.

10.4.2   EMOTIONAL MOMENTS

This section considers the women's emotional awareness gained from viewing and swimming with dolphins. The women talked about the excitement and anticipation of contact with dolphins in the wild. They were highly motivated, animated, and enthusiastic about these very special encounters, which often exceeded their expectations. When asked to describe a special emotional moment relating to their adventure in New Zealand, it wasn't just the physicality of the movement or activity being performed but all that it encapsulated in that moment in time (Myers, 2010). According to McPherson and Beard, women's emotional experiences tend to evoke stronger memories (McPherson & Beard, 1999). Swimming and viewing dolphins were the most popular of the soft adventure activities along with walking in the wilderness. Several women ventured into the water to actually swim with dolphins and on occasions with seals. The positive effects, according to Smith et al. of human/dolphin interaction include enjoyment and a strong feeling of being connected to nature (Smith et al., 2006). In this study, the women's perception of the dolphin as that of a "fun" creature, possessing an image of softness with peaceful attributes being assigned. There was a widespread desire by the women to view dolphins in the wild, an ambition to be fulfilled. The following quote emphasizes the importance of just viewing a dolphin in the wild.

Lis (aged 51) from Australia reflected:

> We saw many blue-nosed dolphins, the captain told everyone to go stand outside at the rail. Don't move. Don't talk, put all cameras away. He shut off the motor, it was incredibly quiet and peaceful. We could hear the water splash from the dolphins and lots of bird songs. Tears welled up. I wished we could have stayed there much longer. The crew must be spiritual or very in touch with nature probably both.

Emotionally charged moments can be stimulated by the interaction of humans and wildlife particularly in their own natural habitats, as is demonstrated in Lis's quote, which also demonstrates the embodied nature of the experience. During participation with wildlife intense emotional moments can occur, these are often referred to as peak or magic moments (Lipscombe, 1999). The following quotes give an insight into the meaning of swimming with dolphins.

Laura aged 27 from England reflected on her interaction with dolphins thus:

> All of a sudden this dolphin like swims past you and you're sort of a bit shocked and the first 20 minutes I think, taking in how big they are and that they're actually really wild. Then I got a little bit more confident and started swimming to the surface with them and holding their eye contact and they actually swim with you so it's really really, it's just amazing to think they're really intelligent and it was really cool, a fantastic really moving experience. They just follow you which is quite funny, yeah like your becoming part of their life or their world I mean. Afterwards, I felt so happy but emotional, so privileged.

Laura momentarily becomes a part of nature, as did other interviewees, their body and emotions were awakened. This awakened emotional state gradually develops into what is termed "flow" reaching an optimum level whereby the focus of the individual on the activity is intense. Such a state can gradually build up through an activity to an "optimal psychological state" (Jackson & Marsh, 1996). Csikszentmihalyi concedes that flow is "the state in which people are so involved in an activity that nothing else seems to matter; the experience itself is so enjoyable" (2003, p. 4). Feeling part of the dolphin's world suggests such a state was achieved, demonstrating complete absorption, focus, and attachment.

Overall, the dolphin swimming encounters tended to begin with a sense of fear and nervousness, a state of self-questioning as to how to act or behave in their presence. Such a physical act draws upon internal strength and determination to perform and succeed. Once over the initial shock of the watery environment and the presence of wild creatures, several women gained in confidence which allowed them to relax and to enjoy and absorb these special intrinsic rewards. Research on human interactions with marine creatures in tourism studies is quite sparse. This study presents new knowledge into women's emotionally charged moments and the detailed meaning of such activities. It is not just what the women chose to do but how they reacted to that experience.

10.4.3 REFLEXIVE MOMENTS

Walking in the bush, or "tramping" in New Zealand, was one of the main physical activities in which the women engaged. This confirms the findings of Richards and Wilson who found that, "walking/trekking and cultural events are most popular among women respondents," while males tend to focus on sports and adrenaline experiences (Richards & Wilson, 2003, p. 26). However, in this study some women, especially the younger ones did also choose the adrenaline rush experiences. There were several references made by the women to the restorative properties of their walking experiences in New Zealand, for example; "it recharges your battery," "it allows you to relax and forget your problems," and "the fresh air and beautiful scenery improves your mood." Being at one with nature was an important element for the women. Yvonne aged 37 from Holland reflected: "I'm sort of in a mid-life crisis and what I need now it's just peace, quiet and beautiful, natural surroundings… it's just I hope I get some time to think and be a bit closer to me instead of always thinking of others."

The walking experiences of the women in this study concur with Edensor's notion that "walking indeed can be particularly suitable for stimulating reflexivity" (Edensor, 2000, p. 102). With reference to his study in the British countryside he explores the idea that walking simultaneously provides the framework for reflexivity is an embodied practice and is a means of escape. He states that walking in the countryside can activate the senses and provoke reflective awareness of the self, leading to a sense of freedom of body and mind, and is "bound up with notions of individuality and self-development and towards a freeing of the body, a rediscovery of childish sensation, aesthetic and moral regeneration" (Edensor, 2000, p. 84). Relating to Brynes' fourth element of reflexivity, many participants in this study emphasized the environmental conditions allowed "time for thought," "time to reflect on my own life," and "I feel free and can think more clearly feel better about myself." Sabine, aged 32 from Germany added:"It's exciting to participate in different activities and see how you cope and you reflect back on your own behaviors and achievements." This quote considers the value of participating; an opportunity to self-assess both reactions to challenges and achievements. Other women gained pride in their achievements and very much appreciated the rewarding views from the mountain tops. Often photographs served as a memento as well as proof of the achievement. Nikki from Australia, talking about high mountain walking, noted: "yeah we climbed for hours, so tiring but it was absolutely amazing but it was 360 degree views around and they were covered in snow there was a lake and Queenstown below, just amazing, absolutely amazing, I was so proud of myself, we took a few photographs to prove we made it."

While walking, the women were traversing unfamiliar paths and often moving from one environmental aspect to another, from a provisional parcel of space; for example from a beach view to a slope on a wooded hillside (Wylie, 2005). In this study the "parcels of space" served as places to relax, reflect, and connect to nature. The women's walking narrative demonstrated a connection with nature, included stopping to listen to "the power of the ocean," or the "the Kia's squawking," to smell the "beautiful flowers," to feel the "smoothness of the rock," or "the bark of the really ancient Kauri tree," to lay in the "soft fine sand," to stop and inspect the "shapes of the ice," or "take another photograph of the unusual landscape." Michelle, aged 24 from Canada, stated: "Walking in the wilderness alone strengthens the trust in yourself, as well as a boost to your self-confidence and self-esteem, a much deeper inner learning; you can be at one with nature." Wylie in particular emphasizes that walking can be an interaction of self, others, and nature and that walking alone allows a visual, tactile relationship with the surrounding nature: the earth, sky, and vegetation (Wylie, 2005). According to Edensor, the attributes of the natural environment have a grounding effect on the individual and Wallace that walking in the natural environment allows an increased awareness of the body in unrestricted space (Edensor, 2000). Yvonne, aged 37, from the Netherlands, further commented: "I had long beautiful walks on my own and loved it. You can walk for miles here without meeting anyone and still feel safe. I loved the time on my own and did a lot of thinking about what I wanted to change in my life." This is a further example of the opportunities in nature for the women to find one of the things they seem to want, a self-reflective space. Being at one with nature was an important element for the women. Quietness and solitude within a beautiful outdoor environment setting can, as Caulkins et al. report, also increase awareness of the self (Caulkins et al., 2006). There was a definite connection with the peace and quiet reported by the women in this study, those women who walked solo commented on this, it gave them "time to think," "me time," and "time to escape." Some older participants also talked about travel as a challenge which extended them both physically, intellectually, and emotionally, as one astute traveler, Liz aged 51 from Australia, pointed out: "With regard to traveling and learning, it's not where you are but who you are—it takes a long time to realize that." Sandra aged 39 from Austria said: "Travel allows my self-development, the freedom to be who you want to be. By traveling I am finding the confidence to be myself the person that I know I am."

As with this study, Desforges notes that young people who had traveled independently returned home with a new found sense of self-identity, because travel is providing them with new stories and narrative which can be re-told presenting themselves in a different light (2000).

10.5 CONCLUSION

Three themes developed from the independent women travelers' interviews with regard to nature-based activities in New Zealand: empowering moments, emotional moments, and reflective moments. Through these

moments the women explored aspects of their self-identity. Empowerment, an increase in confidence, and self-belief were experienced by the
women after successfully completing challenges and negotiating risk,
especially during and after extreme activities. The older women in particular challenged their historical inherited gendered roles and were able
to experience the feeling of empowerment and a strong sense freedom
and personal achievement. Photographs were used as tool to remember
the experience and as a record of achievement. Emotional responses to
New Zealand's environment and to performing some of the activities were
evident in the women's narrative and their enthusiastic responses when
being interviewed. Wildlife encounters and interactions were very special
moments; dolphin watching and swimming with dolphins were explored
with descriptive narratives giving an insight into the importance of such
interactions to the emotional fulfillment of the women travelers. In many
cases, dolphin swimming represented an ambition fulfilled. Self-knowledge involves being conscious of the self, aware of own limits and potentialities and in having a concept of personhood (Byrne, 2003).

Opportunities to be reflexive appeared when walking (tramping) experiences were explored. The naturally beautiful open spaces, the peace, and
tranquility of the environment provided a framework through which the
women could explore their inner feelings and thoughts about their lives.
Such "me-time" allowed the women to explore aspects of their identity.
According to Edensor, the body is believed to come alive in the country
and the quietness and solitude within a beautiful outdoor environment
setting can also increase self-awareness (Edensor, 2000). In this study the
natural environment and adventurous pursuits gave the women an opportunity to participate in new activities, time for self-analysis and reflection,
and to explore identity issues. As Ann from Canada appropriately summarized: "Travel for women means leaving the familiar domain of home and
a comfortable environment to gain freedom to express yourself from the
many constraints. It gives yourself the chance to be who you are and able
to respond to others in that manner." Relating back to Byrne's elements of
self-identity, as a consequence of participating in nature-based activities,
it can be seen that the women gained self-knowledge, became aware of
their own limits and potentialities, gained the opportunity to explore the
emotional and spiritual side of life, and entered parcels of space which
were conducive toward self-reflexive. Such experiences can lead to a new
improved self-identity, a concept which requires further research attention.

Finally, this study is unique in that it attempts to link the elements gained from activity choices of independent women travelers to the positive gains to their self-development and self-identity. The rich and in-depth narratives provide evidence about what were regarded as the important moments and reach a little further into the women travelers' feelings and emotions. Study limitations include a relatively small sample size of one specific group of independent women travelers which does not allow for generalized statements about women and travel. Suggestions for future research include using the internet to interview respondents a few months after their journey to gather more reflective data about any identity changes they have noticed as a result of their travel experiences. In this study, the researcher noted the differences in response between mature women (over 50s) and younger women (under 30s) from different social eras, a comparative study may produce interesting results.

KEYWORDS

- **independent women travelers**
- **nature-based activities**
- **adventure**
- **wildlife tourism**
- **empowerment**

REFERENCES

Beard, C.; Wilson, J. P. *The Power of Experiential Learning: A Handbook of Trainers and Educators;* Kogan Page: London, 2002.

Bowen, H. E. Special Issue: Female Travelers: Part I. *Tour. Rev. Int.* **2005,** *9*(2), 119–227.

Byrne, A. Developing a Sociological Model for Researching Women's Self and Social Identities. *Eur. J. Women's Stud.* **2003,** *10,* 443–464.

Cater, E.; Cloke, P. Performativity of Adventure Tourism' Bodies in Action. *Anthropol. Today.* **2007,** *23,* 6.

Caulkins, M. C.; White, D. D.; Russell, K. C. The Role of Physical Exercise in Wilderness Therapy for Troubled Adolescent Women. *J. Exp. Edu.* **2006,** *29*(1), 18–37.

Cave, J.; Ryan, C. Gender in Backpacking and Adventure Tourism. In Gender, Framing and Travelogues. Pan, S.; Ryan, C., Eds.; *J. Travel Res.* **2005,** *45,* 464–474.

Consalvo, C. *Outdoor Games for Trainers;* Gower: Aldershot, England, 1995.

Csikszentmihalyi, M. *The Psychology of Happiness;* Rider Press: London, 2003.

Dawson, D. *The Tourists of Early New Zealand: Lady Travelers;* Penguin Books: Wellington, NZ, 2001.

Desforges, L. Travelling the World: Identity and Travel Biography. *Ann. Tour. Res.* **2000,** *27*(4), 926–945.

Edensor, T. Walking in the British Countryside: Reflexivity, Embodied Practices and Ways to Escape. *Body Soci.* **2000,** *6*(3–4), 81–106.

Elsrud, T. Time Creation in Travelling: The Taking and Making of Time among Women Backpackers. *Time Soci.* **1998,** *7*(2), 309–334.

Elsrud, T. Risk Creation in Travelling: Backpacker Adventure Narrative. *Ann. Tour. Res.* **2001,** *28*(3), 597–617.

Elsrud, T. Recapturing the Adventuress: Narratives on Identity and Gendered Positioning in Backpacking. *Ann. Tour. Res.* **2005,** *9*(2), 123–137.

Falconer, E. Risk, Excitement and Emotional Conflict in Women's Travel Narratives. *RASAALA.* **2011,** *1*, 2.

Green, E. 'Women doing Friendship': An Analysis of Women's Leisure as a Site of Identity Construction, Empowerment and Resistance. *Leis. Stud.* **1998,** *17*(3), 171–185.

Haldrup, M.; Lawson, J. The Family Gaze. *Tour. Stud.* **2003,** *3*(1), 23–46.

Harris, C.; Wilson, E. 'Travelling Beyond the Boundaries of Constraint: Women, Travel and Empowerment'. In *Tourism and Gender: Embodiment, Sensuality and Experience;* Pritchard, A., Ateljevic, I., Morgan, N., Harris, C., Eds.; CAB International: Oxfordshire, UK, 2007; pp 235–250.

Henderson, K. Breaking with Tradition: Women and Outdoor Pursuits. *JOPERD.* **1992,** *63*, 49–51.

Humberstone, B.; Collins, D. Ecofeminism, Risk and Women's Experiences of Landscape. *Leis. Stud. Asso.* **1998,** *63*, 137–150.

Jackson, S. A.; Marsh, H. W. Development and Validation of a Scale to Measure Optimal Experience: The Flow State Scale. *J. Sport Exerc. Psychol.* **1996,** *18*, 17–35.

Kellert, S. R. The Biological Basis for Human Values of Nature. In *The Biophilia Hypothesis;* Kellert, S. R., Wilson, E. O., Eds.; Island Press: Washington, DC, 1993.

Lightfoot, C. *The Culture of Adolescent Risk-Taking;* The Guildford Press: New York, 1997.

Lipscombe, N. The Relevance of the Peak Experience to Continued Skydiving Participation: A Qualitative Approach to Assessing Motivations. *Leis. Stud.* **1999,** *18*, 267–288.

McDermott, L. Exploring Intersections of Physicality and Female-Only Canoeing Experiences. *Leis. Stud.* **2004,** *23*, 283–301.

Mcpherson, M.; Beard, C. M. The Selection, Design, Use of Individualized Training Methods. In

Human Resource Development; Wilson, J. P., Ed.; Kogan Page: London, 1999; pp 307–318.

New Zealand Tourism International Visitor Survey 2009–2013 (online). http://www.tourismnewzealand.com/media/1768/tourism-profile-walking-and-hiking.pdf (accessed Aug 26, 2015).

Myers, L. Women Travelers' Adventure Tourism Experiences in New Zealand. *Ann. Leis. Res.* **2010,** *13*(1–2), 116–142.

Myers, L. M.; Hannam, K. Adventure Tourism as a Series of Memorable Events: Women Traveller's Experiences of New Zealand. In *International Sports Events;* Shipway, R., Fyall, A., Eds.; Routledge: London, 2012.

Richards, G.; Wilson, J. *Today's Youth Travellers: Tomorrow's Global Nomads.* A Report for the International Student Travel Federation (ISTC) and Association of Tourism and Leisure Education (ATLAS), International Student Travel Confederation (ISTC): Amsterdam, 2003.

Rodaway, P. *Sensuous Geographies;* Routledge: London, 1994.

Shaw, S. M. Gender, Leisure, and Constraint: Towards a Framework for the Analysis of Women's Leisure. *J. Leis. Res.* **1994,** *26*(1), 8–22.

Small, J. Women's Holidays: The Disruption of the Motherhood Myth. *Tourism Rev. Int.* **2005,** *9*(2), 139–154.

Smith, A. J.; Lee, D.; Newsome, D.; Stoeckl, N. Production and Consumption of Wildlife Icons: Dolphin Tourism at Monkey Mia, Western Australia. In *Tourism Consumption and Representation;* Meetham, K., Anderson, A., Miles, S., Eds.; CABI Press: London, 2006; pp 113–139.

Swarbrooke, J.; Beard, C.; Leckie, S.; Pomfret, G. *Adventure Tourism: The New Frontier;* Butterworts-Heinemann: Oxford, UK, 2003.

Veijola, S.; Jokinen, E. 'The Body in Tourism'. *Theor. Cult. Soci.* **1994,** *11*(3), 125–151.

Wilson, E.; Little, D. E. A "Relative Escape"? The Impact of Constraints on Women who Travel Solo. *Tour. Rev. Int.* **2005,** *9*, 155–175.

Wylie, J. A Single Day's Walking: Narrating Self and Landscape on the South West Coast Path. *Trans. Inst. Br. Geogr.* **2005,** *30*, 234–247.

CHAPTER 11

TRAVELERS, TOURISTS, MIGRANTS, OR WORKERS? TRANSFORMATIVE JOURNEYS OF MIGRANT WOMEN

AGNIESZKA RYDZIK

Lincoln International Business School, University of Lincoln, UK

E-mail: ARydzik@lincoln.ac.uk

CONTENTS

FIGURE 11.1   First page of Natalia's artwork.

[M]y life in the UK started when my adult life started too. I didn't leave Poland when I had my own house, family, work and was independent. But I left as a teenager, from my little room where I had a desk and a bed, from Mummy's house. So it was a big jump. Straight away, going to an unknown city, without knowing anyone or anything…. I was walking in sneakers, destroying my sneakers to get to know the city and find out where is what…. I dealt with everything on my own. And nobody helped me. Maybe it took me more time, but at least I have the satisfaction that I

achieved it by myself. (Natalia reflecting on the cover photo of her photo reportage)

11.1 INTRODUCTION

Worldwide, women of many nationalities, backgrounds, professions, ethnicities, and age groups are on the move. Traveling for diverse reasons, they benefit from these experiences as well as experiencing a range of constraints (Harris & Wilson, 2007; Jordan & Aitchison, 2008; Wilson & Little, 2008). However, to date, the body of research on female travelers has focused largely on the experiences of women from more affluent societies, something this book challenges by demonstrating the diversity of female travelers. This chapter's contribution is bringing to the fore the perspective of migrant women. It argues that migrant women from less affluent nations, in this case Central and Eastern Europe (CEE), are also inscribed within this global mobility of women and their journeys should be valued rather than overlooked when recognizing women's travel.

This chapter gives visibility to the transformative journeys of migrant women and their mobile lives. The complex, multifaceted and gendered mobilities of migrant women are often overlooked in gender blind analyzes of migratory movements. Nonetheless, migration is a gendered process (Mahler & Pessar, 2006), with experiences, motivations, and trajectories of migrant women differing substantially to that of migrant men (Nawyn, 2010). Until relatively recently, migrant women and their active participation in global migratory movements have been marginalized in academia, overshadowed by that of men, and associated mainly with family reunification (Morokvasic, 1983; Nawyn, 2010). Yet, far from being passive and merely followers of men, migrant women can be independent and active agents of change, in control of and actively shaping their lives post-migration. This chapter thus moves away from considering migrant women predominantly in the context of family or labor market participation, and toward the transformation and meaningful mobility they undergo post-migration as independent actors and solo travelers. With the feminization of migration and over 105 million migrant women worldwide (UN The World's Women, 2010), it is vital to give voice, visibility and value to their experiences and trajectories, and challenge the often victimizing portrayals of migrant women.

Drawing on the mobilities of CEE women tourism workers in the United Kingdom, this chapter explores their migrant trajectories and, in doing so, it shows the transformative and meaningful nature of their mobility as well as the blurring between travel, tourism, migration, and work; between being tourists and providing for tourists. The transition to market economies post-1989 in CEE countries made women particularly vulnerable, leading to "a considerable decline in women's labor force participation, in many cases accompanied by a reversion to more traditional gender role attitudes and gender relations" (Schmitt & Trappe, 2010, p. 262). The 2004 accession of eight[1] CEE countries to the EU and the subsequent opening of labor markets, led to mass mobility of citizens from these countries to the United Kingdom. Women from these nations—predominantly young, educated, single, and childless—actively participated in this phenomenon.

The focus here is on those women who took the decision to migrate at a relatively young age and migrated independently as autonomous migrants, with no dependents. This approach allows the capturing of their individual migration journeys as young women, before they started relationships and families, focusing on subjective motivations and experiences on an individual level. The trajectories and experiences of solo female migrants are often marginalized in migration literature—for example, within studies on Polish migrant women, the focus is often on women as mothers and in the context of families (Pustulka, 2012; Ryan, 2009; White, 2011)—and little is known about this group. While they are often perceived in the host country through the lens of labor migration and predominantly conceptualized as economic migrants, there is an under-appreciated aspect of their mobility which forms an integral part of their identities, and which is discussed in this chapter. When exploring women's trajectories on an individual level, other aspects of their migration come to the fore, demonstrating that one's mobility is a complex and fluid process, and most importantly for solo young female migrants, one that is transformative and empowering. Thus, the focus on the economic

---

[1]Czech Republic, Estonia, Hungary, Latvia, Lithuania, Poland, Slovakia, and Slovenia are the eight Central and Eastern European countries (CEE) that joined the European Union on the 1st of May, 2004.

side of their migration is limiting and overlooks the richness of their journeys and self-development.

11.2 METHODOLOGY

This chapter draws on findings from a wider study into the mobilities, migrant trajectories, and employment experiences of CEE migrant women tourism workers in the United Kingdom. This qualitative multi-method study adopted an innovative visual and participatory methodology (Rydzik et al., 2013). While scholars recognized the potential of visual methodologies for knowledge creation and dissemination (Banks, 2001; Pink, 2001; Rakić & Chambers, 2010, 2012; Scarles, 2010), these approaches remain marginal in tourism scholarship. This remains particularly the case when it comes to participatory and arts-based approaches to visual research, where research is conducted *with* participants rather than *on* participants, and where participants are actively involved in creating visuals and their meaning are given prominence.

As part of the research process, as well as being interviewed, participants developed visual representations of their migrant trajectories, which were then exhibited during a community event. Several images of participants' artworks are integrated within the chapter together with narratives of their experiences. In this way, the chapter draws on the visual and verbal narratives of migrant women to illustrate the complex nature of their trajectories post-migration, with experiences of inequality as well as empowerment. Drawing on visual and verbal narratives of 10 women, this chapter challenges the stereotyped image of migrant women as passive and immobile, and presents a more complex and multi-layered portrayal of their realities and journeys of transformation post-migration. The participatory and visual nature of this research project is not without significance. Taking part in the project and creating visual representations of their experiences allowed women to pause and reflect on their achievements from a distance, and had an empowering effect on them; leading to increased confidence, self-understanding, and awareness of the meaning of their journeys (benefits of the methodological approach for participants are discussed in Rydzik et al., 2013).

11.3 VISUAL AND VERBAL NARRATIVES OF SOLO MIGRANT WOMEN'S JOURNEYS

11.3.1 MULTI-LAYERED MOTIVATIONS

FIGURE 11.2   Tina's artwork.

> *[W]hat are the reasons behind the decision of many Latvian women to leave the country of their origins and whether or not this really is a choice? Is it a simple desire to earn more money, and what does it mean when women say that they left in search for a better life for themselves and their children? And finally, what does it mean to leave your past behind and step into the unknown, arrive to the place where you are seen as nothing more, but one of the millions and, at the age of 20 (30? 50? 70?) start building your identity from scratch, growing a new life on a foreign ground.* (Tina, in the commentary to her artwork)

Motivations to migrate are gendered (Mahler & Pessar, 2006). Yet little is known about the differences in motivations between CEE women and men. Women's motivations to migrate are often discussed in the context of family or for economic reasons as low-skilled workers. However, migrant women's reasons for migration are multi-layered, heterogeneous, and interconnected. While securing employment to support themselves financially is important, the study participants highlight other reasons for their migration, which differentiates them from the typical image of a "strongly labour-motivated migrant group" (Sumption & Somerville, 2010, p. 24). The economic aspect of migration is often eclipsed by the experiential aspect and more intangible factors related to acquiring new knowledge, experiencing something new or improving English. In their migration, economic factors do play a role but are often secondary to experiential or educational factors and are means to achieve these goals. Indeed, as participants' trajectories show, women search for better life opportunities or migrate out of curiosity. One participant, Iza, arrived in the United Kingdom in 2006. She had been working in a factory in Poland when her friend encouraged her to migrate and offered help in finding work. Her motivation was partly experiential, partly encouraged by her friend but also economic, as she earned little:

> I came here because I had never been abroad and I had always wanted to see how the life as an émigré looks like…so I thought why not come and give it a go. I took six-month unpaid leave from my work. In Poland I worked in poultry factory, where I was sticking expiry date and other labels on frozen products which were ready to be exported to Germany and Holland. My plan was to stay here six months and then go back to Poland.

Several participants came to the United Kingdom at a very young age, soon after finishing their A-levels, as 19-year-olds, or while at university. Natalia finished her A-levels and took a gap year before university. Seeking new experiences and an independent life, she came to the United Kingdom on her own in 2005:

> I knew I wanted to go back to England for a gap year as I didn't know what I wanted to study. It was supposed to be just a year abroad where I think about my choice of degree and then go back to Poland to study….

At the time of leaving Latvia, Signe was also 19-years-old. One of her colleagues suggested coming to the United Kingdom. Wanting to experience something new, she saw it as an opportunity to change her life. Her motivations were partly influenced by the friend, the lack of an interesting job and her openness to adventure:

> I had a friend who asked me if I wanted to go and work in England. I said why not it's a great opportunity. I wanted to go away from Latvia and experience something new. I was quite young as well and I like new experiences and stuff like this. So why not.... I was working one and a half years after I had left school.... It was quite hard, you know. I was working in an office, just cleaning offices and also I was working as a shop assistant.

Lidia always wanted to travel and live abroad. Initially, she came to the United Kingdom in 2005 on a work placement from a Polish institution where she was studying hospitality. She then went back to Poland to finish her studies and returned to the United Kingdom after graduating. For her, the desire to experience life abroad emerged in her teens:

> It all started when I finished my high school. I was a teenager and really wanted to go abroad. But obviously when you are 19 your parents don't want to let you go into the big world. So, my best friend told me about this School of Hotel Industry and Gastronomy in Poznań which has placement schemes abroad during the university course. I went through major arguments with my parents. My mum is well educated.... She tried to discourage me from going to such a school but I really wanted to travel and thought that this would be a great idea. This would sort of open the door to a new world abroad.... After the first year of university I went to Greece for three months. It was so great without my parents that when I got back I started to organize the trip to England after the first semester of my second year. It all worked out well and I went to live in a country house hotel with a restaurant for a year.

Since 2004, Olga has experienced three phases of migration, stimulated primarily by educational and experiential reasons. She first came to the United Kingdom during university summer holidays to work seasonally on a farm, which was a popular trend post-EU accession for Latvians. She then went back to Latvia to continue her studies. As she had always dreamt about studying abroad, she returned to the United Kingdom on an Erasmus exchange program:

One of my teachers suggested to take this opportunity and to study as an exchange student in the UK. Because I really wanted to study here, not work. It was my dream since school. I just grabbed it.... It was a whole year.... I found some good friends and traveled a lot as well.

After one year at a British university, Olga returned to Latvia to graduate and in 2006 she decided to move back to the United Kingdom to start another degree, and then settled in the United Kingdom.

At the core of participants' mobilities and engrained in their idea of migration, is seeking new experiences and self-development. As young solo women, they decide to migrate on their own, asserting their will to experience life abroad and being open to new opportunities. Their motivations to migrate are multi-layered and complex, with individual development and acquisition of new experiences more important than financial motivations. Similar patterns have been observed in a study on Polish migrants where migrants were "determined to realize their own migratory project" (Isański et al., 2014, p. 15). Ryan notes that migration of those migrants who arrived when young, childless, and single was "specifically linked with education, an opportunity to travel abroad, enhance their skills and gain new experiences" and they "rarely drew upon family narratives" (Ryan, 2011, p. 93). Indeed, participants do not perceive themselves as migrant workers, but as independent women who seek new opportunities. While work becomes an integral part of their experience (they need to support themselves financially when abroad, often by working in low-skill, low-paid roles), the financial element is not their ultimate goal. Indeed, as Parutis argues, "for some migrants enhancing their cultural capital may be more important than economic gains" (Parutis, 2014, p. 38). For young, single, and childless women, migration becomes a choice, a journey and an adventure and not an escape or survival strategy. With an increasing trend of individual migration, the decision to migrate can be perceived "as an empowerment strategy and well planned development of their knowledge, education and skills" (Isański et al., 2014, p. 15). Over time, this initially perceived short-term adventure, turns into a long-term transformative life experience of meaningful mobility.

11.3.2   MOBILE WORKERS

FIGURE 11.3   Image of Lidia's artwork "Postcards to My Family: Exploring the Journey to Who I Am Today."

> *This is a series of postcards to my family exploring the journey to who I am today. The journey that I embarked on has been marked on the map and each place where I stayed is signposted by a postcard. An account about me on my own building my identity from scratch, learning to live in the country where I don't know anyone, struggling to communicate because of the language barrier and getting to the point where I am now, completely independent with the ability to speak English fluently, employed, in my final year of English BA. It's a personal reflection about my life, ups and downs, people that I met and situations that I had to find myself in. My rocky road to maturity* (Lidia explaining the concept behind her map of mobilities).

In more affluent societies, there is a trend of young people going on a gap year abroad (Lyons et al., 2012). This was not an option for the participants due to economic factors, such as weaker currencies or lack of funds. Instead, the best opportunity for them to experience life abroad, and achieve their experiential and educational goals was through employment. Although financial factors were not decisive, the opportunity to work and earn even the United Kingdom minimum wage, enabled them to fulfill other, more meaningful, goals. They needed to gain economic capital first to be then able to build up their human and social capital (Hellermann, 2006). In this way, they entered tourism, an industry that has historically been open to migrants due to constant labor shortages and high staff turnover (Janta & Ladkin, 2009). The jobs available for migrant women are often limited to low-skilled, low-paid gendered roles, such as waitress, receptionist, housekeeper, or flight attendant, and exploitative and discriminatory treatment of women is not uncommon (Rydzik, 2014). Yet, despite their jobs being low-skilled and low-paid, they allowed participants to gain financial independence, gave them flexibility to combine work and study, improve their English, and work and interact with diverse people. These are some of the advantages of working in the industry also identified by scholars (Szivas et al., 2003).

As jobs in tourism are considered relatively easy to find, this gave participants flexibility, resulting in increased spatial and occupational mobility. Figure 11.3 illustrates Lidia's mobility in the United Kingdom over six years, demonstrating how her tourism employment facilitated and influenced her mobility as well as showing the benefits of this for her development. With participants relocating relatively easily for jobs and being open to further relocations, mobility becomes "a way of living," with women "constructing more fluid lifestyles" (Ignatowicz, 2011, p. 43). Signe explains: "Here you have more freedom. In Latvia it's really hard to find jobs. Here you can change jobs all the time. If you don't like it, you go and take another one. In Latvia it's quite hard."

For Signe, migration has provided her with an opportunity to fulfill her dream of working as a flight attendant: "In Latvia I couldn't do it. I applied for AirBaltic but they said no. There was no school providing training. There is nothing for flight attendants. So I decided I was going to leave it. So I came here to Scotland and I thought why not Ryanair?" She feels fulfilled in her career: "I like it. Actually, it was and still is my dream. I like flying, meeting different people every single day, the experience of different nationalities." Work in tourism opens up opportunities for travel, resulting in the blurring of the boundaries between travel, leisure, and migration (Cohen et al., 2015). Karolina explains: "I started in the restaurant and then I thought that if I became a croupier, it would open up opportunities for me like traveling all over the world. With this profession you can work in any country in the world." Tourism working environments encourage women's participation in tourism. Their curiosity toward traveling and getting to know new places is awakened by working with a diverse range of people and providing for tourists. They learn about travel behavior from their customers and co-workers or as they, through their work, participate in tourism and become traveling migrants.

11.3.3   TRAVELING MIGRANTS

FIGURE 11.4   Image from Natalia's artwork.

> *Meanwhile she was building her social life. Working wasn't the main part of her life any longer….She started living her own life, taking advantage of youth, freedom and financial independence. Her dreams about traveling came true.* (Text from Natalia's photo reportage)

Leisure participation, specifically travel, is important for migrants. Lifestyles of migrants undergo significant changes during the post-arrival period (Stodolska, 2000). Yet, only limited attention has been given to migrants' leisure participation patterns. These are often discussed in the context of constraints that limit migrants' participation in leisure (Rublee & Shaw, 1991) or the role of leisure in migrants' integration into the host community (Horolets, 2015). Participation in recreational mobility can reduce uncertainty among migrants and lead to empowerment, aiding integration and negotiation of one's identity in a new environment (Horolets, 2015). However, scholars have also argued that post-migration, migrants often experience constraints to leisure participation, such as lack of time, limited language skills, demanding work schedules, financial limitations and family responsibilities (Juniu, 2000). While some migrants experience a decrease in leisure participation and cease some leisure activities, others gradually discover emerging new leisure opportunities (Stodolska, 2000). Of interest here is how young solo female migrants engage in leisure, specifically travel, post-migration.

Benefits of travel are well documented and include relief and renewal, broadening experiences, social interaction, developing independence, and strengthening family relationships (Hazel 2005, p. 228). Migrant travel behavior is predominantly associated with visiting friends and relatives (VFR). VFR has attracted some attention from scholars (Janta, Cohen and Williams, 2015), who highlight the importance of family networks for migrants and the emotional aspect migrants and the emotional aspect of "traveling home" (Ignatowicz, 2011). VFR mobility is not the scope here and instead the focus is on solo migrant women's mobility for purely recreational purposes, which to date received limited attention. The study participants regularly travel "home" to visit their relatives. However, they do not consider these visits as holidays because they play a different role in their mobility (Rydzik et al., 2012).

Outside of VFR visits, embracing the post-2004 freedom of movement, participants engage in travel across, mostly European, borders and begin to participate in tourist activities. Indeed, travel starts to play an important role in their lives post-migration. Despite certain constraints, migration becomes the first step toward their increased leisure mobility (Rydzik et al., 2012). It opens up new opportunities for tourism and allows women to fulfill their pre-migration dreams of traveling. Iza reflects:

> [W]hen I came here I met my friend with whom I started traveling, something I was always dreaming of....I would like to return to Poland one day and I promise myself all the time that I'll start saving up money to buy a flat there and go back one day. But I often hear stories about people who returned and didn't make it, and came back to England. All

this tells me that maybe instead of saving up, I should travel more and stay here a bit longer.

Travel was something that most participants did not consider attainable for those on lower incomes back in their countries of origin. There was a common perception among participants that back in their countries a number of constraints made traveling abroad beyond their reach. According to Olga: "If you have a lower salary in my country, you can't really do anything. Here you can even travel, buy yourself stuff". It was migration that lifted these constraints and opened up new opportunities for recreational mobility. Indeed, for Signe, migration is "like freedom. In Latvia you can't do the things I'm doing here. I mean money wise. Here, you can do whatever you want. I love traveling. I've been in quite a few places: Many places in Italy, Spain, Sicily…" As Stodolska argues, "it is the removal of constraints that triggers participation" because "people who could not engage in certain activities because of economic and social barriers, or other barriers such as lack of knowledge or lack of facilities, exhibit a latent demand for these activities" (Stodolska, 2000, p. 58).

The introduction of cheap air travel revolutionized mobility patterns of new EU migrants, resulting in development of flexible migration trajectories and opportunities for enhanced mobility (Ignatowicz, 2011). Indeed, it has been shown that Polish migrants have embraced low cost airlines, leading to the development of the infrastructure and the mushrooming of low cost flight connections between Poland and United Kingdom (as well as other CEE countries), with migrants embarking not only on journeys visiting friends and family (Burrell, 2011) but also traveling across European destinations. This has led to the creation of a culture of hypermobility among post-2004 migrants, traveling "home" as well as inscribing themselves within the Western ideas of travel and tourism. Natalia reflects on this:

When you go traveling abroad, you see Polish people traveling (…) and it's normal that they go back to England after their holidays. For example, we had a flight canceled and we were stranded at the airport. We met some Polish people and where were they going? Obviously, they were going back to London. When you live in Poland you can't afford to travel.

Far from being immobile and constrained in their participation in travel post-migration, participants become increasingly mobile in their private as well as working lives, inscribing themselves within Western trends of travel behavior. This adoption of Western trends has been described as the demonstration effect, where migrants adopt certain leisure activities and behavior which they associate with people of high status and a desirable way of life (Stodolska, 2000, p. 60). Although predominantly employed in low-skill, low-paid jobs, these roles do not limit their mobility. On the contrary, their employment often facilitates their mobility as they become more open to relocation, changing employment and confident in exploring new opportunities.

11.3.4   TRANSFORMATIVE JOURNEYS

FIGURE 11.5   Final postcard from Lidia's artwork.

Transformation: *The shaping of my Identity throughout the time when I have been living, working and studying in Bristol.* (Lidia's description of one of the postcards from her artwork)

The last photo is the photo of my transformation.... Over the three years I have transformed a lot. In the beginning, I was this blonde, crazy girl. I was going to parties, drunk a lot and didn't care about work.... Then I went to uni and started to change. The middle photo is a bit artier photo.... The third part is a photo from this year's holidays, one of my latest photos when I think that I am a mature and adult woman. I have completely transformed. That's why I have butterflies around me because a butterfly is a symbol of transformation.... [The image] was made out of three photos each taken with a different camera. One is made by an old rubbish camera at a party; second one with my manual camera and the third was taken with a very good camera of my boyfriend where every parameter was set very well. So all three faces were of a different quality.... You can see the upgrade in my life through the cameras these photos were taken with. (Lidia describing the postcard).

Migration can be a transformative and meaningful experience for women migrating solo at a young age. Through interconnected mobilities post-migration—occupational, spatial, educational, and leisure mobility—and the experiences that emerge through these, on an individual level, women undergo a transformation. With time and experience, they grow confident in their abilities and in voicing their opinions. Kasia's words reflect this: "As time was passing by it was much easier for me to stand up for myself. Life abroad is a great lesson to shape the character". Looking back, the women could see the benefits of the decision they made to leave their country and the transformative impact it had on their lives, and saw migration as a learning process. V. says: "When you start earning, you start feeling more comfortable and you want to see more and you want to see further more and to see how much more can I achieve, what else can I do?" Iza also appreciates the learning opportunities and lifestyle enabled by migration:

Here in the UK I saw that you can live an easier life. And you can live this life not only working. Of course you can go to work but you can afford to rest and relax and not just work, work, work. Also, here I finally got access to the Internet. There was Internet in Poland but I didn't have a computer or access to it. Here I could read a lot and I discovered many new things. So I can say that England opened my eyes to the world.

This was not an easy process and often required strength and the development of resilience, particularly in relation to their working lives. Poor working conditions, exploitative and discriminatory work practices are not uncommon in United Kingdom tourism working environments (McDowell et al., 2007; Wright & Pollert, 2006), and migrant women are often at risk of triple discrimination for being foreign, female and employed in low-status roles (Rydzik, 2014). Indeed, most participants experienced unfair and discriminative treatment at work. Yet, through their active confrontation of unfair treatment, they emerge stronger, determined to achieve more and fight for their rights. Wiola reported bullying by her manager: "What is really happening is people resigning and looking for different jobs because they don't want to hassle themselves with fighting for their rights. They simply want to avoid problems. I fight for my rights therefore I am still at the same place". Similarly, Kasia took an unfair dismissal case to her employer:

> I'm not a marionette to shuffle me from one place to another. I decided to appeal because I thought that it was not fair what they did. I wanted to appeal not because I wanted to go back to work but more to have a chance to say what I think about it…. I wanted to hear a response to my questions and explanations of the unfair accusations made against me. They had no evidence, and each question I asked the reply was: 'Well, no'. I didn't have to go there again. They paid me my monthly salary as they paid others who got made redundant.

While the employment experiences they gained in tourism roles range from positive to very negative, the women emerge from these experiences not as passive victims but as active agents in control of their lives. With time and experience, they gain knowledge about their working rights, improve their English and develop networks. They begin to challenge unfair treatment, rejecting the label of easily exploitable victims. Iza reflects:

> I started to understand that it's not like that Polish friend of yours told you to "just work and keep quiet" but that you are in a more civilized country, and that you can change your attitude a bit and your approach. The language school helped me a lot and I realized that I don't have to be this housekeeper squashed by the rest but even if I am this housekeeper I deserve something better.

Even though many of them continue working in similar environments, their awareness grows, they become more confident in negotiating situations and defending their rights. Although constraints and feelings of under-appreciation by employers are very much present in their lives, participants do not let these overtake their sense of achievement.

Just like independent travel for women can offer "a unique and important way of building their sense of self, confidence and empowerment" (Wilson & Harris, 2006, p. 164), for young solo migrant women, independent migration can become a transformative, life-changing experience and one of meaningful mobility. Exploring experiences of solo women travelers, Wilson and Harris conceptualized the term "meaningful travel" (2006). This chapter takes this concept a step further by opening it up to include the transformative and meaningful mobilities of migrant women. Too often, migrant women are overlooked in the analysis of women's travel. Yet, as women find meaning and fulfillment through migration, theirs are life changing and long lasting journeys of self-empowerment and transformation. Migration thus becomes a platform for self-development and building confidence, going far beyond financial gains.

11.4   CONCLUSION

This chapter explored the diverse ways in which CEE solo female migrants undergo transformation post-migration and engage in meaningful mobility. Little is known about the impact of migration on young solo women. Giving visibility to their transformative journeys, enabled by migration, tourism employment and travel, and highlighting the value of their interconnected mobilities was at the core of this chapter. Their migration journeys are ones of meaningful mobility, with learning and self-development central. Explored on an individual level, these rich narratives challenge the perception of migrant women as passive victims and followers of men. Migration for them is a journey and a road to personal transformation, often taking place in parallel to entering womanhood, transitioning from teenagers to independent women, as well as providing an opportunity for women to redefine and renegotiate their gender roles (Duda-Mikulin, 2013).

Migrant women are on the move and their multiple and intersecting mobilities should not be overlooked and under-appreciated, as their mobile lives constitute an important manifestation of contemporary society and are inscribed within lifestyle mobility (Cohen et al., 2015). While CEE migrant women are perceived primarily as economic migrants employed in precarious jobs, their motivations to migrate are of an experiential and educational nature, and their experiences post-migration transformative and empowering. Employed in low-paid gendered tourism roles, they often endure poor working conditions and uneven power relations. However, they reject the label of passive victims of exploitation, by negotiating constraints and constructing their identities as active agents of change and in control of their lives.

Theirs are hypermobile lives, where work, life, travel, leisure, and migration are blurred, and where women actively participate in mobility— providing for those on the move and discovering travel for leisure for themselves. Through verbal and visual narratives, female migrants emerge as independent actors with agency, increasingly mobile and confident, with intention "to move on, rather than move back" (Cohen et al., 2015, p. 159), as Natalia concludes in her artwork (Fig. 11.6). Theirs is a meaningful mobility, a mobility that is empowering and results in one's transformation on an individual level, leading to self-development, gaining confidence and a voice to achieve one's goals.

Sometimes she looks back and thinks 'what could have happened if...not emigration?' No answer. She left her family home, childhood and lots of memories in the country. Now she is here, adult and knows what she wants – moving on.

FIGURE 11.6   Image from Natalia's photo reportage.

KEYWORDS

- solo female migrants
- mobilities
- migration
- transformation
- visual methodologies

REFERENCES

Banks, M. *Visual Methods in Social Research;* Sage: London, 2001.

Burrell, K. Going Steerage on Ryanair: Cultures of Migrant Air Travel Between Poland and the UK. *J. Trans. Geogr.* **2011,** *19*(5), 1023–1030.

Cohen, S. A.; Duncan, T.; Thulemark, M. Lifestyle Mobilities: The Crossroads of Travel, Leisure and Migration. *Mobilities.* **2015,** *10*(1), 155–172.

Duda-Mikulin, E. Migration as Opportunity? A Case Study of Polish Women: Migrants in the UK and Returnees in Poland. *Problemy Polityki Społecznej.* **2013,** *23*(4), 105–121.

Harris, C.; Wilson, E. Travelling Beyond the Boundaries of Constraint: Women, Travel and Empowerment. In *Tourism & Gender: Embodiment, Sensuality and Experience;* Pritchard, A., Morgan, N., Ateljevic, I., Harris, C., Eds.; CABI: Wallingford, CT, 2007; pp 235–251.

Hazel, N. Holidays for Children and Families in Need: An Exploration of the Research and Policy Context for Social Tourism in the UK. *Child. Soc.* **2005,** *19,* 225–236.

Hellermann, C. Migrating Alone: Tackling Social Capital? Women from Eastern Europe in Portugal, *Ethnic Racial Stud.* **2006,** *29*(6), 1135–1152.

Horolets, A. Finding One's Way: Recreational Mobility of Post-2004 Polish Migrants in West Midlands, UK. *Leis. Stud.* **2015,** *34*(1), 5–18.

Ignatowicz, A. Changing Construction of Mobility: Traveling Home and 'New' Polish Migrants n England. *Migr. Stud.* **2011,** *1,* 33–47.

Isański, J.; Mleczko, A.; Seredyńska-Abou Eid, R. Polish Contemporary Migration: From Co-Migrants to Project ME. *Int. Migr.* **2014,** *52*(1), 4–21.

Janta, H.; Ladkin, A. Polish Migrant Labor in the Hospitality Workforce: Implications for Recruitment and Retention. *Tour. Cult. Comm.* **2009,** *9*(1–2), 5–15.

Jordan, F.; Aitchison, C. Tourism and the Sexualisation of the Gaze: Solo Female Tourists' Experiences of Gendered Power, Surveillance and Embodiment. *Leis. Stud.* **2008,** *27*(3), 329–349.

Juniu, S. The Impact of Immigration: Leisure Experience in the Lives of South American Immigrants. *J. Leis. Res.* **2000,** *32,* 358–381.

Lyons, K.; Hanley, J.; Wearing, S.; Neil, J. Gap Year Volunteer Tourism: Myths of Global Citizenship? *Ann. Tour. Res.* **2012,** *39*(1), 361–378.

Mahler, S. J.; Pessar, P. R. Gender Matters: Ethnographers Bring Gender from the Periphery Toward the Core of Migration Studies. *Int. Migr. Rev.* **2006,** *40*(1), 28–63.

McDowell, L.; Batnitzky, A.; Dyer, S. Segmentation, and Interpellation: The Embodied Labors of Migrant Workers in a Greater London Hotel. *Eco. Geogr.* **2007,** *83*(1), 1–25.

Morokvasic, M. Women in Migration: Beyond the Reductionist Outlook. In *One Way Ticket: Migration and Female Labour;* Phizacklea, A., Ed.; Routledge & Kegan Paul: London, 1983; pp 13–31.

Nawyn, S. Gender and Migration: Integrating Feminist Theory into Migration Studies. *Sociol. Compass.* **2010,** *4*(9), 749–765.

Parutis, V. 'Economic Migrants' or 'Middling Transnationals'? East European Migrants' Experiences of Work in the UK. *Int. Migr.* **2014,** *52*(1), 36–55.

Pink, S. *Doing Visual Ethnography;* Sage: London, 2001.

Pustulka, P. Polish Mothers on the Move: Transnationality and Discourses of Gender, Care and Co-Residentiality Requirement in the Narratives of Polish Women Raising Children in the West. *Studia Sociol. IV.* **2012,** *2*(2), 162–175.

Rakić, T.; Chambers, D. Innovative Techniques in Tourism Research: An Exploration of Visual Methods and Academic Filmmaking. *Int. J. Tour. Res.* **2010,** *12*, 379–389.

Rakić, T.; Chambers, D. *An Introduction to Visual Research Methods in Tourism*; Routledge: London, 2012.

Rublee, C. B.; Shaw, S. M. Constraints on the Leisure and Community Participation of Immigrant Women: Implications for Social Integration. *Soc. Leis.* **1991,** *14*, 133–150.

Ryan, L. How Women use Family Networks to Facilitate Migration: A Comparative Study of Irish and Polish Women in Britain. *His. Family.* **2009,** *14*, 217–231.

Ryan, L. Transnational Relations: Family Migration among Recent Polish Migrants in London. *Int. Migr.* **2011,** *49*(2), 80–103.

Rydzik, A.; Pritchard, A.; Morgan, N.; Sedgley, D. Mobility, Migration and Hospitality Employment: Voices of Central and Eastern European Women. *Hosp. Soc.* **2012,** *2*(2), 137–157.

Rydzik, A.; Pritchard, A.; Morgan, N.; Sedgley, D. The Potential of Arts-Based Transformative Research. *Ann. Tour. Res.* **2013,** *40*(1), 283–305.

Rydzik, A. (In)visible Lives: A Visual and Participatory Exploration of the Female Migrant Tourism Worker Experience. Ph.D. Dissertation, Cardiff Metropolitan University, Cardiff, 2014.

Scarles, C. Where Words Fail, Visuals Ignite: Opportunities for Visual Autoethnography in Tourism Research. *Ann. Tour. Res.* **2010,** *37*(4), 905–926.

Schmitt, C.; Trappe, H. Introduction to the Special Issue: Gender Relations in Central and Eastern Europe – Change or Continuity? *J. Family Res.* **2010,** *22*(3), 261–265.

Stodolska, M. Changes in Leisure Participation Patterns after Immigration. *Leis. Sci.* **2000,** *22*, 39–63.

Sumption, M.; Somerville, W. *The UK's New Europeans. Progress and Challenges Five Years After Accession.* Equality and Human Rights Commission Policy Report. [Online] 2010 http://oppenheimer.mcgill.ca/IMG/pdf/new_europeans.pdf (accessed May 1, 2015).

Szivas, E.; Riley, M.; Airey, D. Labour Mobility into Tourism. Attraction and Satisfaction. *Ann. Tour. Res.* **2003,** *30*, 64–76.

UN The World's Women 2010. United Nations Trends and Statistics, Department of Economic and Social Affairs. [Online] 2010, http://unstats.un.org/unsd/demographic/ products/Worldswomen /WW_full%20report_color.pdf (accessed May 2, 2015).

White, A. *Polish Families and Migration since EU Accession;* The Policy Press: Bristol, CT, 2011.

Wilson, E.; Harris, C. Meaningful Travel: Women, Independent Travel and the Search for Self and Meaning. *Tourism.* **2006,** *54*(2), 161–172.

Wilson, E.; Little, D. E. The Solo Female Travel Experience: Exploring the 'Geography of Women's Fear'. *Curr. Issues Tour.* **2008,** *11*(2), 167–186.

Wright, T.; Pollert, A. *The Experience of Ethnic Minority Workers in the Hotel and Catering Industry: Routes to Support and Advice on Workplace Problems* – Final Report. Acas Research Paper 03/06, Acas: London. [Online] 2006 http://www.acas.org.uk/media/ pdf/0/b/03-06_1.pdf (accessed May 1, 2015).

CHAPTER 12

HOME HOLIDAYS AS REAL HOLIDAYS? MIDLIFE SINGLE WOMEN'S EXPERIENCES

BENTE HEIMTUN

Department of Tourism and Northern Studies, UiT, The Arctic University, Norway

E-mail: bente.heimtun@uit.no<ABS>

CONTENTS

12.1 INTRODUCTION

Tourism researchers often argue that travel for pleasure is a social necessity in Western societies (Frew & Winter, 2010), and that "the modern subject is a subject on the move" (Urry, 1995, p. 141). Further, "travel has become an automatism, a kind of habitual mobility" (Krippendorf, 1989, p. 136). Such discourse suggests that "normal adults" will travel for pleasure and "to stay at home is to be pitied" (Urry, 1988, p. 36). Thus, the concept of a home holiday—or what has been alternatively labeled as a "staycation" (Fox, 2009)—is widely perceived to not be a "real" holiday (Frew & Winter, 2010). Consequently, tourism researchers focus on extraordinary experiences rendering tourists' ordinary, everyday-like experiences relatively invisible (Urry, 1990). The everyday-like experiences of tourism have received increasing attention, whereas holidays spent at home are still relatively neglected as an area of scholarly study (McCabe, 2002).

Home holidays can be defined broadly as leave from work (in Norway the Holiday Act entitles employees 25 working days leave each year), when the nights are spent at home and the days are spent in the home area. Home holidays thus contrast with traditional understandings of tourism which often are defined as holidays with overnight stays away from home (Leiper, 1979). The concept of a home holiday offers an alternative approach for understanding the tourist experience, which opens up for the possibility to engage in "tourism," and follows McCabe's notion that tourism is better understood as a "lay construct" rather than as a normative act (McCabe, 2009b, p. 40). For the purposes of this chapter, it is argued that home is both a physical entity and the surrounding places (Mallett, 2004), which makes it possible to feel away even at home (Uriely, 2010), for instance when being a tourist in the home area (Shani & Uriely, 2012). I also argue that holiday time contrasts with leisure time in the sense that is constitutes a greater break from daily/weekly routines (Deem, 1996), and thus is embedded with greater freedom of choice of what to do and when (Wang, 2000). In this way, this chapter responds to Haukeland's call for greater focus on people who do not leave their home in the holidays (Haukeland, 1990). In order to rectify this knowledge gap, and from a feminist perspective, I explore midlife single women's home holidays; in doing so, the dichotomies inherent in the concepts of "home" and "away," and of "leisure" and "tourism," are explored and problematized.

Midlife is defined as the period from age 35 to 55 (Ogle & Damhorst, 2005), and single refers to a person without a partner and who lives alone. Further, "single" is a term which encapsulates singles, widows, and divorcées (DePaulo & Morris, 2005). A survey on singles in Norway states that a lack of travel partner explains why 48% stay at home in the holiday; the same survey also showed that summer holidays are more difficult than other annual holidays (Dragland, 2011). However, it is not only singles that spend summer holidays at home; many married and coupled people in Norway do not take longer trips (Granseth, 2010). For men, the main reasons for staying home are lack of time and interest, and for the women, it is a lack of money and time. Moreover, 10% of the total population is constrained by lack of travel partner (Haukeland, 1990). Traveling for pleasure is thus imbued with unequal access to diverse forms of capital (Bourdieu, 1986). Although research has identified reasons for non-traveling, little is known about how people reflect upon their home holidays, what they do and the (potential) constraints they negotiate. With this focus, I add to the growing literature on women's holidays across the life course (e.g., Wilson & Little, 2008; Small, 2002; Sedgley et al., 2006).

12.2   HOME AND HOLIDAYS

Home is "(a) place(s), (a) space(s), feeling(s), practices, and/or an active state of being in the world" (Mallett, 2004, p. 62). Home is a multidimensional concept which includes the physical structure of the house and its positive and negative qualities as a dwelling place and space, as well as the surrounding neighborhood and town, city, or region. The concept of home may also refer to the family birth home and one's own homeland (the former understanding is used here in this chapter). Home is thus understood as a starting point for engaging in holiday (tourism) activities such as eating out, going to the beach, visiting a museum, doing outdoor recreation, going shopping and so on. Home holidays have been described as "staycations," defined in the Merriam-Webster Dictionary as "a vacation spent at home or nearby" (Merriam-Webster.com, 2014). To Hay, a staycation is a form of domestic tourism (Hay, 2010) and to Dodds it is the ultimate slow tourism (Dodds, 2012). Used in the first sense it includes second home tourism and caravanning in own country (Davidson, 2012).

Nevertheless, the concept's popularity boomed after the Global Financial Crisis in 2007 as many people lacked money for traveling (Fox, 2009). In the aftermath of the crisis there was a growth in handbooks on what activities to pursue locally. To prevent staycations from becoming "fake-cations," Wixon suggests advice on how to make this time memorable, educational, and fun (Wixon, 2009, p. 21).

Home holidays blur the distinction between leisure studies and tourist studies. One traditional difference between the two is the spatial environment, or the distinction between home and away (Carr, 2002). This distinction is also based on different social and cultural constructions of free time, linked to daily rhythms and routines (Wang, 2000). However, by including immobilities, the new mobility turn rejects the opposition of home/away (Hannam et al., 2006). Immobilities are linked to difference and power relations, but also to virtual and imaginative forms of tourism mobility, done at home (Gale, 2009). In recent theories, leisure and tourist studies are merged and the spatial differences are less important (Ryan & Glendon, 1998). Daytrips, for instance, are taken both from home and when staying in a tourist resort (Ryan, 1994). Moreover, although everyday activities and obligations are also part of (home) holidays, the temporal freedom is greater in the home holiday than in everyday leisure.

In spite of a growing awareness of home as more than a merely a point of departure for the holidays (Leiper, 1979), the literature on holidays taken at home is scarce. Haukeland, however, identified a typology of non-travelers; those who did not want to travel in their holidays; those who were obliged to stay at home; those who had social welfare problems; and those constrained by social obligation and welfare issues (Haukeland, 1990). Those without a choice missed visiting family, experiencing something different and the time to rest and relax. Moreover, they were deprived of the social right to travel and the social well-being imbuing tourism (see also McCabe, 2009a). Minnaert argued that poor teenage mothers without prior travel experiences were uncertain and anxious about how to enact the tourist role; it felt scary, unsafe for the child and the mothers lacked a support system (Minnaert, 2014). In particular, single mothers were reluctant toward traveling. Their degree of uncertainty was also connected to other spheres of life such as lack of confidence in decision-making, constraining them more than lack of economic capital.

Deem explored "holidays at home" as engendered leisure and discussed how female residents consumed the home city in time and space (Deem, 1996), thereby challenging the tourist gaze (Urry, 1990). These women's home holidays were similar to pleasure travel, although child care and household work responsibilities continued and it was difficult to take advantage of the tourist gaze. Still, holidaying at home gave "less intensive and less time-aware experience than being at home at any other time," even when engaged in similar activities (Deem, 1996, p. 115). The break from paid work was thus more important than the break from domestic work, and the separation from paid work did not rely upon mobility, or "going away." Yet a sense of domestic place was always present. While many of the women interviewed by Deem did not consider home as very different from holidays involving travel (Deem, 1996), holidays at home are embedded in a discourse where traveling is considered socially accepted and expected (Frew & Winter, 2010). Poor mobility therefore increases people's a sense of social exclusion and a "real holiday" is construed as something that can only be taken away from home. In Frew and Winter's study few tourists found staying at home attractive and most of them pitied those who missed out on traveling. To increase the value of staying at home, people's attitudes thus had to change. Krippendorf's notion then that the "new tourist" would want to act more sustainably by traveling less, to take "a safari in the neighborhood rather than one in the jungle," seems utopian (Krippendorf, 1986, p. 134).

Molz's (2009) and Sharma's (2009) analysis of United States popular media's representations of staycations during the economic crisis also showed how immobility was embedded in a negative value discourse. Molz argued that mobility and immobilty were imbued with moral, ethical or political values related to pace and stillness, which were made meaningful through intersecting practices and discourses (Molz, 2009). With a few exceptions, the United States media discourse constructed stillness as something discomforting, as a substitute to the real thing. This discourse thus devalued home as a space for recuperating and for escaping the hectic of everyday life, thereby marginalizing the stillness of home holidays. Moreover, the discourse did not encourage reflections on ideologies of capitalism and consumerism. It was a white middle class discourse, constructed by the big media houses, which encouraged home investments and a new form of domestication by excluding local economy and community (Sharma, 2009).

12.3 METHODOLOGY

This chapter is based on a feminist study of 30 midlife single women in Norway. This study used a qualitative, feminist methodology to explore the interrelationship between holiday making and gender/single/midlife identities (Heimtun, 2007). The data, which was collected in 2005, resulted in several publications on these women's experiences. However, one part of the data was never analyzed, and when working on this chapter, I realized that I had silenced the experiences of the women who spent much/parts of their holidays at home. Similar to other tourism researchers, perhaps, I had also been blinded by the assumption that tourism knowledge is restricted to experiences away from home. I was interested in re-visiting that data as there still is a need to open up our understanding of the holiday experience as multifaceted, partly due to the financial crisis, but also from a gendered perspective.

The data was collected before, during and after the summer holiday. In the first and last phase I conducted focus group interviews as a way of empowering the participants to interact and reflect with each other, thereby giving me less control over the conversations (Wilkinson, 1998, 1999). Seven focus groups were held in April with three to six participants; and nine between September and October, then with two to four women in each group. Twenty-six of the thirty women partook in both interviews which suggested a commitment to the research. Each meeting lasted about two hours and I transcribed all interviews verbatim. To ensure that the women's identities were kept anonymous they selected pseudonyms of choice, and these are provided here with the quotes.

During the holidays the women wrote solicited diaries, which were explicitly designed for this research (Meth, 2003) as a way of getting access to their multiple holidays without my presence. The women were thus given the control over when and how to participate (Bell, 1998). The diaries were handed out at the end of the first focus group meetings and contained small questionnaires (DeLongis et al., 1992) mapping the women's holidays; where they went, with whom, for how long, and so on. It also consisted of open questions about one daily activity; positive and negative thoughts and feelings and reflections on being a midlife single woman in this context. Twenty-eight of the women kept a diary for up to 14 days during the holidays. After being copied the diaries were returned to the women.

The participants (35–55 years old), recruited through snowball sampling (Schutt, 1999), had different single statuses; 15 were divorcees/widows and 15 were always singles. Ten of the divorcees/widows had adult children. All were heterosexual. The always-single women tended to be 35–45 years old, whereas most of the divorcees/widows were aged between 45 and 55. Only one woman could not afford to travel. Nine women had small and five had very large budgets. The remaining half had standard budgets, compared to other Norwegians (Aulid, 2012).

I drew upon "constant comparison" of data (Glaser & Strauss, 1977); first by open, initial coding and the emergence of as many categories as possible, and later by focused coding and the making of connection between categories (Charmaz, 2006). I used the logic of grounded theory to locate empirical realities similar to the constructivist grounded theory. I also drew upon narrative analysis of individual cases (Reissman, 2008). Based on careful and sensitive readings I selected three stories which were rich and varied in content. When constructing the narratives I searched for the starting point, what happened where, when and with whom, important incidents, main messages and themes, and how the narrator evaluated the situation (Labov, 1972). This approach allowed for deeper insights into their personal stories (Sedgley et al., 2006), due mainly to the richness of their diaries.

12.4 TOURISTS AT HOME

Twenty-two of the women spent the summer holiday at home and two of them did this with company only. The rest spent their holiday at home, partly alone and partly with family and friends. Some of these women divided their summer holidays in two or three breaks. The number of women spending time at home increased if they took a second and a third holiday. In this section, I explore how this time was perceived by the women, before telling Doris, Nichola, and Paris' stories of home holidays. These stories were imbued with the complexities of home holidays, as also voiced by many of the other women. The stories demonstrate the blurring lines of leisure and tourism, and of how these holidays, in various degrees, were shaped by joy, amusement, satisfaction, sightseeing, dread, loneliness, conflicts, sociability, commitment, work, and responsibilities, which can be part of most holidays.

12.4.1   PERCEPTIONS OF REAL HOLIDAYS

Most of the women were excited about exploring other environments in the holidays and felt that a sense of temporal and spatial otherness was lost at home; thus the days off became part of everyday life, and not real holidays. "It is as if time disappears" and "as if the days go very, very slowly", as put by Eve and Daisy, respectively. If faced with staying at home, some of the women would rather go to work, in particular if the weather was bad. Moreover, even if they were too tired to deal with the hassles of travel, after a short time the boredom and restlessness would set in. When talking about staying home in the holidays the women discussed that if friends were away, it would be a very quiet and lonely time and spending the holidays at home was not necessarily cheaper than traveling:

> DAISY – If you're bored and start to spend money (laughter)
> ADA – Start going to the shopping mall every day (laughter)
> JUNE – Withdrawal symptoms. All days are the same, few new experiences. No sense of holiday. … You mentioned that the time would feel long; at the same time I think three weeks at home… It wouldn't feel as long a time.
> DAISY – No, when you get back.
> JUNE – When you haven't experienced anything.
> DAISY – To work, then it has been a waste. What have you done in the holiday? Whoosh, then that holiday was gone.
> JUNE – Yes.
> ADA – Nothing really happened.
> JUNE – No. There is something about movement, seeing new things.

Some of the women, however, found much pleasure in staying home. This was particularly the case with Bess, who preferred familiar surroundings and did not need to travel to feel as though she was taking time from work; for her, home holidays were indeed very real. At home she engaged in favorite leisure activities without being controlled by the clock. She loved the freedom of choice and the comforts of home. The other women in the focus group were surprised by Bess's lack of interest:

> BESS – I can paint the house or something like that. I don't need to travel.
> JANE – Is holiday synonymous with free time, then? In a way that it is OK?

BESS – I have to be physical active.
TINA – When you think about July, when the general staff holidays are on, don't you have any dreams?
BESS – No. (Laughter)
TINA – I just had to ask. (Laughter)
BESS – No, I don't. I take it as it comes.

Seventeen of the midlife single women had negative views on home holidays, two had ambivalent feelings, and eleven were positive, thus considering them as "real" holidays. In particular, those who lacked travel companions and feared traveling alone (Heimtun, 2010a), and who could not afford or disliked group package tours stayed at home, at least for some of the days (Heimtun, 2010b). Even the women with negative attitudes still enjoyed most activities on home holidays.

12.14.2 DORIS'S HOME HOLIDAYS

Doris (38-years-old), who was unfamiliar with spending summer holidays at home, usually traveled alone to urban destinations. This summer, however, she spent seven days alone at home (half the holidays). Home was located in a small municipality in Eastern Norway, mostly known as a winter ski resort and a place for outdoor recreation. She had lived there for one year. The days were filled with domestic activities and day trips. The two days allocated to domestic chores were not perceived as duties, but as nice activities on rainy days: "A lot of people think this is work, I find it cosy. Nice to make it pretty, watch TV and listen to the radio while doing it. Grab a beer. What a good day. Wandering around, cleaning the shower and the floors, watching Oprah. It smells nice everywhere" (Day 8).

On most good weather days Doris did day trips involving hiking in and gazing at scenic nature and landscapes. To her own and her friends' surprise, she liked using her body when exploring local nature/landscapes. Still, Doris was aware of the necessity to be self-disciplined, to uphold positive spirits and attitudes, not to think "I am so alone" (day 11) and "work is my life" (day 8). At the same time, by the end of this holiday her desire for these activities was also a way of avoiding a sense of stagnation, and that she missed the rewards of an interesting job. She easily became bored: "I have become an outdoor person to the extreme – uhh! Hiking all the time. Without it I would have lost it on these free days. The free days are a bit dangerous.... Work makes me tic. Everybody say that I work too much, but it is through work that I confirm myself. Although, I, like everybody else, enjoy the holidays, I soon get tired and bored." (Day 14).

To Doris these holidays were real and she challenged herself by engaging in outdoor activities that were not part of her self-identity. Moreover, as an experienced solo traveler, solitude did not constrain her actions, at least not during the day. The evenings, however, were spent at home. In the diary she expressed a wish to go out for a meal or drink, but as all her friends were away, she stayed at home. Public solitude at home at night was thus something she avoided, but when traveling alone she enjoyed going out for a meal in the evenings.

12.4.3   NICHOLA'S HOME HOLIDAYS

Nichola (37-years-old), who lived just outside a medium sized seaside town in Eastern Norway, had these last 10 years spent most summer holidays here. Besides two trips to Crete and Spain, she had never traveled much abroad. Lack of money was never an issue and Nichola longed for experiencing new places and cultures. Lack of travel companions and fears of traveling alone, however, made her stay at home. Over the years this had made Nichola dread the holidays, and in some years she replaced vacation days with work. The main challenge was uncertainty about how to fill the days. Inspired and encouraged by this research, Nichola went alone to Dublin for four nights, conquering her fears of loneliness. The rest of this holiday (five weeks in total) was spent at home. One result of traveling to Dublin was that the home holiday felt more satisfying in comparison.

At home, Nichola embarked on day trips with friends and parents, such as visiting Oslo with a friend. It turned out to be a "dream vacation day" (Day 1). Another day she drove, with her mother and her friend, to an artisan site of crafts and history. As they avoided the main high ways, and got lost while driving back, it felt like a "road trip" (Day 13). The days at home were also filled with enjoyable shorter outings in nearby towns with friends and home visits. Still, these longer and shorter outings made Nichola reflect upon solitude and feelings of loneliness. In the diary she wrote about taking more control over her mind set, questioning her actions, feelings and reasoning: "It is easy to ask the parents, they always say yes. Can become like a pillow (nobody wants to do this, so I call mummy!). Can improve at asking others, not only think that they don't have the time.... You never know before asking.... They can surprise you with a YES! I'll do that next time!" (Day 13).

Nichola predominantly described shared experiences, but also how she felt when spending time alone working in the garden. This was both a satisfying and boring activity which awoke a desire for partner and family. Such feelings were also voiced on her birthday and when she spent a few hours visiting a married friend with two children: "I also want to experience this unity/community. Feel like I miss out on that as single. Must be nice to have someone around, who are as fond of and attached to you as children are.... My holidays are almost over and I'm going back to work in the nursery. But it's not the same as having one's own family." (Day 14).

Nichola spoke of a desire to change her largely negative views on home holidays and to find support to change her habits and mindset about these holidays not being real. Her diary and the second focus group, where she shared her joy and pride of traveling to Dublin alone, suggested that this experience empowered her also at home. At the same time her wishes for connectedness, in particular with a partner/children, remained just as strong.

12.4.4 PARIS'S HOME HOLIDAYS

Paris, a 43-years-old single woman, lived in and originated from the capital of Norway. Her four week summer holiday was spent at home (12 days) and at the family second home a few hours' drive away. As a younger woman Paris traveled quite extensively to short and long haul destinations, both alone, and with friends and partners. The last five years, however, she stayed predominantly at her second home and at home. The latter was related to ailing parents in need of support and to lack of money, given that she had recently finished a university degree. She felt that her energy to travel was returning.

At home, Paris sometimes enjoyed exploring the city's natural and cultural attractions. She spent time with friends, parents, former colleagues, and a potential new partner. She also looked after the neighbor's cat and enjoyed gardening alone. With a friend she had an "exotic day" (Day 14) exploring one of the multicultural neighborhoods in the city. Here they bought inexpensive fabrics and amused themselves by gazing at the locals and being in each other's company. This outing "felt like traveling."

The main activities undertaken, however, were related to caring for her parents. As Paris's mother was moving back home after five years in a nursing home some changes to the parental home were required. Paris thus spent a lot of time decorating a new kitchenette. Moreover, she also had to arrange a Sunday dental visit for her mother as one of the nurses, by mistake, had thrown away her denture. Additionally, she visited her father for a joint meal. These visits occurred weekly and were highly appreciated. At the same time spending holiday time caring for her parents was also a duty, and Paris believed that with her own family they would expect less of her, that the "family claws" would have been less sharp (Day 9). Emotionally, she was tired of her parents' problems and acting as their "servant." Her holidays seemed to drift away and a partner seemed unacceptable:

> I feel tired and do not really have time to accompany her to the dentist and to lose a vacation day. Father is in terrible mood and I'm now everyone's chopping block. … I am most eager to get it over, get some distance to my angry feelings. In neighboring gardens a lot of couples sit in candle lights and grill. I feel like I'm in a horror movie, my time just flows away and I'm stuck in the fox trap. It feels like I'm the family's maid and that my parents and brother are very against me having a boyfriend. (Day 9)

Although able to fill the holidays with tourist experiences, domestic pleasurable activities and a budding flirtation, Paris's ambivalent relationship to her parents casted a shadow over her enjoyment. By holidaying home, she got little rest from the ongoing parental duties; it only occasionally felt like a real holiday.

12.5   DISCUSSION

These midlife single women's narratives challenge the discourse of tourism as temporal and spatial mobility. In some cases, their stories also transgress the notion that home holidays are not "real" holidays (Frew & Winter, 2010; Molz, 2009). Moreover, they suggest that the tourist role is not constant, but appears when engaging in activities outside the house. To achieve a real holiday at home these women have to accept the fluidity of tourism and everyday life (Aitchison et al., 2000). They have to use the comforts of home as a starting point for indoors and outdoors activities. Doris is a good example; alone she enjoys domestic chores and daytrips in the home area. This is not always easy and Doris has to engage in positive thinking to keep a sense of loneliness at bay. Her success is based on many lessons learned in negotiating tourism places/spaces as a midlife single woman on her own (Heimtun, 2010a). Maturity and previous experiences thus give agency also on home holidays.

Nichola is not yet there. Her inexperience and uncertainty shape her home holidays in more negative ways (Minnaert, 2014); they become boring, dreaded times full of stillness, which makes her feel socially excluded (Molz, 2009; Mallett, 2004). Travel experience is thus a form of cultural capital which, when embodied, serves as an asset also on home holidays (Bourdieu, 1986). Yet inexperience and lack of cultural capital do not completely explain Nichola's uncertainty; she also longs for traveling away, and from home. Contrary to Bess who is content at home, Nichola, desires new places but is constrained by fears of solo traveling and lack of travel partner (Wilson & Little, 2008). She is subdued by singlism and gender power relations imbuing tourism spaces (DePaulo & Morris, 2005; Jordan & Gibson, 2005). The short solo trip she took to Dublin, however, is a first step of resistance.

Like Doris, Paris is not constrained by inexperience and uncertainty. When not supporting her parents she enjoys being a tourist in her own back yard (Shani & Uriely, 2012). The social obligations toward her ailing parents, however, turn these home holidays more into spaces and times for unpaid social work. This elder care is a mix of duty and pleasure which is a constant presence in her life, holidays or not. Like many women she feels strong obligations toward her family and believes that her lack of partner and children intensify expectations. Being single thus adds to the gendering of nurture when it comes to caring for parents (Brody, 2004). However, compared to motherhood this caretaking is not 24 h a day, seven days a week (Deem, 1996), whereby single women have more opportunity to step back and to enjoy the tourist gaze. Then again, elder care can sometimes result in greater stress than childcare and it can be harder to manage (Smith, 2004).

Home holidays could also further exacerbate these single women's lack of a partner. This is not evident in other types of holidays such as traveling with friends or alone (Heimtun, 2007, 2010a), where in the former the focus is more on bonding with friends and in the latter, on issues of loneliness and fear of the tourist gaze upon them. On solo holidays the midlife single women miss travel companionship *per se*, not specifically a partner/boyfriend. The longing for a partner on home holidays is particularly evident when engaging in domestic activities such as gardening and other house projects. However, most of these women appreciated the freedom imbuing singlehood (Reynolds & Wetherell, 2003); some situations at home thus made them feel more vulnerable and less independent in the holidays.

12.6   CONCLUSION

By exploring the concept of "home holidays," this chapter has argued that tourist activities co-exist with everyday life, and that it is also possible to be a tourist in the home area (Shani & Uriely, 2012). This study has also demonstrated that holiday time gives a sense of freedom to choose what to do when (Wang, 2000), whether it be domestic chores, gardening, or sightseeing. Straightforward and simplistic definitions of tourism therefore do not capture the complexities of holiday making and taking. Through uncovering the subjective nature of the women's home holidays, this study has challenged stereotypical assumption that only travel constitutes real holidays, although some of the midlife single women's perceptions were also shaped by this dominant discourse. This exploration has also revealed that further research on other demographic categories of people is required to broaden our understanding of holiday making, and how it shapes and is shaped by the tourist industry and society at large.

KEYWORDS

- midlife
- women
- temporal
- spatial mobility
- annual holiday
- home holidays

REFERENCES

Aitchison, C.; MacLeod, N. E.; Shaw, S. J. *Leisure and Tourism Landscapes: Social and Cultural Geographies;* Routledge: London, 2000.

Aulid, B. O. Nordmenn på ferietopp i Norden. [Online] May 7, 2012. http://www.dinepenger.no/bruke/nordmenn-paa-ferietopp-i-norden/10086885 (accessed Oct 24, 2014).

Bell, L. Public and Private Meanings in Diaries: Researching Family and Childcare. In *Feminist Dilemmas in Qualitative Research: Public Knowledge and Private Lives;* Ribbens, J., Edwards, R., Eds.; Sage Publications: London, 1998; p 72.

Bourdieu, P. The Forms of Capital. In *Handbook of Theory and Research for the Sociology of Education;* Richardson, J. G., Ed.; Greenwood Press: New York, 1986; p 241.

Brody, E. *Women in the Middle: Their Parent Care Years;* Springer Publishing Company: New York, 2004.

Carr, N. The Tourism - Leisure Behavioural Continuum. *Ann. Tour. Res.* **2002,** *29,* 972–986.

Charmaz, K. *Constructing Grounded Theory: A Practical Guide through Qualitative Research;* Sage Publications: London, 2006.

Davidson, L. In *'Staycations': What are the Drivers to Holidaying at Home?,* Proceedings of the ITRN, Ulster, Ireland, Aug 29–30, 2012. http://www.itrn.ie/uploads/PC206_Davison_2012.pdf (accessed Oct 20, 2014).

Deem, R. Women, the City and Holidays. *Leis. Stud.* **1996,** *15,* 105–119.

DeLongis, A.; Hemphill, K. J.; Lehman, D. R. A Structured Diary Methodology for the Study of Daily Events. In *Methodological Issues in Applied Social Psychology;* Bryant, F. B., Edwards, J.; Tindale, R. S., Posavac, E. J., Heath, L., Henderson, E., Suarez-Balcazar, Y., Eds.; Plenum Press: New York, 1992; p 83.

DePaulo, B. M.; Morris, W. L. Target Article: Singles in Society and in Science. Psychological Inquiry. *Int. J. Adv. Psychol. Theory.* **2005,** *16,* 57–83.

Dodds, R. Questioning Slow as Sustainable. In *Critical Debates in Tourism;* Singh, T. V., Ed.; Channel View Publications: Bristol, 2012; p 380.

Dragland, E. Rapport Fra Singelundersøkelsen. 2011. http://www.singelnett.no/?catid=1&ItemID=590 (accessed Aug 17, 2011).

Fox, S. Vacation or Staycation. In *The Neumann Business Review;* Neumann University: Aston, PA, 2009. http://www.neumann.edu/academics/divisions/business/journal/review09/fox.pdf (accessed Oct 20, 2014).

Frew, E.; Winter, C. Tourist Response to Climate Change: Regional and Metropolitan Diversity. *Tour. Rev. Int.* **2010,** *13,* 237–246.

Gale, T. Beaches, Virtual Worlds and 'The End of Tourism'. *Mobilities.* **2009,** *4,* 119–138.

Glaser, B. G.; Strauss, A. L. *The Discovery of Grounded Theory: Strategies for Qualitative Research;* Aldine Publishing Company: Chicago, 1977.

Granseth, T. Nordmenns Feriereiser om Sommeren: Vi Ferierer Oftest i Norden. *Samfunnsspeilet.* 2010, *3,* 21. [Online] 2010 https://www.ssb.no/kultur-og-fritid/artikler-og-publikasjoner/vi-ferierer-oftest-i-norden (accessed Oct 21, 2014).

Hannam, K.; Sheller, M.; Urry, J. Editorial: Mobilities, Immobilities and Moorings. *Mobilities.* **2006,** *1,* 1–22.

Haukeland, J. V. Non-Travelers: The Flip Side of Motivation. *Ann. Tour. Res.* **1990,** *17,* 172–184.

Hay, B. What's in a Name: In *A Review of Popular New Words to Describe Holidays - A Clever Marketing Ploy or a Pointless Waste of Time?* Proceedings of the CAUTHE 2010, Feb 8–11, 2010. http://eresearch.qmu.ac.uk/1502/1/eResearch_1502.pdf (accessed Oct 20, 2014).

Heimtun, B. Mobile Identities of Gender and Tourism: The Value of Social Capital. Ph.D. Dissertation, University of West of England, Bristol, 2007.

Heimtun, B. The Holiday Meal: Eating Out alone and Mobile Emotional Geographies. *Leis. Stud.* **2010a**, *29*, 175–192.

Heimtun, B. The Group Package Tour and Sociability: Contesting Meanings. *Tour. Rev. Int.* **2010b**, *14*, 3–15.

Jordan, F.; Gibson, H. "We're not Stupid...but we'll not Stay Home either": Experiences of Solo Women Travelers. *Tour. Rev. Int.* **2005**, *9*(2), 195–211.

Krippendorf, J. The New Tourist Turning Point for Leisure and Travel. *Tour. Manage.* **1986**, *7*, 131–135.

Krippendorf, J. *The Holiday Makers: Understanding the Impact of Leisure and Travel;* Heinemann Professional Publishing: Oxford, 1989.

Labov, W. *Language in the Inner City: Studies in the Black English Vernacular;* University of Pennsylvania Press: Philadelphia, PA, 1972.

Leiper, N. The Framework of Tourism: Towards a Definition of Tourism, Tourist, and the Tourist Industry. *Ann. Tour. Res.* **1979**, *6*, 390–407.

Mallett, S. Understanding Home: A Critical Review of the Literature. *Sociol. Rev.* **2004**, *52*(1), 62–89.

McCabe, S. The Tourist Experience and Everyday Life. In *The Tourist as a Metaphor of the Social World;* Dann, G. M. S., Ed.; Cabi Publishing: Wallingford, Oxon, 2002; p 61.

McCabe, S. Who Needs a Holiday? Evaluating Social Tourism. *Ann. Tou. Res.* **2009a**, *36*, 667–688.

McCabe, S. Who is a Tourist? Conceptual and Theoretical Developments. In *Philosophical Issues in Tourism;* Tribe, J., Ed.; Channel View Publications: Bristol, 2009b; p 25.

Merriam-Webster.com. 2014, 'Staycation'. http://www.merriam-webster.com/dictionary/staycation (accessed Oct 20, 2014).

Meth, P. Entries and Omissions: Using Solicited Diaries in Geographical Research. *Area.* **2003**, *35*, 195–205.

Minnaert, L. Social Tourism Participation: The Role of Tourism Inexperience and Uncertainty. *Tour. Manage.* **2014**, *40*, 282–289.

Molz, J. G. Representing Pace in Tourism Mobilities: Staycations, Slow Travel and the Amazing Race. *J. Tour. Cult. Change.* **2009**, *7*, 270–286.

Ogle, J. P.; Damhorst, M. L. Critical Reflections on the Body and Related Sociocultural Discourses at the Midlife Transition: An Interpretive Study of Women's Experiences. *J. Adult Dev.* **2005**, *12*, 1–18.

Reissman, C. K. *Narrative Methods for the Human Sciences;* Sage Publications: Thousand Oaks, CA, 2008.

Reynolds, J.; Wetherell, M. The Discursive Climate of Singleness: The Consequences for Women's Negotiation of a Single Identity. *Fem. Psychol.* **2003**, *13*, 489–510.

Ryan, C. Leisure and Tourism: The Application of Leisure Concepts to Tourist Behaviour - A Proposed Model. In *Tourism: The State of the Art;* Seaton, A., Ed.; John Wiley & Sons: Chichester, 1994; p 294.

Ryan, C.; Glendon, I. Application of Leisure Motivation Scale to Tourism. *Ann. Tour. Res.* **1998,** *25,* 169–184.

Schutt, R. K. *Investigating the Social World. The Process and Practice of Research;* Pine Forge Press: Thousand Oaks, CA, 1999.

Sedgley, D.; Pritchard, A.; Morgan, N. Understanding Older Women's Leisure: The Value of Biographical Research Methods. *Tourism.* **2006,** *54,* 43–51.

Shani, A.; Uriely, N. VRF Tourism: The Host Experience. *Ann. Tour. Res.* **2012,** *39,* 421–440.

Sharma, S. The Great American Staycation and the Risk of Stillness. *M/C J.* [Online] Mar 2009, *12,* 1. http://journal.media-culture.org.au/index.php/mcjournal/article/view-Article/122 (accessed Oct 20, 2014).

Small, J. Good and Bad Holiday Experiences: Women's and Girls' Perspectives. In *Gender/ Tourism/Fun(?);* Swain, M. B., Momsen, J. H., Eds.; Cognizant Communication Corporation: New York, 2002; p 24.

Smith, P. R. Elder Care, Gender, and Work: The Work-Family Issue of the 21st Century. *Berkeley J. Empl. Labor Law.* **2004,** *25,* 351–400. http://ssrn.com/abstract=1087688 (accessed Oct 20, 2014).

Uriely, N. 'Home' and 'away' in VFR Tourism. *Ann. Tour. Res.* **2010,** *37,* 854–857.

Urry, J. Cultural Change and Contemporary Holiday-Making. *Theory Cult. Soc.* **1988,** *5,* 35–55.

Urry, J. *The Tourist Gaze: Leisure and Travel in Contemporary Society;* Sage: London, 1990.

Urry, J. *Consuming Places;* Sage: London, 1995.

Wang, N. *Tourism and Modernity: A Sociological Analysis;* Pergamon: Amsterdam, 2000.

Wilkinson, S. Focus Groups in Feminist Research: Power, Interaction, and the Co-Construction of Meaning. *Women's Stud. Int. Forum.* **1998,** *21,* 111–125.

Wilkinson, S. Focus Groups: A Feminist Method. *Psychol. Women Quart.* **1999,** *23,* 221–244.

Wilson, E.; Little, D. E. The Solo Female Travel Experience: Exploring the 'Geography of Women's Fear'. *Curr. Issues Tour.* **2008,** *11,* 167–186.

Wixon, M. *The Great American Staycation: How to Make a Vacation at Home Fun for the Whole Family (and your Wallet!);* Adams Media: Avon, MA, 2009.

CHAPTER 13

WOMEN TRAVELING FOR HEALTH TOURISM: RESULTS FROM FOCUS GROUPS IN AUSTRIA

MARGRET JAEGER[1], MAGDALENA HOFFMAN[2], and
MARIA OPRODOVSKY[3]

[1]Health Tourism Consultant, Austria

[2]Medical University Graz, Austria

[3]Campus Social Medical Center, Vienna, Austria

*Corresponding author. E-mail: margretjaeger@yahoo.com

CONTENTS

13.1 INTRODUCTION

Tourism is one of the world's growing markets and moves people and money for different reasons. In Austria, tourism constitutes 5.3% of GDP, which, in 2012, amounted to 15.09 billion Euro (Smeral, 2010). Health is increasingly seen as a crucial personal, economic, and political commodity which is founded in the dynamic interaction of demographics, economy, and advanced medicine. Among the most important growth sectors are located in the health-industry; the term "Gesundheitsgesellschaft" ("health-society") is often being used (Kickbusch, 2012). The current accelerated lifestyle of many people causes changes in the living, working, and surrounding circumstances which in turn can lead to health problems. Health problems and the search for cure, rehabilitation, or relief, or the wish to promote one's own health were, and still are, some of the primary motivators for traveling for health (Konu, 2010; Konu & Laukkanen, 2009; Hall, 2011; Smith & Puzcko, 2010). Fortunately, patients have early access to health care systems. One significant issue remains reduced accessibility of the system for individuals of lower socioeconomic standing (Cassens et al., 2012). For women this could be a hindrance due to the difference in their income as compared to men (Statistik Austria, 2013).

The target market for health tourism is primarily customers seeking to escape their rapid, demanding lifestyles while at the same time attaining positive effects on their health (Con.os, 2011; Smith & Puczkò, 2010). Internationally, visitors to health tourism establishments are mostly healthy women between 35 and 55 years of age (Con.os, 2011;). The International Spa Association (ISPA) describes the typical spa visitor as female, employed, between 30 and 49 years of age, but notes that the segment of customers under 30 years of age is increasing. Among the younger visitors to health tourism establishments, women constitute up to 73% of this target group. ISPA cites surveys from Australia, Austria, Germany, Japan, Singapore, Spain, and Thailand (Smith & Puczkò, 2010). Consumers of health tourism will be the focus of the research results in this chapter, with particular regard to their preferences and attitudes concerning lifestyle-concepts and topics of relevance to health. The main goal here is to provide a deeper insight into, and understanding of, women's motivations regarding the usage of health tourism establishments (Smith & Puczkò, 2010).

Women have not yet been explored as a distinct target group for tourism in Austria, nor have thelinks between women, tourism andand health been widely explored in the Europen context. It is difficult to understand why, perhaps, given the changed social, cultural and economic circumstances of middle/western European women. Indeed, the German business consultant Diana Jaffè describes women as "crucial enterprise assets" (Jaffè, 2005). By virtue of their communicative and demanding manner as customers they offer major potential for modern businesses to expand and specify their products (Jaffè, 2005). The hotel industry has already made some first attempts at approaching women as a target audience, for example in the form of women-friendly hotels or hotel floors, primarily tailored toward traveling businesswomen. It is worthy of note that the expression "women-friendly" is not considered very appealing as it carries the implicit negative connotation for all those not declaring themselves equally. Not only do women distinguish themselves as customers with clear notions and concise expectations regarding hotel services and features, they remain, if satisfied by the services offered, loyal and lasting customers with high recommendation rates (Brandes, 2010).

In Austria, 980 companies comprise the health tourism sector, 78% of which are focused on the wellness segment. Wellness facilities, like saunas, swimming pools, and massage services, are being offered as additional features in many cases, especially in the Western parts of Austria although the original motives for travel, such as winter sports, do not fall into the traditional health tourism sector. The research regarding Austrian guests of health tourism establishments is negligible. While there are surveys being conducted every other year in the scope of the Tourismus Monitor Austria (T-MONA), a deeper understanding of the subject matter cannot be reached by pure statistical analysis. In this context preferences regarding vacations in cities or the countryside, relaxation or adventure are surveyed—the findings are not, however, sufficiently put in relation with sociocultural, and respectively, gender-specific aspects (Österreich Werbung, w.y.). A cluster-analysis by Bässler shows the typical consumers of health tourism establishments to be 57% female, in the 36–50 years of age-range. Furthermore, 51% are couples without children, 26.5% constitute families, and 23.5% report being single (Bässler, 2003). In literature and in practice, women's health behavior and consumption of health products are interpreted as having a higher health-awareness (Mueller & Kaufmann, 2001; Zemp & Ackermann-Liebrich, 1988).

Accordingly, women are identified specifically in the scope of diversification of the products and services available in health tourism

(Smeral, 2010). The opportunities for international growth in health tourism are in the creation of unique, specialized destinations with a clear profile. In particular, differentiation from competitors and high service quality are considered essential criteria for success in health tourism (Rulle, 2008; Smeral, 2010).

This chapter aims to outline the perceptions and experiences of Austrian women regarding health tourism services (primarily hotels and treatments). The results presented were part of a wider study about health tourism in Austria. The research project "Gender Perspectives in Health Tourism" (lead author: Jaeger), took place between 2013 and 2015, and aimed to analyze the potential of women-only health hotels in the world. As an example, one women-only hotel in Austria was analyzed by a team of six women (five of them master students of health sciences and health professionals) in a mixed-methods approach and resulted in recommendations for improvement for the owner group (the study having been requested by them). One part of the project focused particularly on exploring whether women-only health hotels fulfill women's desires and needs. Worldwide, health hotels had been identified which focus on different aspects of women's health, physical and psychological wellbeing, and benefits and limitations of this area are discussed. The methodological approach for this part of the project consisted of two focus groups conducted with women in 2013, combined withqualitative content analysis. The comparison with current products from hotels shows how the desires and needs of women differ from the hotels perspectives of health and the created offers. The results may serve as base-line for a discussion about the meaning of health for women and the reaction of the tourism world to it.

13.2 THEORETICAL BACKGROUND

The operating definition for health tourism for the overall project was taken from a study from the Austrian Ministry of Economics, Family and Youth in 2011. This decision was taken because there exist many definitions, and the Austrian authorities contracted a consulting company to do research on that and extract a definition for use in the Austrian tourism industry. This project team took the decision to apply a local definition of health tourism and evaluate institutions and products based on that. Their definition is that:

> Health tourism constitutes all relations and manifestations of voluntary, self-financed, multiple day, non-permanent, change of venue, outside of their work or hometown for the purpose of restoration, stabilization and advancement of their social, mental and bodily wellbeing by consuming health-services provided by third parties (Con.os, 2011, p. 17).

Ultimately, very little research has been carried out on the demand for health tourism services in relation to socio-demographic factors such as gender, for example. The available data do, however, point toward specific differences in health tourism consumers' preferences (Illing, 2009). Ryan et al. (w.y.) and Sherman et al. (2007) could, in their research, identify clear divides between men and women in their respective process regarding selection of the holiday destination, its attributes, and their preferences regarding services offered for spa-visitors. Both studies were conducted outside Europe, in Australia and United States, respectively. Accounting for cultural differences of each country, living conditions are relatively equal in Europe (with the exception of Eastern Europe). A case can be made for an assumption that the needs and expectations with regards to health tourism establishments might diverge along similar gender lines in Austria, too.

13.2.1 TOURISM AND GENDER

As a result of the social upheavals of the last century the realities of women's lives in the Western world have changed fundamentally. The effects of these changes become apparent when looking at the traveling activities of women (Bhimji, 2008; Gibson et al., 2013; Harris & Wilson, 2007; Kinnaird & Hall, 1996; Norris et al., 1994; Wilson & Harris, 2006). It is thus only a natural consequence to include gender as a further dimension when analyzing the phenomenon that is "tourism." In relation to both supply-side and demand-side considerations a gender-specific approach is relevant. Many employees in the tourism-related service sector are female, found in strongly segregated functions and underprivileged positions. Women working in tourism largely perform services that are close in nature to those of the housewife, and do not require advanced training, such as cleaning functions (Cukier et al., 1996; Redclift et al., 2013). Two noteworthy demand-side phenomena that call for a gender perspective in studying tourism are, that it is largely women who act as initiators and managers of the family leisure, and that women tend to have less free time (and often also money) at their own disposal (Hudson, 2000; Kattiyaporn-pong & Miller, 2008; Kinnaird & Hall, 1996; Wilson & Harris, 2006).

Almost four decades ago, Smith referred to women as the "taste-makers" in tourism; that is, it is women who make the majority of deci-sions about the couple's or family's holiday destination (Smith, 1979). She noted important implications for marketing experts with regards to the role that women take in tourism. Marketing strategies should be expressly tailored to women, given that they are the ones, who apparently initiate the traveling decision, are open for new destinations and choose the informa-tional material they present to fellow travelers.

Mottiar and Quinn arrive at similar results concerning the role of women in initiating journeys, with respect to the eventual travel decision, such as choosing the destination, in which they describe a highly shared decision process with the couples studied (Mottiar & Quinn, 2004). Considering in particular those journeys tend to require significant budgetary deci-sions, such concerted decision making seems understandable. Insofar as the sources for travel information are concerned, the authors could discern clear patterns in men's and women's behavior. The latter primarily turned to travel agencies, the internet, and friends for information, while men mainly asked family and colleagues at work for advice. Also, bookings were largely performed by women. In effect, women play a substantial role at the beginning of the touristic process, for they already pre-select when gathering information, and are thus essential to the final decision.

The motivational factors for women to travel can be summarized around five points: gaining distance from the home and workplace, overcoming emotional problems, experiencing adventures, reaffirming their capabili-ties, and gaining knowledge. Changes in their personal situation, such as the ending of relationships, or the death of close relatives, as well as gaining independence from the family, can lead to forced travel of women (Riley, 1988; Russell, 1986). After a review of publications, one may conclude that gender (as in sex difference) is of great importance in relation to tourism research, and that the differences described are noteworthy in the develop-ment of new touristic products and services. In light of the ever-changing living environments of women the goal of research must be to align as close to reality as possible in order to be able to meet the needs of the target group (Aitchison & Reeves, 1998; Byrne Swain, 1995; Gibson et al., 2013; Kinnaird & Hall, 1996; Ryan et al., w.y.; Smith, 1979).

13.2.2 WOMEN AND THEIR SPECIFIC USE OF HEALTH TOURISTIC INSTITUTIONS

Marked gender-specific differences in the motives for and expectations of traveling are apparent in the results of the interviews conducted as part of tourism-monitoring in 2006 and 2008. For example, Bässler found several relevant results in a secondary data analysis on the topic of "wellness as behavioral pattern" (Bässler, 2006). Further, women were more interested in wellness vacations than men, with this form of tourism being most popular among those under 29 years of age, while those aged 50–69 years report having the most experience with wellness tourism. An above average use of wellness tourism services was found in groups with a higher than average education and income (post-secondary education and monthly income above €2180). The prevailing motive among women aged 29 or below was to "indulge oneself," which highly correlates with an interest in wellness and the objective to repeatedly experience wellness vacations (Bässler, 2006).

Differences between women and men with regards to spas in Florida wre studied by Sherman et al. and reveal that the typical spa-visitor had a high level of education, was of middle age, and most likely married (Sherman et al., 2007),. Significant gender-related differences were found in the evaluation of services according to their necessity. Women preferred services relating to their appearance, such as facial treatments, manicures, and pedicures. The physical program was asked to be less demanding, for example, yoga and pilates. Sherman et al. highlighted the implications of their results for the (commercial) success of spas.

The consideration of the specificity in women's use of their free time is important in this context. Moore et al. suggest that behavior in tourism and in leisure can and should be conceptualized, even though the authors iden-tify ideological differences in the two approaches (Moore et al., 1995). While tourism is considered primarily from a commercial perspective, approaches in studying leisure and regeneration developed along a welfare tradition. Nevertheless, a joint conceptualization of tourism and leisure, close to real life, can offer a holistic understanding of behavior.

13.2.3 WOMEN, HEALTH, AND TOURISM IN AUSTRIA

Rulle refers to Austria as the "big player of the modern spa and wellness business under distress," locating it among countries with a long tradition of bathing (Rulle, 2008). Its "strain" is due to the decrease in services financed by health insurers. This problem is trying to be solved by continued development with holistic approaches of the brand "Tourismusland Österreich – tourism country Austria" (Rulle, 2008). The Austrian Report on Women's Health specifically takes into account the issue of "women and time" (2011). The overarching conclusion is that due to many women's multiple burdens (e.g., professional life, household, and child care), they have less time at their disposal for leisure activities. As a target group for health tourism they appear nevertheless of interest, because complementary medical treatments are consumed largely by women. For example, massages are explicitly named in this respect (Bundesministerium für Gesundheit, 2011) given that women possessing a higher education are the larger group among consumers of complementary and alternative medical services; analogies to internationally described customers of health tourism facilities are evident (Bässler, 2006; Bundesministerium für Gesundheit, 2011; Smith & Puzkó, 2010).

In summary, it can be said that women travel for different reasons than men and when they travel they do so differently, in terms of motivation, places, activities, company, and so forth. Their behavior in general has changed dramatically in the last decades since Western societies have changed and women have garnered more independence. They have their own income and can decide where and when to go. The motivation for taking care of their own health has grown and illness prevention as travel motive is becoming increasingly important. The tourism industry has not yet widely acknowledged the needs and desires of women as special target group for their products.

13.3 METHODS

The first aim of this study was to find out if, where and with what focus women-only health hotels exist. Second, the research should give insight into which specific needs and expectations Austrian women have with regards to health tourism providers. Furthermore, we wanted to discover these women's previous experiences in health tourism institutions and their recommendations for improvements and changes. This study utilized a multi-mixed approach with desktop research, questionnaires, participant observation, interviews, and document analysis part, respectively. In this chapter, two focus groups were conducted and qualitative content analysis of the transcripts was performed by the authors.

13.3.1   DATA COLLECTION

A desktop research stage (of the AQR homepage) was conducted to identify women-only health hotels in the world to compare their products and presentation in general. For the exploration of women's needs and expectations two focus groups comprising six people each were conducted. Especially in the area of perception and insights regarding the research topic innovations were expected by using this specific method. Focus groups give the unique chance to bring different opinions and experiences together allowing us to study participants' reactions to each other's comments.

The choice of participants was based on criteria derived from insights following from guest questionnaires conducted by the ISPA (Smith & Puczkó, 2010), studies of German citizens and health tourism (Rulle, 2008), and results of the cluster-analysis according to Bässler (Con.os, 2011). Participants were female and between 25 and 65 years of age. They distinguished themselves with respect to their personal situation, income, level of education, and working status. The objective was to achieve a high level of diversity. Focus groups were conducted and observed by project members Oprodovsky and Guttmann, following moderation and observation guidelines developed by the team.

13.3.1.1   WOMEN OF THE FIRST GROUP (JULY 2013)

Out of the six participating women, five lived in Vienna. They were aged between 28 and 56 years. Three out of six had a high school diploma as highest educational level, one a post-secondary education, one with university diploma, and one with a professional education diploma. All of them were employed: two teachers of nursing schools, on self-employed, one hotel employee, and two of them with small employments (under 405 €/month).

13.3.1.2   WOMEN OF THE SECOND GROUP (AUGUST 2013)

The second group consisted of six women, all living in Vienna, aged 30–49 years. Their educational level was that two of them had a university diploma, two had a post-secondary education, one had a high school diploma, and one had a professional education diploma. All the women were in full-time employment: two nurses with leading duties, one nurse, and three with employee status. The study was approved by the Committee of Research Scientific and Ethical Questions at the University of Health and Life Sciences UMIT, Hall in Tyrol, where the authors worked and studied. An informed consent was signed by all of them and data was kept anonymous.

13.3.2   DATA ANALYSIS

Following the interview, protocols were written and transcribed verbatim. The transcripts serve as a source of knowledge for research. The written texts underwent an analysis by using qualitative content analysis, based on Mayring carried out by the authors together (Mayring, 2010, 2012). This form of analysis starts with an identification of keywords based on the focus group's questions which are later summarized into categories and sub-categories. Important text fragments are summarized under these categories and the most important ones are quoted in original. The categorization offers the possibility to order the material and create a system while the second step of summarizing helps to compromise it.

13.4   RESULTS

The findings from the desk research to identify hotels reveals that very few health hotels exist that rely upon the women-only label to promote their offers. The products show considerable difference in scope, ranging from addressing one or two health problems as observed in big hotels in the United States or France, and hotels which offer a range of treatments and wellbeing activities like the one in Austria. Altogether six hotels could have been identified through an extensive desktop research and were classified as women-only health hotels within the criteria of the research projects: one in France, two in the United States, one in Austria, one in Saudi Arabia, and one in South Korea (with no homepage accessible). There exist in New Zealand some very small guest houses with a holistic approach that addresses mainly mental health and wellbeing. Those were excluded also because access to detailed information was not possible via internet requests. Health issues such as obesity, diabetes, and high blood pressure are addressed directly as the main reason for (long term) stays in hotels in France and the United States, while the Austrian and Saudi Arabian hotels address more wellbeing, lifestyle changes, and beauty treatments. Analysis of the information on the hotels homepages shows in general a big variety of many offered treatments per house, some with specific programs others not. The ethnographic experience and quantitative data from questionnaires in the Austrian establishment showed discrepancies between offers and women's use of services and their given answers in the questionnaires about services. In concert with the reviewed literature, this led to the questions for the focus groups. The focus group results are organized in two dimensions with some sub-categories to facilitate the comprehension of it.

13.4.1 WELLNESS, SPA, AND HEALTH TOURISM INSTITUTIONS

Women were asked about their previous experiences with regards to health tourism-related services, and about the level of quality standards they demanded from wellness facilities. Each participant had a rather large wealth of experience in using wellness and spa facilities. They all shared a clear idea of the concept of "wellness," and what they demanded to optimally enjoy a wellness experience.

13.4.2 "WELLNESS INSTITUTION" FROM A SUBJECTIVE, FEMALE PERSPECTIVE

Significant attributes of wellness are found by women in wellbeing, in a suitable location, and in having time for themselves. Wellness is not exclusively searched for, and found, in health tourism institutions, but also in, for example, taking a warm bath on a Saturday, looking after oneself, and simply enjoying oneself. A participant described a wellness vacation as a "private holiday," an occasion for one to consider nobody except oneself. Nature has been named as an important factor in this respect. Participants stated that they often seek to "be in nature" in order to relax. Ascriptions vary up to an almost meditative character of nature stays. All women had gathered significant experiences with health tourism and identified themselves as frequent users of thermal baths. Having visited different institutions, they could distinguish between what each market had to offer.

In the second focus group meeting, the topic "spirituality and wellness" was discussed, given that one participant had stayed several times at Catholic cloisters and at an institution of a Sinyasi-community with the objective of gaining greater calm and enlightenment. Several women named "expanding oneself" in a spiritual sense as a substantial aspect of wellness. In this regard, personal crises were brought up, which they were attempting to resolve, in part by using health tourism services. Participants described leaving old tracks behind, both mentally and physically, and experimenting, for example creatively.

Two participants mentioned balancing multiple burdens as mothers, wives, and in their professional functions, through rest as a form of wellness. Switching off electronic devices such as cell phones and laptops was judged by several participants as wellness. Being unavailable and offline was an important and valuable function with regards to wellness.

> I want to relax, leave old experiences behind, and this takes some time. For this reason, three days of wellness mean just being lazy, but if it takes longer - a week or so - then I have two days with which I start to leave things behind and get quieter.

On the contrary, other women in the focus groups wanted to participate in unique activities and to try out new exercise types in order to be able to relax. They confessed to getting a little bored after spending some time in health tourism institutions. In particular, stays in thermal baths were named in this respect. Women asked for exercise programs with a varied range of physical activity, comprising new sports and fitness trends.

> I also think each health tourism institution should offer many different types of things to do, but not too *clichéd*. ... not only yoga or belly dancing and stuff like that, but also things to try that you normally do not try out.

The different interpretations each woman gave to wellness resulted in different levels of interest at these places. A vital demand seems nevertheless to be that institutions should offer clear and structured concepts. Several participants were critical of the current number of offers and derived from that a lack of expertise on the providers' side.

To summarize, it is possible to distinguish two main approaches to wellness. On the one hand, physical activity, and discovering and trying out new types of exercise are judged as important, while on the other hand, wellness is associated with calmness, indulging oneself, and reading a good book.

13.4.2.1 EXPERIENCES WITH FACILITIES AND OFFERS OF HEALTH TOURISM INSTITUTIONS

Women's experiences with health related hotels and holidays were heterogeneous and differentiated. Overall, smaller institutions, regardless of type, were better received than larger ones, because the latter are perceived to be overcrowded, with a high level of noise pollution and possibly children using the facilities. Architectural qualities of an institution were also discussed, and the participants voiced the wish for rural environments, which were judged as important. They clearly preferred smaller health tourism institutions with an architectural concept that integrated them well into their surroundings.

> I like an ambiance of wellbeing; also water I, need too. Saunas, healthy nutrition, and being able to leave the house, to see nature.

The pricing policies of health tourism institutions were discussed extensively in both groups. Given that a wellness vacation was seen as a short, additional, and occasional weekend trip, in general, women were not prepared to spend more than €70 per night per person. Only one participant declared herself willing to pay for expensive (more than €150/night) trips if the hotel provided high quality services and facilities, and explained that she went on wellness trips once or twice a year at most. Several women preferred package prices that included the use of spa facilities, food and drinks, and a cosmetic treatment or massage.

Both noise and children in health tourism were judged negatively and when asked, participants actively denied the compatibility of children and wellness. Negative experiences were recounted with regards to hygiene and cleanliness of health tourism institutions, among others, the carpet flooring in a relatively new hotel with spa facilities and joint use of a thermal bath was critically discussed. One participant said that the flooring was unhygienic and stained. The rooms themselves were rarely discussed; women did not want to spend much time in their rooms, although both the spa areas and rooms should fulfill the highest standards of cleanliness. Towels should be abundant and easy to replace. Body care products that were provided, sometimes of a renowned brand, were well received.

The pool area was also noted as important; the size of the pool should be generous and allow for swimming, and smell of chlorine should be avoided. Salt water pools were attributed a health promoting function in "detoxing the body." Food smells arising from the spa facilities' connection with the hotel and restaurant areas were experienced as unpleasant. Another issue regarding the booking of health and wellness services was discussed. One participant described her experience when attempting to book massage treatments, whereby she was told she would have to book a month in advance before her actual stay. The participant viewed this as unacceptable and reportedly considered canceling her stay.

The topic of service quality was discussed extensively, as clear conceptions about what constitutes appropriate behavior toward customers were visible. Participants noted a certain reserve, but also a caring attitude as important. They were critical of the qualifications of some fitness trainers, who could clearly not be as qualified in all forms of exercise they led (ranging from yoga to Zumba), and thus would need to increase their expertise in some areas.

The diet and food offered was judged with varying importance, depending on the length of the stay. In both focus groups food was classified as less important on short stays up to three days, with vegan and vegetarian diets being highly-regarded as welcome by both groups. High quality food, as well as regional and seasonal sourcing was demanded. Women judged the level of management and organization of an institution by its thoughtful and diligent use of food. In summary, a slightly smaller range of higher quality was preferred by participants.

13.4.2.2   WOMEN-SPECIFIC TRAVEL ASPECTS

The discussion groups were asked to describe their experiences regarding the differences in usage of health tourism facilities by men and women. Women were consistently seen as more frequent users of health tourism services, and even if accompanied by men, as the initiators of the stay.

Women are more conscious, perhaps listen more tothemselves, and come to rest. Men are always in some sporting activities, [pushing] the limits; they are more active.

Offers specifically targeting women were discussed with, for example, single-sex areas being judged positively, apparently from an aesthetical perspective as "the view of sweaty men" was considered as unpleasant. One participant articulated an interest in women-only health tourism institutions as a new experience.

Wellness stays were mostly spent in groups of women or with female friends, but also with partners. The difficulty in selecting suitable companions was described by a participant as follows: *"Thus, take care with whom you spend your vacations!"* In general, participants did not object to men or women as companions, for it depended only on the compatibility of the travelers with regards to the wellness program. This is paralleled in the different demands for physical activities of the participants. However, spending a wellness vacation by oneself was perceived by all but two participants as difficult, with only one being willing to go on a day stay alone, having done so before. All others were worried especially about having to dine by themselves, something they perceived as not enjoyable. One participant recounted the solo stay of a recently widowed friend, who was unable to engage with other guests and found this rather traumatic.

13.4.3 MOTIVATION AND NEED FOR WELLNESS VACATIONS

In a second topic group participants were asked for their reasons for undertaking a wellness stay. Health related expectations toward wellness vacations were also discussed. In particular here, the term wellness was used by the authors to stimulate the discussion and was also applied by the group participants to talk about the topic, even though they mentioned sometimes the word health.

13.4.3.1 FREQUENCY AND LENGTH OF WELLNESS VACATIONS

The frequency of using health tourism services and facilities varied in the focus groups between a weekend every two years, to two or three times per year. The women's personal circumstances were of significant importance in determining the frequency of stays. For instance, childcare and caring for elderly relatives were stated as a major obstacle, as these would limit the time resources available. Wellness stays were almost unanimously categorized as short vacations. Participants also did not want to make long journeys, as the strain of traveling seemed to diminish the effect of the wellness experience. Only three participants said they had been on stays abroad (Germany, Greece, and Turkey).

The length of wellness stays was in part dependent on the expectations of the health benefits to be gained from the stay, in part on the choice of destination. In fact, the location was usually within a short distance from participants' homes, as detailed above. As diverse as the interviewed women, their definitions of wellness and approaches to health tourism were their motives for visiting health tourism facilities. The choice of destinations is influenced by women's expectations of offered services and facilities, their wish for new experiences, and their financial means. The majority thus sees Austria as the main destination for health tourism journeys. Although the overwhelming part of the wellness stays were short and/or weekend vacations, one-week stays with different aims were also discussed. One woman told about her positive experiences in a cloister: she stayed to fast, remain silent, and distance herself from daily life.

13.5   DISCUSSION

Dunn wrote in an article entitled "High-level Wellness for Man and Society" (Dunn, 1959, p. 786): "...we will realize that the state of being well is not a relatively flat, uninteresting area of 'unsickness' but it is rather a fascinating and ever-changing panorama of life itself, inviting exploration of its every dimension." This statement is affirmed in view of the multitude of information received in the focus groups on the concept of wellness held by Austrian women. Attitudes toward health, wellness, and healthy behavior seem important in the use of health tourism institutions. Nevertheless, these results are not to be taken as static, for continuous changes in social and personal circumstances imply also changes in women's approaches and experiences.

Different dimensions of spirituality, seen by Dunn also as an axis of the high-level wellness concept, were articulated by participants of the focus groups as a need, and a motivation for health tourism journeys (Dunn, 1959). Similar experiences were described by participants as part of health tourism journeys such as stays in cloisters for meditation, or recreation in nature for personal reflection far from distracting experiences of daily life. Leaving familiar surroundings, being unavailable, and reflecting upon one's own existence and its meaning is paralleled by the trend in pilgrimage, yoga journeys, and stays in cloisters (Smith & Puzkó, 2010; Willson et al., 2013).

Brandes describes women's preferences regarding hotel rooms when traveling professionally, with the rooms as a "type of castle, a shelter reminding of home and providing undisturbed retreat from curious glances," and further "for many women, the hotel is a refuge" (Brandes, 2010, p. 37). Some would want certain spaces to be designated as "women-only" areas. The more intimate, or body-related, the more women wished to stay among themselves, for instance in saunas. The furnishings and atmosphere of the rooms were not discussed much in the focus groups, because a wellness stay was seen clearly as a short vacation, and women were ready to trade lower prices against comfort. The parts of health tourism facilities reserved for women were evaluated differently by participants, and judged more attractive especially with regards to traveling alone. Men in nude areas were described as unpleasant by some participants. It is worth noting here that only one woman regularly uses health tourism facilities alone. Brandes' results show that furnishing and atmosphere of rooms is important to women, but her interview where women on business travel who reported to spent more time in the room in the evening (Brandes, 2010).

In their study of women-specific preferences for hotel stays in Malaysia, Marzuki et al. found that women travelers placed importance on factors such as the "cleanliness of hotel", "friendly services of hotel staff" as well as "bathrobes and towels in bathroom" (Marzuki et al., 2012). In the present study, the topic of cleanliness and hygiene were discussed frequently in focus groups, especially in relation to negative experiences participants had had. This is perhaps surprising given the defined and controlled hygiene standards imposed particularly on thermal baths. On the other hand, an abundance of towels and dressing gowns in rooms was judged positively. With regards to service quality, a clear desire for friendliness coupled with a certain professional distance was evident.

Sherman et al. found in their analysis regarding the preferences of men and women for services used in spas a difference in types of activities selected: "women were more prone to select less rigorous activities (i.e. yoga, pilates)" (Sherman et al., 2007). In this study, focus group participants were less unanimous in this regard, with those travelers seeking more physical activity rejecting the idea of "softer" sports as *clichéd*. Nevertheless, all opted for cosmetic treatments in accordance with the results presented by Sherman et al., preferring offers such as facial treatments, manicures, pedicures, and massages (Sherman et al., 2007).

Bässler describes thermal baths or traditional Austrian spa locations as the most popular destinations among Austrian health tourists, and identifies a preference for comprehensive package offers due to transparent prices (Bässler, 2006). Results in focus groups diverged only slightly from each other. Women had almost exclusively traveled to locations in the vicinity of their homes, and complete packages were judged positively both for their clear pricing and for including booked treatments and services.

13.6   CONCLUSION

Based on the results presented in this chapter, we would argue that it is necessary to differentiate the range of health tourism offers with regards to gender (sex difference). Women are conscious customers, and able to value well-designed offers especially in health tourism. Products ranging too broad are not well received, nor are concepts perceived as insisting on female stereotypes. Women's desires in the focus groups hint on two interest clusters. On the one hand, travelers seeking tranquility, rest, and reading, on the other, those women looking for change, new activities, and occupations. To accommodate for both groups, clear concepts and innovations from the managerial side of health tourism institutions are necessary. From a research perspective, more inquiry is needed to test these hypotheses in broader studies.

KEYWORDS

- **health tourism**
- **spa**
- **focus group**
- **Austra**
- **wellness**

REFERENCES

AQR. – The Association for Qualitative Research. *Desk Res.*. http://www.aqr.org.uk/glossary/ desk-research (accessed July 25, 2015).

Aitchison, C.; Reeves, C. Gendered (Bed)Spaces: The Culture and Commerce of Women Only Tourism. In *Gender, Space and Identity: Leisure, Culture and Commerce;* Aitchison, C., Jordan, F., Eds.; Leisure Studies Association: Bolton, UK, 1998; pp 47–68.

Bässler, R. *Qualitätsniveau und Gesundheitskompetenz im Österreichischen Kur- und Wellness-Tourismus;* Österreichisches Bundesministeriums für Wirtschaft und Arbeit: Wien, 2003.

Bässler, R. Verhaltensmuster "Wellness". In *Wellness und Produktentwicklung. Erfolgreiche Gesundheitsangebote im Tourismus;* Krczal, A., Weiermair, K., Eds.; Erich Schmidt Verlag GmbH & Co: Berlin, 2006; pp 70–71, 75–77, 85–86.

Bhimji, F. Cosmopolitan Belonging and Diaspora: Second-Generation British Muslim Women Traveling to South Asia. *Citizenship Stud.* **2008,** *12*(4), 413–427.

Brandes, U. *Frauenzimmer im Hotel. Wie Geschäftsfrauen Sich Hotels Wünschen;* Erich Schmidt Verlag: Berlin, 2010.

Bundesministerium für Gesundheit 2011; Österreichischer Frauengesundheitsbericht 2010/2011. Eigenverlag: Linz, Austria, 2011.

Byrne Swain, M. Gender in Tourism. *Ann. Tour. Res.* **1995,** *22,* 247–266.

Cassens, M.; Hörmann, G.; Tarnai, C.; Stosiek, N.; Meyer, W. Health Tourism: Increasing Importance of Touristic Settings for Public Health and Medical Prevention. *Prävention Gesundheitsförderung.* **2012,** *7*(1), 24–29.

Con.os. Tourismus Consulting GmbH. *Grundlagenstudie: Der Gesundheits- und Wellness- Tourismus in Österreich: Status–Potentiale–Ausblick;* Bundesministerium für Wirtschaft: Wien, 2011.

Cukier, J.; Norris, J.; Wall, G. The Involvement of Women in the Tourism Industry of Bali, Indonesia. *J. Dev. Stud.* **1996,** *33*(2), 248–270.

Dunn, H. L. High-Level Wellness for Man and Society. *Am. J. Public Health.* **1959,** *49*(6), 786–792.

Gibson, H.; Jordan F.; Berdychevsky, L. Women and Tourism. In *Leisure, Women and Gender;* Freysinger, V. J., Shaw, S., Henderson, K. A., Bialeschki, D., Eds.; Venture Publishing: PA, 2013

Hall, C. M. Health and Medical Tourism: A Kill or Cure for Global Public Health? *Tour. Rev.* **2011,** *66*(1)–2, 4–15.

Harris, C.; Wilson, E. Traveling Beyond the Boundaries of Constraint: Women, Travel and Empowerment. In *Tourism and Gender: Embodiment, Sensuality and Experience;* Pritchard, A., Ateljevic, I., Morgan, N., Harris, I., Eds.; CAB International: Wallingford, CT, 2007; pp 235–250.

Hudson, S. The Segmentation of Potential Tourists: Constraint Differences Between Men and Women. *J. Travel Res.* **2000,** *38,* 363–368.

Illing, K. T. *Gesundheitstourismus und Spa-Management;* Oldenbourg Wissenschaftsverlag: München, Germany, 2009.

Jaffè, D. *Der Kunde ist weiblich: Was Frauen Sich Wünschen und wie sie Bekommen was Sie Wollen;* Ullstein Buchverlag GmbH: Berlin, 2005.

Kattiyapornpong, U.; Miller, K. E. A Practitioner's Report on the Interactive Effects of Socio-Demographic Barriers to Travel. *J. Vacat. Mark.* **2008,** *14*(4), 357–371.

Kickbusch, I. Die Gesundheitsgesellschaft. [Online] 2012, http://www.ilonakickbusch.com/kickbusch/gesundheitsgesellschaft/index.php (accessed Aug 12, 2012).

Kinnaird, V.; Hall, D. Understanding Tourism Processes: A Gender-Aware Framework. *Tour. Manage.* **1996,** *17*(2), 95–102.

Konu, H. Identifying Potential Wellbeing Tourism Segments in Finland. *Tour. Rev.* **2010,** *65*(2), 41–51.

Konu, H.; Laukkanen, T. In *Roles of Motivation Factors in Predicting Tourists' Intentions to Make Wellbeing Holidays – A Finnish Case*, Conference Proceedings ANZMAC. 2009.

Marzuki, A.; Chin, T. L.; Razak, A. A. What Women Want: Hotel Characteristics Preferences of Women Travelers. Strategies for Tourism Industry. In *Strategies for Tourism Industry – Micro and Macro Perspective;* Kasimoglu, M., Aydin, H., Eds.; InTech: Rijeka, Croatia, 2012; pp 143–164.

Mayring, P. *Qualitative Inhaltsanalyse. Grundlagen und Techniken. 11. Aktualisierte und überarbeitete Auflage;* Beltz Verlag: Weinheim und Basel, 2010.

Mayring, P. Qualitative Inhaltsanalyse. In *Qualitative Forschung, Ein Handbuch. 9. Auflage;* Flick, U., Ed.; Rowohlts Taschenbuch Verlag: Hamburg, Germany, 2012.

Moore, K.; Cushman, G.; Simmons, D. Behavioral Conceptualization of Tourism and Leisure. *Ann. Tour. Res.* **1995,** *22*, 67–85.

Mottiar, Z.; Quinn, D. Couple Dynamic in Household Tourism Decision Making: Women as the Gatekeepers? *J. Vacat. Mark.* **2004,** *10*, 149–160.

Mueller, H.; Kaufmann, E. L. Wellness Tourism: Market Analysis of a Special Health Tourism Segment and Implications for the Hotel Industry. *J. Vacat. Mark.* **2001,** *7*(1), 5–17.

Norris, J.; Wall, G.; Cooper, C. P. Gender and Tourism. In *Progress in Tourism, Recreation and Hospitality Management;* Cooper, C. P., Lockwood, A., Eds.; 1994; p 6, 57–78.

Österreich Werbung: *Was sind die Motive für einen Urlaub in Österreich?* SU Tourismusforschung, without year.

Redclift, N.; Sinclair, M. T.; Sinclair, M. T. *Working Women: International Perspectives on Labour and Gender Ideology.* Routledge: London, 2013.

Riley, P. J. Road Culture of International Long-Term Budget Travelers. *Ann. Tour. Res.* **1988,** *15*(3), 313–324.

Rulle, M. *Der Gesundheitstourismus in Europa, Entwicklungstendenzen und Diversifikationsstrategien, 2nd ed.;* Profil Verlag: München, Wien, 2008.

Russell, M. *The Blessings of a Good Thick Skirt: Women Travelers and Their World;* Collins: London, 1986.

Ryan, M.; Henley, N.; Soutar, G. *Gender Differences in Tourism Destination Choice: Some Implications for Tourism Marketers;* Edith Cowan University: Joondalup, Western Australia, without year, 2306–2317.

Sherman, L.; Clemenz C.; Philipp, S. Gender-Based Service Preferences of Spa-Goers. *Adv. Hosp. Leis.* **2007,** *3*, 217–229.

Smeral, E. *Tourismusstrategische Ausrichtung 2015, Wachstum durch Strukturwandel, Kurzfassung;* Österreichisches Institut für Wirtschaftsforschung: Wien. [Online] 2010, http://www.bmwfj.gv.at/TOURISMUS/Seiten/Tourismus strategie.aspx [accessed Aug 10, 2012].

Smith, M.; Puczkó, L. *Health and Wellness Tourism;* Elsevier: Oxford, UK, 2010.

Smith, V. L. Women: The Taste-Makers in Tourism. *Ann. Tour. Res*. **1979,** 49–60.

Statistik Austria. Soziales: Personeneinkommen. 2013. http://www.statistik.at/web_de/statistiken/menschen_und_gesellschaft/soziales/personen-einkommen/index.html [accessed Aug 5, 2015].

Wilson, E.; Harris, C. Meaningful Travel: Women, Independent Travel and the Search for Self and Meaning. *Tourism*. **2006,** *54*(2), 161–172.

Zemp, E.; Ackermann-Liebrich, U. Geschlechtsunterschiede in Gesundheit und Gesundheitsverhalten. *Sozial-und Präventivmedizin*. **1988,** *33*(3), 186–192.

SECTION V
Industry Perspectives

CHAPTER 14

FEAR AND LOATHING: WOMEN TRAVELERS AND SAFETY IN INDIA

SUE BEETON

William Angliss Institute, Australia

E-mail: s.beeton@outlook.com

CONTENTS

14.1   INTRODUCTION

Media reports of attacks on women tourists in India in 2013 received a high level of attention around the world, with numerous countries releasing official warnings for women traveling to India to take extra care and observe stringent security, some of which remain in force today, including Australia, the UK, the USA and, more recently, Japan. As noted in the popular news and social media site Scroll.in and taken up by many other online news outlets:

> Before the December 2012 Delhi gang rape case, most reports about women's safety in India focused on the plight of Indian women. But since then, spates of sexual assaults against visitors to the country have been reported as well: A Swiss cyclist in Madhya Pradesh, an Irish charity worker in Kolkata, a German teenager on a Mangalore-Chennai train, and a Danish woman in Delhi (Narayanan, 2015).

Safety fears are always a major deterrent for travel, but the reports can be exaggerated or mis-represented, particularly in these days of 24 h news and the associated need for "stories." Regardless of their efficacy, they all contribute to one's perceptions and attitudes toward a destination. This chapter looks at how women in particular are responding to the reports, and the effect similar situations have had on tourism in other parts of the world. While not playing down the safety issues, ways to ameliorate the perceptions of danger are proposed, while also creating safe places for foreign travelers, by actually asking those surveyed—the potential female visitors.

14.2   TOURIST SAFETY

There are various forms of attacks that affect tourist safety, including animal attacks, political instability (terrorism, kidnapping, war), and personal attacks (theft, physical, sexual, psychological). But it is often difficult to find data on such events, particularly the more personal sexual based attacks. This can be due to non-reporting, and even when they are reported, such data is often suppressed and not publicized primarily due to fears of negative repercussions. This is not surprising, as when the attacks are made public, the outcomes are often direct and immediate. For example, in Acapulco in March, 2013, it was reported that up to 80% of hotel bookings were canceled after six Spanish tourists were gang-raped in Acapulco. "Instead of five thousand tourists who booked their stay in Acapulco's coast hotels, there are now only 300 reservations.... [*after*] the unfortunate incident.." (Tourism Review, 2013). More recently, attacks on the Bardo museum in the Tunisian capital, Tunis in March 2015 killed 17 international tourists and two Tunisians. Immediately, two major cruise ship companies canceled their stops at Tunis, drying up a major source of tourists to the region (Squires, 2015). An Italian tour operator who had block-booked a 170-room hotel for five months over the summer period (May to October) canceled the reservation at an estimated loss to the hotel of 1.4 million euros (Larbi, 2015).

Certainly, crime committed against tourists is not a new phenomenon and has been considered in some detail by researchers such as Fujii and Mak (1979) in relation to Hawaii, Elliot and Ryan (1993) in Corsica, Tarlow and Muehsam (1996) and Dimanche and Lepetic (1999) in relation to New Orleans, who all have considered the effect that threats to safety has on tourism demand. There is also a body of literature that looks more specifically on tourism victimization by criminals, including Harper (1983), Schiebler et al. (1996)), Crotts (1996), De Alburquerque and McElroy (1999), and more recently Baker and Stockton (2014).

Issues of safety took on greater public prominence post September 11, 2001, particularly from the perspective of terrorism and civil unrest. For example, in a study of tourists' perceptions of the risk of visiting New York after the World Trade Center terrorist attacks, Floyd et al. (2004) found that they were most concerned regarding their personal safety and social risks, along with the impact on their travel experience. As Mansfeld and Pizam note, "...these incidents cause an imbalance in global tourism systems, forcing this highly important yet fragile global industry to operate under high uncertainty and risk levels" (Mansfeld & Pizam, 2006, p. 13). However, in spite of the prevalence of violent crime against tourists and the immediate effects as reported in the media, the high majority of research to date in relation to tourist safety and risk remains focused on health, crime, natural disasters, crises, and terrorism (e.g., Becken & Hughey, 2013; Floyd et al., 2004; Hall, 2010; Korstanje et al., 2014; Michalko 2004; Ritchie, 2009; Wilkes & Page, 2003) rather than personal attacks such as rape and assault. Yet, in a study of the impact of violent crime (homicide, rape, robbery, and assault) on international tourism revenue,

Altindag (2014) found the impact to be economically significant. A 10% increase in violent crime in a country with a population of 25 million could lead to around US$140 million decline in tourism revenue.

14.2.1 PERCEPTIONS OF SAFETY

While the reality of a situation may be quite different to one's perception of that place, our perceptions drive much of our decision-making behavior, particularly in terms of travel and tourism. Certainly, the fear of crime, while out of proportion to the actual risk of crime, is a major deterrent for tourists, which is often magnified by news reports of certain crimes. This fear is not entirely unfounded, as increased crime rates are common in tourist areas. This, combined with non-reporting and over-sensualization tend to obfuscate many of the research attempts to find a clear, direct, causal connection between tourism, crime, and safety (Brunt et al., 2000; Harper, 2001).

Not surprisingly, numerous studies, including a relatively early study by Pearce (1988), found that concern with personal security is a major decision-making factor, with Roehl and Fesenmaier (1992) concluding that uncertainty relating to the safety of a destination affects the decision to travel there. In their work on terrorism and tourism, Sönmez and Graefe conclude that, "[w]hether real or perceived, risks associated with international tourism place serious constraints on tourist behavior" (Sönmez & Graefe, 1998, p. 140). In a 2008 examination of "megatrends" affecting the future of tourism, Dwyer et al. note that, "[s]ince tourist behavior is as constrained by perceived risk as it is by actual risk, operators need to address perceptions of risks as well as the risks themselves" (Dwyer et al., 2008, p. 51). In a study designed to identify the elements that drive tourists' concerns ("worries") Larsen et al. found that, while tourists overall do not worry too much, "the more risky respondents perceive a destinations to be, the more they worry" (Larsen et al., 2009, p. 264) and, importantly, that this was different from the non-tourist population. Their major concerns were petty crime and accidents rather than violent crime. However, the authors note that their study was undertaken in the relatively safe Nordic region, which may have influenced their findings.

In spite of increasingly negative reports from both the media and via government advisories regarding the safety of women travelers in certain countries, the effect of sexual assaults on women on female tourists' perceptions of a destination has received little if any academic attention. One of the few studies on women travelers' perceptions of safety was undertaken in relation to Kuala Lumpur, which found that while Malaysia is considered to be a safe destination, their perceptions of safety reduced at night time (Amir et al., 2015); however there were no directly expressed questions regarding sexual attacks.

14.2.2 ATTACKS ON WOMEN TOURISTS IN INDIA DURING 2013

During 2013, various media reports on violent attacks on women tourists in India received a high level of attention around the world, with some countries releasing official warnings for women traveling to India. Narayanan (2015) provides a summary of such attacks which include a South Korean tourist being allegedly drugged and then raped in a hotel in January 2013, and Swiss tourist gang raped in front of her boyfriend in April that year. As a sober reminder of the fear that such attacks can bring, an English tourist broke her leg when she jumped from her hotel window in fear of being raped by the hotel manager, who claimed to actually be checking up on her wellbeing. Furthermore, a series of highly publicized vicious and fatal attacks on Indian women, such as that of Jyoti Singh Pandey (known as "braveheart" due to Indian laws not allowing the press to identify rape victims) also occurred around this time, highlighting what many see as an endemic negative attitude toward women in India (Narayanan, 2015).

A study by the Indian based Associated Chambers of Commerce and Industry found that, in the first three months of 2013, the number of foreigners traveling to India dropped by 25%, while the number of women tourists dropped even further, by 35%. The sample comprised 1200 tour operators from across the country who concurred that "concerns about the safety of female travelers" had impacted how foreign travelers viewed India. They also found that travelers opted for other Asian countries such as Malaysia, Thailand, Indonesia, and Vietnam (Associated Chambers of Commerce and Industry, 2013). However, figures and reports produced by the Indian government disputed this, with a statement from the Tourism Minister claiming that foreign tourist arrivals to India grew by 2.1% during January and February, 2013 (NewsWala, 2013).

The attacks and the conflicting travel data noted above raise a number of questions, with a major one being "how do women feel about these reports and does it influence their travel decisions?" This was of such concern to certain areas of the Indian tourism industry such as inbound tour operators and agents that the Indian Chapter of the American Society of Travel Agents (ASTA) convened a seminar in New Delhi on this topic in 2014 (*Incredible India: Will India's Tourism be tarnished by attacks on women travelers?*). My keynote speech for this event introduced the outcomes of the research outlined in this chapter, along with discussions from a panel of high-level Indian women in the tourism industry. As the keynote presenter and regular (female) traveler to India, I found this to be a very interesting seminar due to its currency and controversy, and was impressed with the concern this male dominated industry was expressing by convening and attending this seminar. However, government representatives refused their invitation to attend, allegedly due to a concern of being quoted in the media as being concerned about this issue, therefore making it "real," and little seems to have changed.

14.3   RESEARCH STUDY

In order to address the above question and to assist the inbound tourism industry in India in its quest to address issues of violence against women and understand its impact, a primarily qualitative online survey of 108 women from around the world was conducted using a snowball technique to recruit participants. After removing those who did not meet the study requirements, 94 usable questionnaires remained. Due to the referral nature of this approach, the respondents were primarily Australian and American (with some from the United Kingdom and Europe), over 35 years old, tertiary educated and experienced travelers. In other words, they came from developed, primarily Westernized nations. This group is a high yield market often targeted by tourism authorities (Dwyer & Forsythe, 2008), and was purposefully solicited for this study.

In a desire to investigate this issue in some depth and to uncover as much information as possible, the majority of the questions were open-ended, considering the perceptions, opinions, and feelings the women had toward traveling in India in light of the attacks on women, both local and tourists. By leaving them free to express their thoughts, rich interesting and useful data arose.

Nearly three quarters were aware of the attacks against women. Among those who have been to India (over 70%), most (95%) want to return; but as well as expressing concern about issues of personal safety, they noted that these attacks influenced their overall opinion of the country, in particular its male dominated culture. The comments were all thoughtfully articulated, with some presenting strong opinions:

> It made me more aware of the injustices suffered by Indian women and the danger to female tourists.

> With this knowledge, I would be much less likely to visit India because I am afraid as well as disgusted.

Furthermore, many governments issued travel warnings or advisories relating to women traveling in India, including Australia, Canada, the United Kingdom, and the USA. For examples:

> We continue to advise Australians to exercise a high degree of caution in India overall because of the risk of terrorism, civil unrest, crime and vehicle accidents. Australia: http://smartraveler.gov.au/zw-cgi/view/Advice/India [April 11, 2013].

> Women should avoid traveling alone, particularly at night, on public transportation, taxis and auto-rickshaws....Canada: http://travel.gc.ca/destinations/india [April 11, 2013].

> Women should use caution when traveling in India. Reported cases of sexual assault against women and young girls are increasing; recent attacks against female visitors in tourist areas and cities show that foreign women are also at risk. British women have been victims of sexual assault....UK: https://www.gov.uk/foreign-travel-advice/india/safety-and-security [April 11, 2013].

> Women should observe stringent security precautions, including avoiding use of public transport after dark without the company of known and trustworthy companions....USA: http://travel.state.gov/travel/cis_pa_tw/cis/cis_1139.html [April 11, 2013].

The issuing of travel warnings by national governments has often been criticized as over-reactionary and counter-productive, particularly in relation to natural disasters, with many in the affected areas believing that, by over-stressing dangers and discouraging travel at a time when the support and income from tourists is most needed, the destination suffers even more, and that the media over sensationalizes such stories (Beirman, 2003). Certainly tourism and hospitality operators along with local and national governments have been known to downplay dangers or simply not report criminal activities in an attempt to limit their financial exposure to a negative economic situation. As well as being a risky strategy, trying to ignore the situation is rarely successful in tourism terms. Certainly, the survey participants took great stock in these advisories stating that:

> Smart Traveler (the Australian government's travel advisory) is not exaggerating or blowing anything out of proportion, so don't lay any blame on these warnings. It is true, from everything I've heard, and therefore a needed service.

They also commented that the advisories did directly affect their perceptions of the country, more so than potentially sensationalist news responding that:

> It makes me feel…that India is quite an unsafe place, remains so, and only I can really regulate my safety.

> Fearful, disinclined to go, ultra-vigilant and careful if I did travel there.

However, there are still those whose travel plans were not deterred by the advisories, but noted that it does encourage them to take more care of their personal safety, which can be seen as a constructive and positive use of such warnings:

> I would, as the warnings suggest, exercise due caution. I would consider where I was staying, the most suitable form of transport and would try to make sensible decisions, not actively putting myself in harm's way.

It was clear that simply denying that such a danger exists would not be enough to encourage these women to change their perceptions nor travel intentions. As most are well educated and traveled, they are more likely to continue to access what they consider to be the more reliable information from sources such as their own government and selected media outlets.

14.4   WHAT CAN BE DONE?

It was clear that it was important to ascertain what could be done to encourage and support women traveling in India as so many were still keen to, but increasingly wary. So, instead of simply leaving the study at this point, they were asked as to what could be done to support their travel, resulting in some very positive suggestions. These suggestions centered around presenting clear and unbiased information, which can be easily adopted by travel organizations and authorities.

Furthermore, quite specific suggestions were provided. Many wanted to see information that demonstrated cultural change such as reduced corruption, which they indicated would be a powerful way to alter their perceptions and desire to travel to India. This may be a longer-term strategy, but necessary as these are recognized as long-term issues.

> If it could be proven to me that sexual assault is less common, frowned upon by Indian society and taken more seriously by Indian authorities. This would indicate to me that women's rights in India had improved and I would then consider visiting

> Better standard of policing and support...a major overwhelming shift in attitude towards women in India but this not likely in short term

> If there was visible change to police corruption, rates of women going to school, and domestic violence, as well as some indication that Western women were no longer publicly groped if they weren't with a man.

It was very clear that the women wanted information on actionable strategies as opposed to simply warning them to take care or be vigilant. Many did not want to go elsewhere, but to be able to travel safely in India. Consequently, their comments surrounding this were particularly interesting and suggest that some cultural information from India would assist. In addition, the need to change their own behavior when traveling solo in India was noted, with some female travelers even pretending that they were meeting male relatives. While this may seem extreme, others found that understanding the need to curb their natural friendliness to be important.

> Suggested strategies would be more useful than general warnings.

It took me a while to work out not to engage with men when on my own. To ignore questions.

One respondent also noted that she felt the travel industry itself could be an agent for change, rather than simply reacting to such events:

As such, even though its impact on my own behavior is not huge I do think this is something that India should take seriously and for which women around the world (and especially those in the travel industry) should hold them to account. But that would be more on account of local Indian women than our own account.

However, due to the enormity of the issue and some perceptions that the law does not support women, respondents believed that change needs to come from the top and that the Indian government has an important role to play, not only in taking some action but also in informing the wider community that there are such developments.

I am hoping that this will be an incentive for the Indian government and people to try to make a change.

I think the Indian government needs to do something about this. It is not a small issue to be treated with little attention.

I would like to hear that the Indian government is taking action and reforming laws regarding attacks on women in India.

14.5 RECOMMENDATIONS AND CONCLUSIONS

As discussed earlier, this study focused on a specific, high yield market of developed, primarily Westernized nations. Such a group is also highly articulate and prepared to express their thoughts and opinions, which can be used constructively by tourism authorities. By asking women travelers what they think and how they feel, we get a sense of what is really going on in relation to their decisions and what is important, rather than relying on confusing "data." While many are fearful and may not travel to India, they also made a number of constructive suggestions as to what could be done in the short term to encourage them to visit. However, this is a longer term, broader, and more complex issue than simply an immediate reaction to such attacks, with the women surveyed raising issues of respect, independence, and women's rights.

Some suggestions that have come out of this study and the literature include elements of planning and training as well as the suggested changes to law. For example, it is key that the situation should never be downplayed, but presented as realistically as possible and that travelers need to be provided with information and resources to support them, reinforced by Beirman (2003) and Dwyer et al. (2008). Front line staff, the majority of whom are male, need to be trained regarding the needs of women travelers, especially those traveling alone (Tarlow & Muehsam, 1996). An example is that entering women's rooms uninvited is not appropriate, and while not noted specifically in my research, was discussed at the industry seminar in light of the reported case of the woman jumping out of her hotel window as reported by Narayanan in the Introduction (Narayanan, 2015). Avoiding giving women ground floor rooms is accepted practice in some hotels and was discussed at the industry seminar on this topic by the female manager of a major Indian hotel, where she noted that it is welcomed by many women.

In terms of regulation, Tarlow and Muehsam argue that a high level of security and/or police presence in tourist areas needs to be provided, and where there are tourist police stations, they need to be manned with both female and male officers (Tarlow & Muehsam, 1996). To date, this is not the case in India, in spite of calls for such support since the 1990s by Tarlow and others (Roehl & Fesenmaier, 1992).

However, media reports also need to be managed, and the needs of today's media understood—24 h news cycles are always looking for stories, so instead of the sensationalized negative reports, there is a chance to provide follow-up positive, recovery style reports (Beirman, 2003). In fact, the Indian media has been driving much of the cultural change toward women, such as the NDTV (New Delhi TV) India of the Year Awards which were given entirely to women in 2013, including Braveheart's family. Also in 2013, the station established a campaign, "Our Girls, Our Pride," with the aim to create awareness in India surrounding the four main issues relating to female children in the country, namely nutrition, education, health feticide, and infanticide (http://www.ndtv.com/micro/uniteforgirls/).

Furthermore, the dearth of academic literature into this area of tourist safety, namely attacks on women travelers, is indicative of a general reluctance to approach such sensitive issues, but certainly requires more attention. The findings of this small research project underline the level of importance that travelers place on impressions of safety and security.

Since this study was undertaken, attacks on Indian women have not received such wide media attention as they did in 2013; however, they persist, with young women committing suicide due to sexual attacks and abuse. Unfortunately, it may well take more high profile attacks on female tourists to bring some momentum to this issue, but there are certainly some women who are not waiting for this and are "voting with their feet," as one respondent stated:

> Why put your life at risk when the rest of the world is waiting to be visited?

KEYWORDS

- tourist safety
- women tourists
- fear
- travel warnings
- India

REFERENCES

Altindag, D. T. Crime and International Tourism. *J. Labor Res.* **2014,** *35*(1), 1–14.

Amir, A. F.; Ismail, M. N. I.; See, T. P. Sustainable Tourist Environment: Perception of International Women Travelers on Safety and Security in Kuala Lumpur. *Procedia-Soc. Behav. Sci.* **2015,** *168,* 123–133.

Associated Chambers of Commerce and Industry. 'Atithi Devo Bahava' Takes a Hit: ASSOCHAM; 25% Decline in Foreign Tourists' Inflow, ASSOCHAM Press Release March 31, 2013. http://www.assocham.org/prels/shownews.php?id=3947

Baker, D., Stockton, S. Tourism and Crime in America: A Preliminary Assessment of the Relationship Between the Number of Tourists and Crime in Two Major American Tourist Cities. *IJSSTH.* **2014,** *1*(5), 1–25.

Becken, S.; Hughey, K. F. Linking Tourism into Emergency Management Structures to Enhance Disaster Risk Reduction. *Tour. Manage.* **2013,** *36,* 77–85.

Beirman, D. *Restoring Tourism Destinations in Crisis: A Strategic Marketing Approach;* McPherson's Printing Group: Maryborough, Australia, 2003.

Brunt, P.; Mawby, R.; Hambly, Z. Tourist Victimisation and the Fear of Crime on Holiday. *Tour. Manage.* **2000,** *21*(4), 417–424.

Crotts, J. C. Theoretical Perspectives on Tourist Criminal Victimisation. *J. Tour. Stud.* **1996,** *7*(1), 2–9.

De Alburquerque, K.; McElroy, J. Tourism and Crime in the Caribbean. *Ann. Tour. Res.* **1999,** *26*(4), 968–984.

Dimanche, F.; Lepetic, A. New Orleans Tourism and Crime: A Case Study. *J. Travel Res.* **1999,** *38*(1), 19–23.

Dwyer, L.; Forsyth, P. Economic Measures of Tourism Yield: What Markets to Target? *Int. J. Tour. Res.* **2008,** *10*(2), 155–168.

Dwyer, L.; Edwards, D. C.; Mistilis, N.; Roman, C.; Scott, N.; Cooper, C. *Megatrends Underpinning Tourism to 2020: Analysis of Key Drivers for Change;* Sustainable Tourism Cooperative Research Centre, CRC for Sustainable Tourism Pty Ltd: Gold Coast, Australia, 2008.

Elliot, L.; Ryan, C. The Impact of Crime on Corsican Tourism: A Descriptive Assessment. *WTTC.* **1993,** *3,* 287–293.

Floyd, M. F.; Gibson, H.; Pennington-Gray, L; Thapa, B. The Effect of Risk Perceptions on Intentions to Travel in the Aftermath of September 11, 2001. *JTTM.* **2004,** *15*(2–3), 19–38.

Fujii, E. T.; Mak, J. The Impact of Alternative Regional Development Strategies on Crime Rates: Tourism Vs. Agriculture in Hawaii. *Ann. Regional Sci.* **1979,** 13(3), 42–56.

Hall, C. M. Crisis Events in Tourism: Subjects of Crisis in Tourism. *Curr. Issues Tour.* **2010,** *13*(5), 401–417.

Harper, D. *The Tourist as Crime Victim. Paper Read at the Academy of Criminal Justice Science Meetings.* San Antonio: TX, 1983.

Harper, W. Comparing Tourists Crime Victimization. *Ann. Tour. Res.* **2001,** *28*(4), 1053–1056.

Korstanje, M. E.; Tzanelli, R.; Clayton, A. Brazilian World Cup 2014: Terrorism, Tourism, and Social Conflict. *Event Manage.* **2014,** *18*(40, 487–491.

Larbi, K. Tunisia is Desperately Trying to Convince Tourists to Come Visit after Attacks. Business Insider, AFP. [Online] May 22, 2015. http://www.businessinsider.com/afp-tunisias-sunbeds-and-souks-empty-after-museum-attack-2015-5?IR=T (accessed August 11, 2015).

Larsen, S.; Brun, W.; Øgaard, T. What Tourists Worry About: Construction of a Scale Measuring Tourist Worries. *Tour. Manage.* **2009,** *30*(2), 260–265.

Mansfeld, Y.; Pizam, A. *Tourism, Security and Safety: From Theory to Practice;* Butterworth-Heinemann: NY, 2006.

March, S. Families Devastated after Report Claims Suicide, Not Murder of Two Indian Girls Hanged from Tree. *The Age.* [Online] November 29 2014. http://www.abc.net.au/news/2014-11-29/suicide-not-rape-and-murder-in-case-of-indian-girls-report/5927622 (accessed August 3, 2015)

Michalko, G. Tourism Eclipsed by Crime. *J. Travel Tour. Mark.* **2004,** *15*(2-3), 159–172.

Narayanan, N. 'Exercise Extreme Caution': What Countries Around the World Tell Women Planning to Visit India, Scroll.in. [Online] February 12, 2015. http://scroll.in/

article/706025/%27Exercise-extreme-caution%27:-What-countries-around-the-world-tell-women-planning-to-visit-India (accessed May 8, 2015)

NewsWala. Government Clarifies Tourist Data, NewsWala. [Online] April 3, 2013 http://www.newswala.com/India-National-News/Government-clarifies-tourist-data-34293.html

Pearce, P. L. *The Ulysses Factor. Evaluating Visitors in Tourist Settings;* Springer-Verlag: New York, 1988.

Ritchie, B. W. *Crisis and Disaster Management for Tourism*; Channel View Publications: Bristol, UK, 2009.

Roehl, W. S.; Fesenmaier, D. R. Risk Perceptions and Pleasure Travel: An Exploratory Analysis. *J. Travel Res.* **1992,** *30*(4), 17–26.

Schiebler, S.; Crofts, J.; Hollinger, R. Florida Tourists' Vulnerability to Crime. In *Tourism Crime and International Security Issues;* Pizam, A., Mansfield, Y., Eds.; Wiley: Chichester, UK, 1996; pp 37–50.

Sönmez, S.; Graefe, A. R. Influence of Terrorism Risk on Foreign Tourism Decisions. *Ann. Tour. Res.* **1998,** *25*(1), 112–144.

Squires, N. Tunisia attack: Tourists Disappear After Killings at Museum. *The Telegraph.* [Online] March 21, 2015. http://www.telegraph.co.uk/news/worldnews/africaandindianocean/tunisia /11487222/Tunisia-attack-Tourists-disappear-after-killings-at-museum.html

Tarlow, P.; Muehsam, M. Theoretical Aspects of Crime as They Impact the Tourism Industry. In *Tourism, Crime and International Security Issues;* Pizam, A., Mansfeld, Y., Eds.; John Wiley & Sons: Hoboken, NJ, 1996.

Tourism Review. Security Problems: 80% of Hotel Bookings in Acapulco Cancelled. [Online] March 25, 2013. http://www.tourism-review.com/80-of-hotel-reservations-in-acapulco-canceled--news3629#i8ZF879rjJkEY1kd.99

Wilkes, J.; Page, S. *Managing Tourist Safety in the New Millennium;* Elsevier Science Ltd: Oxford, UK, 2003.

CHAPTER 15

THE ROLE OF A FEMALE-ONLY ONLINE HOSPITALITY NETWORK IN THE CHANGING WORLD OF WOMEN'S INDEPENDENT TRAVEL

MANDY ROWE

Founder, Broads Abroad Travel Network

E-mail: mandy@broadsabroad.net

CONTENTS

As the sun set behind the Arabian sands, my Saudi friend - a descendent of King Saud -spoke of her Bedouin heritage. "When a stranger arrives at our door we offer them food, water and accommodation for three days; they are the guest - we the host". Why, I ask? "Because one day I might find myself in the desert in need of shelter. Then it will be my turn to be the guest, another the host. For survival we need to know that hospitality is reciprocal."
Anonymous, pers. comm, 2000, Al-Ghat, Saudi Arabia

15.1 INTRODUCTION

For centuries, Bedouins have been opening their doors to strangers—giving them unconditional shelter, security, and sustenance for three days. Traditional Islamic *hadiths* states this about hospitality, "if the guest stays longer than the 'three days' it becomes charity" (O'Gorman, 2010). One wonders if this ancient Bedouin tradition should be considered one of the first hospitality exchange networks. In 1949 SERVAS International—one of the first hospitality exchange networks—was founded to promote world peace. Members' contact details were printed and distributed on paper, and homestays were arranged with the host either by the telephone or the written word. The advent of the Internet made this form of communication almost obsolete and new online hospitality networks emerged—Hospitality Exchange, BeWelcome, and Global Freeloaders. The most well-known is Couchsurfing, and by 2013, was estimated to have over 5.5 million global members (www.couchsurfing.org). Membership of these hospitality exchange networks is mixed gender. These computer-mediated hospitality networks, born of the sharing economy—a new socio-economic system built around the sharing of resources—are growing in popularity. Gansky believes the world is in the midst of an economic shift which involves less owning and more sharing (Gansky, 2010). Developments in the digital age, coupled with this shared economy phenomenon, has led to a global movement whereby people are sharing their cars, their wi-fi and even their spare bedrooms.

This chapter provides a contemporary case study of an enterprise addressing the needs of a specific tourism market segment. The role of a female-only online hospitality network, *Broads Abroad Travel Network* (BATN)—a global travel community which moves seamlessly from the virtual world to real life connections—has a valid place in the growing body of knowledge on women's travel. The BATN initiative emerged from the author's own experience as an Australian psychologist, traveler, and entrepreneur. It denotes a new approach to tourism study. Small suggests that despite developments in the field of gender and tourism studies, there are noticeable gaps in the knowledge base, especially among older women tourists (Small, 2003). This investigation focuses on the evolution of a particular network and addresses the behavior of the BATN online community of women travelers.

15.1.1 *BROADS ABROAD TRAVEL NETWORK (BATN)*

Launched in Australia in 2013, BATN is the only online female hospitality exchange network in the world (www.broadsabroad.net). Its aim is to link—at levels from the local to the international—women who want to offer each other free accommodation in their homes, or meet and show fellow-members their city. Both types of experiences/encounters seem to be changing the way women are traveling. For independent women wishing to derive extra benefit from engagement with destination insiders, the network provides experiences gleaned from interaction with residents who are the custodians of the local knowledge. By visiting and/or staying with women in other places there are opportunities to explore and experience landscapes and lifestyles safely and uniquely.

Social media uptake by mature independent women is manifested in BATN members' interaction. By marketing herself, setting up public profiles through blogs, Facebook, and Twitter, the author is attracting a growing number of members. The public face of the network is the BATN Facebook page. Its principal message—that there are alternative approaches to singles' travel—seems well understood by potential members. This defined idea allows for a brand to emerge while the content produced is monitored and personalized as traction is developed. The habit of regularly sharing updates expands the network's reach and appeal. The illustrative material featured is sourced from members as well as the author. This consistent engagement with the public forum is essential to the sense of community that BATN is trying to create.

15.1.2 MEMBERSHIP OF BOARDS ABROAD

To register, a prospective member must provide their full name and address, and some form of identity document. Once verified, they are given access to the network, and are able to complete their profile information and upload a photograph. Members are asked to provide biographical demographic material (age, hometown, marital status, vocation, languages spoken) and a 100-word description about who they are (interests, philosophy on life, travel experiences).

Members (potential guests) can navigate the database of hosts geographically. An internal message-sending mechanism enables members to contact each other. Individuals are free to arrange their own conditions for the exchange within the guidelines of Broads Abroad. Currently membership to BATN is free. After using the service, members are encouraged to review their experience. After these reviews are approved by BATN staff, they are published on the BATN website. For members who cannot offer accommodation, they are expected to offer another activity. For example, some offer to pick a member up from the airport while others meet for a meal at a cafe. Activities appear to be many and varied. A private Facebook forum allows members to upload photos of their encounters with other members.

15.2 WOMEN TRAVELERS

The establishment of the BATN emerged as the growing academic literature addressed the changing needs of independent women travelers. This new phenomena of people connecting online and then meeting face-to-face is piquing the interest of many (Rosen et al., 2011). In 2001, Wittel coined the term "network sociality," which allowed Molz to ponder "the way individuals perform hospitality in a mobile…and networked society" (Wittel, 2011). Molz continues with "new hybrid spaces of social interaction…redefining who counts as a 'friend' or a 'stranger'" (Molz, 2011). Like many scholars, she wants to know "what is at stake when complete strangers encounter and accommodate one another online, on the move and in one another's homes" (Molz, 2011). Zuev suggests hospitality exchange networks—having emerged from the sharing economy—are not only about "recycling" residential space but are about intangibles gained from the "rhythms" that define a culture (Zuev, 2011). These "rhythms of everyday life can be more important than physical characteristics of places and become collective representations and memories of them" (Wunderlich 2008). Zuev also suggests these intangible resources such as a "sense of place" come from the sharing of local knowledge by the host (Zuev, 2011). Sharing local knowledge is an "essential ritual" of these networks; whereby the "information bureau is replaced by the institution of the host" (Zuev, 2011). The Broads Abroad philosophy mirrors these statements: "Imagine being based at the home of a fellow member who can tell you about the best local haunts" (www.broadsabroad.net).

Wilson suggests "the solo woman traveler represents a growing market segment, with research showing that increasing numbers of females are choosing to travel alone, without the assistance or company of partners, husbands or packaged tour groups" (Wilson, et al., 2009). Small studied women over 65 and found that these women value the simplicity of life and the essence of the everyday. A holiday offered new experiences and the women were open to these experiences (Small, 2003). There was an expansion of the women's lives, rather than a contraction. Investigation of the *BATN* modus operandi provides a model that satisfies this demographic from the supply side. Chiang and Jogarantnam used a factor analysis with five motivational dimensions: experience, escape, relaxation, social, and self-esteem (Chiang & Jogarantnam, 2006). Their study highlighted implications for the significant factor of "experience" as essential under-standing of marketers (Chiang & Jogarantnam, 2006). While their study indicated significant differences between respondents on demographic and trip characteristics, the researcher was keen to test such observations with the current cohort of respondents for her study.

The aim of this study therefore, is essentially from an industry perspec-tive—that is, to research whether a role exists for a female-only hospitality network, and if so, does it change the way this segment of the market travels. The author herself has walked in the same shoes as this travel segment. Her own experience of global travel and residency in large and small international destinations has led her to pursue this initiative. By collecting good data, she is hopefully able to build loyalty and increase frequency of interaction. By members explaining their motivation for undertaking solo travel and engaging with the BATN, a greater under-standing of how benefits can be built into the network can be accrued. This online engagement helps explain how women's travel choices are medi-ated and how the female travel experience is constructed.

15.3   THE STUDY

Since BATN's launch the network appeared to appeal to women who are 50 years of age and over. This is the only trend gleaned from the initial profile information women provided on the website—68% of the members who specified their age upon joining BATN were 50 years plus. Hence, this chapter offers the voices of, predominantly older, women tourists. The data collected for the purpose of this chapter explores the membership in greater depth, leading to a better understanding of the type of woman who is comfortable adopting "on-line social networking platforms and creating new hybrid spaces of social interaction, …redefining who counts as a 'friend' or a 'stranger'" (Molz, 2011). Given that this represents a demographic shift in the market place, it firstly requires a qualitative investigation. The analysis of members' identity, behaviors, motivations, and experiences provides a framework for further exploration. The relationships between members and hosts involved with sharing their homes and communities are examined by monitoring their communication between themselves and their use of social media platforms. This offers evidence of a distinctive shift in travel preferences, growing use of digital interfaces and a commitment to offering quality hospitality.

In addition to the qualitative data, a 35-question self-administered online survey was emailed to all members. The survey included questions about demographic information, the way members travel (who with, why, and where) and members' experience of the network, including their usage of an online forum associated with BATN. BATN currently has 155 members and 58 members completed the survey (a 37% response rate). The mixed methodology engaged members through interviews and an online survey. Multiple data collection techniques avoided bias. The data examined below constitutes analysis of the content of members' reviews, biographical data, and responses to a questionnaire aimed at discovering women's reasons for choosing a solo women-only travel network as a tool for implementing their travel plans. Qualitative information came from a series of open-ended questions. Quantitative data was analyzed using descriptive and inferential statistics, while the qualitative data was analyzed by a process of inspection of responses, whereby key themes and ideas were drawn out and counted.

Of particular interest was whether hospitality exchange networks like BATN were changing the way people travel, and why this network seems to be attracting this demographic. Reviews are an important way of evaluating the hospitality experience for members. These are published on the website for all members to read. Members gave permission to quote from their reviews.

15.4 RESULTS

15.4.1 DEMOGRAPHICS

BATN is women only, and this sets it apart from other hospitality exchange networks. Ninety percent of respondents said it was important that BATN was female-only. Less than 15% would join if the network was mixed gender. Respondent A liked that it is female only "because I don't have to deal with men who are trolling the internet for women." Toeniskoetter interviewed Couchsurfers and most said a person's gender played a minor role when choosing a host or surfer (Toeniskoetter, 2013). Common interests and perceived trust were more important than gender, to this cohort who is younger than BATN members. It seems gender concerns may be age related.

The age of members becomes another unique selling proposition. Without consciously marketing to any particular age cohort, the network seems to be attracting an older demographic. As seen in Figure 15.1, 84% of women joining BATN are 50 years or over; 59% said they find age an important factor in their BATN membership. Respondent B says: "there are few sites where you can connect with middle aged and older people… there are plenty of sites for younger people…. I think we more often seek connections with our contemporaries." Respondent C comments: "coupledom and children restrict many women's freedom…. Broads Abroad is a breath of fresh air to get them back into the world of fun, after decades of serving family." There appears to be much truth in respondent C's observation. For many women, the freedom to travel comes when the children have left home.

It appears women joining BATN are very well educated. About 47% had postgraduate qualifications (Fig. 15.1). Apart from two people, all other respondents had some form of post-secondary education. Members of BATN are a well-traveled cohort. As shown in Figure 15.3, 35 listed ten or more countries visited, 17 had traveled to more than 20 countries, while six said there were too many to list. "I have been to over 320 cities around the world, traveling since I was 19," said respondent D.

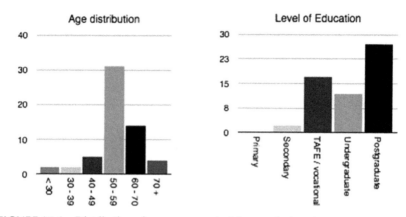

FIGURE 15.1   Distribution of survey respondents' age and education.

15.4.2 MEMBERS' EXPERIENCE OF THE NETWORK

A Broads Abroad travel experience usually involves close contact with a person one has not previously met. Respondents were asked to indicate how much they agreed with certain statements regarding this experience. These were; they approached with an open mind, they found it exciting, they found it daunting. The results seen in Figure 15.2 allow an inference of confidence in BATN and confidence in oneself.

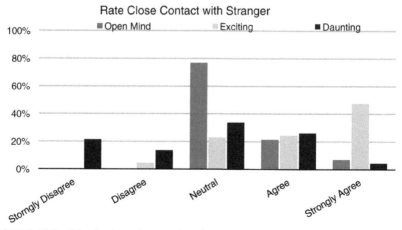

FIGURE 15.2   Distribution of respondents' agreement with three statements regarding close contact with other, previously unknown, members of BATN.

Thirty-eight percent (38%) of women have met another member in person while 81% have communicated with another member either via the BATN messaging platform or private Facebook forum. Many joined BATN because of the information and positive tone of messages posted regularly on the public Facebook page. Respondent E, an Australian, sums up her unwarranted trepidation about using the network. "I had my first Broads Aboard experience in Cape Town. I felt a bit anxious, what if we didn't like each other...? But I like the Broads Abroad concept and desperately wanted to try it. What was I worried about? We never stopped talking...she was clever and fun and courageous and interesting and left me alone enough and involved me enough...she was the perfect host."

15.4.3   MOTIVATIONS FOR TRAVEL

Sixty-four percent (64%) of respondents say the most important reason to travel is to experience other cultures. Instead of sightseeing they prefer "life-seeing"—a term coined by Bosschart and Frick (2006). As respondent F says: "monuments and scenery can be awe inspiring but it is the people you meet that leave an indelible impression. They are the window to humanity's soul." The freedom, spontaneity, and flexibility of solo travel appealed to 47% of the respondents (see Fig. 15.3). Many saying it was easier to mix with the locals if they were on their own. Fifty-two percent liked to make their own travel arrangements, instead of being part of organized tours.

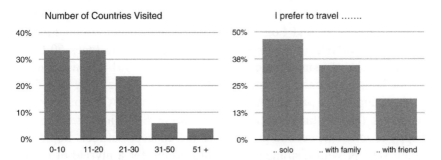

FIGURE 15.3   Distributions of respondents' travel histories and travel preferences.

It was anticipated that BATN would primarily be a source of confidence for the solo traveler. Open and honest discussion and hospitality provides the essential ethos from which BATN is able to provide its service; through correspondence and rendezvous come a commencement or reinvigoration of experiential travel.

15.5   DISCUSSION AND IMPLICATIONS

The study has created a clear profile of the women who would join BATN. On the whole, the network appeals to resourceful, confident, well-educated women who have been "on the road" for decades, long before the internet was invented. From a practitioner's point of view such as my own, this is such useful information. It tells us that any future marketing needs to be tailored to this demographic. At this stage, Facebook is BATN's primary voice. The tone of the posts needs to be a mix of information and inspiration. To date, the most popular posts are photos of colorful, independent older women; women who seem to march to the beat of their own drum. A free spirited woman seems to be very appealing.

From the supply perspective, we now understand that there is a need to determine what publications the demographic reads and then pitch the BATN story to these "editors." At this stage, we can learn more from other hospitality providers, than they can learn from us, especially in terms of how to expand the network. When developing our website we adopted a sharing economy model similar to that used by Couchsurfing. Their demographic is predominately younger than BATNs; they are a cohort who has grown up with the internet and it's plethora of sharing platforms like Uber, Zipcar, and Fon. For them, online sharing communities are the norm. Burbank found only "7 percent of Boomers (ages 50-64) are willing to share" using online platforms (Burbank, 2014). This reluctance by the boomer segment to embrace "the sharing culture" may be reflected in the sluggish growth of BATN. When explaining BATN to prospective members, three distinct reactions usually occur. Some just "get it" and are happy to join. The second group loves the concept but feels trepidations about staying with a stranger. The third group, for a myriad of reasons, prefers hotel accommodation or staying with family or friends. The question for BATN is how do we make the experience of sharing irresistible? Drawing on our share-economy elders, we need to utilize our members as the driving force behind promoting the network. Essentially, the positive experiences BATN members have had need to be promoted on our public Facebook page. Why is BATN a unique experience? Why should I trust this person in my home? These questions need to be answered with real life success stories. Potential members', apprehensive or not, need to see immediately that the experiences available through BATN are indeed safe and fun. To be truly valuable, BATN needs to have a large number of members around the world touting a large amount of experiences to work effectively and expand to its full potential.

A woman from San Francisco joined BATN a few months ago. She decided—after working for 30 years—to have a grown-up gap year traveling the globe with a backpack. In her blog, she says "if I live to be 85 years old, I have fewer than 14,000 days left to live… and I don't imagine I'll be the life of the party at the old folks' home if the only stories I have to tell are about software deals I closed" (BATN, 2015). It appears more and more women—who perhaps have not had the opportunity to travel in their younger years—are now wanting to pack a bag and do something on their own (possibly for the first time). Another BATN member recently posted her solo journey on the private Facebook forum. She drove 3000 km from Cape Town to Namibia staying in remote villages and meeting the local people. The internet makes planning these trips so easy. She was able to find accommodation, hire a car, and Facebook her journey. In the changing world of women's independent travel (and indeed all travel), the use of online platforms is key. Travel has never been easier. Planning itineraries has never been easier. It is time for older women to embrace this new dimension of sociality. A network like BATN is a supportive adjunct to their travels. The world of women's independent travel is changing because our demographic is mastering the internet—leading to a sense of empowerment and confidence. They can go to the places and see the things perhaps they had only ever dreamed about.

15.6   CONCLUSION

While in many regards, the way in which BATN members engage with the network coincides with recent literature regarding trends in women's travel, the demographic results of the current investigation were somewhat unexpected. The key result appears to be that BATN is attracting a distinct cohort of well-traveled and educated women whose main motivation is to experience different cultures. BATN is not necessarily *changing* solo female travel, rather it is attracting women whose unique travel motive is to experience new cultures and get an insider's view of a destination to experience the "rhythms" as Zuez says (Zuez, 2011).

This offers evidence of a distinctive shift in travel preferences, growing use of digital interfaces and a commitment to offering hospitality, which Telfer describes as "the giving of food, drink and sometimes accommodation to people who are not regular members of a household" (Telfer, 2011). BATN, however, appears to be more than a free bed; rather it is growing into a community of like-minded mature-aged women who appear to be reacting against commercial tourism by seeking more authentic travel experiences.

KEYWORDS

- online
- Broads Abroad Travel network
- female travel
- independent

REFERENCES

Bosschart, D.; Frick, K. *The Future of Leisure Travel: Trend Study;* Gottlieb Duttweiler Institut: Zurich, Switzerland, 2006.

Broads Abroad Travel Network. http://broadsabroad.net (accessed May 1, 2015).

Burbank, J. The Rise of the 'Sharing' Economy. 2014. http://www.huffingtonpost.com/john-burbank/the-rise-of-the-sharing-e_b_5454710.html (accessed Apr 27, 2015).

Chiang, C. Y.; Jogaratnam, G. Why do Women Travel Solo for Purposes of Leisure? *J.Vacation Market.* **2006,** *12,* 59–70.

Gansky, L. *The Mesh: Why the Future of Business is Sharing;* Penguin Group (USA) Inc.: New York, 2010.

Molz, J. G. CouchSurfing and Network Hospitality: 'It's not Just about the Furniture'. *Hosp. Soci.* **2011,** *1*(3), 215–225.

O'Gorman, K. D. *The Origins of Hospitality and Tourism;* Goodfellow Publishers Ltd: Oxford, UK, 2010.

Rosen, D.; Lafontaine, P. R.; Hendrickson, B. CouchSurfing: Belonging and Trust in a Globally Cooperative Online Social Network. *New Media Soci.* **2011,** *13*(6), 981–998.

Small, J. The Voices of Older Women Tourists. *Tour. Recr. Res.* **2003,** *28*(2), 31–39.

Telfer, E. The Philosophy of Hospitableness. In *Search of Hospitality: Theoretical Perspectives and Debates;* Lashley, C., Morrison, A. J., Eds.; Routledge: Abingdon, UK, 2011.

Toeniskoetter, C. 'Hospitality Exchange: Overcoming Safety, Trust and Gender Concerns in the Couchsurfing Community. Honors Thesis, University of Michigan, Ann Arbor, Michigan, 2013.

Wilson, E.; Holdsworth, L.; Witsel, M. Gutsy Women? Conflicting Discourses in Women's Travel Guidebooks. *Tour. Recr. Res.* **2009,** *34*(1), 3–11.

Wittel, A. Towards a Network Sociality. *Theory Cult. Soci.* **2001,** *18*(6), 51–76.

Wunderlich, F. M. Symphonies of Urban Places: Urban Rhythms as Traces of Time in Space. A Study of "Urban Rhythms", Koht Ja Paik/Place and Location. *Stud. Environ. Aesthet. Semiot.* **2008,** *6*(6), 91–111.

Zuev, D. CouchSurfing as a Spatial Practice: Accessing and Producing Xenotopos. *Hosp. Soci.* **2011,** *1*(3), 227–244.

INDEX

dilemmas, 25
educational value, 22
feminized interactive tourism, 26
guide book, 23
handbooks, 23
leisure, 21–22, 28
position in public/domestic space, 21
problem of inequality, 24–25
problems, 23
research, 25
romantic encounters, 26
sexual behavior, 27
Taliban rulings, 24
travel writings of, 21–22
visual pleasures, 22
voluntary organizations, 24
Contiki tour, 42
Couchsurfing, 258
"Country bumpkins," 41

D

Dancing Naked, 43
Doris's home holidays, 209–210. *See
also* Home holidays
Down Under in Europe, 44

E

Eat, Pray, Love, 120
Elamite civilization, 88–89
Emotions, 121–122
Erasmus exchange program, 186–187

F

Family leisure, 54
Feminist literature on women's leisure,
54
Fiefer documents, 19
Findings, 166–167
emotional moments, 169–171
empowering moments, 168–169
family holiday experiences for
mothers, 62

fathers as facilitators of mum's own
time, 58–59
gender differences in relaxation needs
for parents, 59–60
mother's own time or relaxation,
57–58
reflexive moments, 171–173
relaxation linked to
less responsibility, 60–61
safety of children, 61–62
relaxation needs for mothers as recognized by children, 60
Flâneur, 19
Flâneur to choraster, 104–107
Foundations of travel phenomenon,
32–33
Four Kiwis and a Falcon, 39

G

Genderaware framework, 4
Gender considerations in tourism litera-
ture, 52–53
Gendered holiday experiences, 52
"Gender ignition," 4
"Gender-stagnation," 4
"Gesundheitsgesellschaft" ("health-
society"), 220
Gilligan's research, 54
Global Financial Crisis in 2007, 204
Grand Tour, 120
Grounded theory methodology (GTM),
56

H

Health tourism sector, 221
Austria, 225–226
discussion, 234–236
methods, 226
data analysis, 228
data collection, 227–228
results, 228
motivation and need for wellness
vacations, 233–234

T - #0131 - 230425 - C75 - 229/152/14 [16] - CB - 9781771884686 - Gloss Lamination